T0301666

Mapping National Innovation Ecosystems

Mapping National Innovation Ecosystems

Foundations for Policy Consensus

Amnon Frenkel

Associate Professor of Urban and Regional Planning and Senior Research Fellow

and

Shlomo Maital

Professor (Emeritus) and Senior Research Fellow

Samuel Neaman Institute for Advanced Studies in Science and Technology, Technion, Haifa, Israel

Edward Elgar
Cheltenham, UK • Northampton, MA, USA

Published by
Edward Elgar Publishing Limited
The Lypiatts
15 Lansdown Road
Cheltenham
Glos GL50 2JA
UK

Edward Elgar Publishing, Inc.
William Pratt House
9 Dewey Court
Northampton
Massachusetts 01060
USA

A catalogue record for this book
is available from the British Library

Library of Congress Control Number: 2014932527

This book is available electronically in the ElgarOnline.com Economics Subject Collection, E-ISBN 978 1 78254 681 8

ISBN 978 1 78254 680 1

Typeset by Servis Filmsetting Ltd, Stockport, Cheshire
Printed and bound in Great Britain by T.J. International Ltd, Padstow

Contents

Figures

Tables

Preface

The standard definition of innovation is "the process of translating an idea or invention into a good or service that creates value for which customers will pay". If we interpret "service" to include processes, this definition embraces virtually everything human beings do in the daily business of life – what they produce and how they produce it.

How we innovate is itself an appropriate domain for innovation. Recent global developments have stimulated growing interest in innovation processes and policies. In their recent study, Reinhart and Rogoff (2010) found that rising public debt, as a proportion of gross domestic product (GDP), is associated with a decline in economic growth.[1] In the aftermath of the global economic and financial crisis, many governments (mainly in Europe and North America) found that the level of public debt rose alarmingly, as slowing economies shrank tax revenues and increased deficits, and as bailouts of banks by governments shifted private debt onto public balance sheets. This has led to a wave of austerity (budget-cutting) programs. The resulting scarcity of resources has put renewed focus on finding creative ways to make existing resources do more, in both the private and public sectors, and on finding ways to stimulate innovation through public policies. The cyclical crisis occurs against a backdrop of a possible alleged secular downward trend in economic growth and innovation, discussed in the Introduction that follows.

What then is the best approach for researching innovation and innovation policies? Most such research has taken a partial approach, focusing on a particular aspect of innovation policy, such as research and development (R&D) tax credits, subsidies, human capital formation, technology transfer, intellectual property, entrepreneurial finance and science and technology infrastructure. This research is valuable and has led to important insights. But in the process of our work with research teams from several European countries, in the framework of a Seventh Framework project known as "PICK-ME",[2] we came to understand that as with many public policy issues, it is vital to adopt a systems-based approach that seeks to understand how the entire nationwide innovation process works. Without understanding the complex interactions among the components of innovation, there is a danger that some public policies, in themselves beneficial, may in fact in the end be counterproductive. What if generous public funding of innovation and R&D, for instance, displaces and discourages private funding? The classic example of the dangers of "partial" policy is the creation of public housing in America's city centers, in the 1960s, to house the poor, in itself laudable, but which crowded out industry and jobs and created vast ghettos of poverty that remain to this day (Forrester, 1969). In Chapter 1, we discuss at length the nature of, and importance of, national innovation ecosystems, in the context of the search for effective pro-innovation public policies and the ongoing tension between "push" and "pull", between market-based innovation driven by demand forces and supply-side policies initiated primarily by various levels of government.

As a result of this insight into the vital need to understand innovation systems, Frenkel adapted a methodology he employed earlier, in the context of regional planning, to the empirical visualization of national innovation ecosystems. (See Chapter 2 for a detailed explanation of the methodology.)

With the assistance and cooperation of our PICK-ME colleagues, we helped organize a series of Experts Workshops that led to grounded field-based visualizations of national innovation ecosystems in Israel (Chapter 3), Poland (Chapter 4), Germany (Chapter 5), France (Chapter 6) and Spain (Chapter 7).

Based on the interesting results obtained in these studies, we chose to expand our research and examine innovation ecosystems at the regional level. Our friends Heather Fraser and Mark Leung, director and deputy-director, respectively, of DesignWorks, part of the University of Toronto's Rotman School of Management, were instrumental in organizing an Experts Workshop to explore Toronto's healthcare innovation ecosystem, described in Chapter 8. Our colleague Marta Garcia de Alcaraz was instrumental in organizing an Experts Workshop in Shanghai's leading entrepreneurial incubator, in Zhangjiang Science Park; Chapter 9 presents the result visualizing the innovation system centered around Shanghai. Finally, Chapter 10 describes Singapore's national innovation ecosystem, thanks to the kind assistance of JD Yap. Singapore, of course, is a nation; but it is also a regional financial and technological hub for Southeast Asia, hence we include it with the other two regional studies.

We summarize and conclude our book in Chapter 11, comparing and contrasting national and regional innovation systems and drawing the implications of these systems for innovation policy, with emphasis on demand-driven and supply-driven innovation.

We wish to thank our Samuel Neaman Institute (SNI) colleague Dr Daphne Getz, who contributed her knowledge and experience to our

PICK-ME research, and our excellent PICK-ME colleagues Dr Yitzchak Goldberg and Haik Zakrzewski from CASE (Center for Social and Economic Research) Warsaw, Poland; Professor Andreas Pyka and Dr Matthias Müller from University Hohenheim, Germany; Professor Jackie Krafft and Professor Francesco Quatraro, Universite De Nice – Sophia Antipolis, France; Dr David Consoli, Dr Pablo D'Este Cukierman, Mr Rodrigo Martinez Novo and Cristian Paulo Matti from the Institute of Innovation and Knowledge Management (INGENIO) Polytechnic University of Valencia (UPV), Spain.

In addition, Dr Eran Leck and Vered Segal supplied efficient and capable research assistance. We also thank former SNI Director Professor Moshe Moshe, who supported this project, along with the current director Professor Omri Rand. We would like to thank all those experts who agreed to take part in the Workshops and impart their wisdom to our project. Finally we wish to thank Dana Landau, who prepared our manuscript for print and dealt with a myriad of small but crucial details with speed, efficiency and grace.

NOTES

1. Herndon, Ash and Pollin (2013) found an Excel error in the Reinhart-Rogoff paper, and other errors, that diminish the empirical impact of debt on growth; but the basic finding that debt and growth are negatively correlated remains.
2. This Project is funded by the European Union under the Seventh Framework Programme: "Policy Incentives for the Creation of Knowledge: Methods and Evidence – (PICK-ME)" Project No. 266959. Research teams are from Netherlands, France, UK, Spain, Poland, Germany, Italy and Israel.

Introduction

BACKGROUND

In this introduction, we explore some of the theory and evidence underlying both policymakers' and scholars' growing concern over the continuing weakness of economic growth in the West and the role innovation must play in strengthening it.

The great British economist A.C. Pigou once wrote that the goal of research is both fruit and light – light, meaning, better understanding of the world, and fruit, meaning, the ability to change the world in a meaningful way.[1] The objective of this book is both light and fruit – to better understand the innovation process within countries and to provide a better basis for shaping pro-innovation policies. But first, we must ask, why is innovation so crucial to the wellbeing of the world and those who live in it? Why is innovation the first link in the causal chain whose end result is economic wellbeing?

PRODUCTIVITY, ECONOMIC GROWTH AND INNOVATION

The teleology (cause and effect) of productivity, economic growth, innovation and economic wellbeing is simple and clear. Economic wellbeing is measured by per capita consumption. Growth in per capita consumption must be driven by growth in per capita output, or output per labor hour, that is by productivity growth. Of course, consumption can outpace productivity, for a time, but only at the cost of growing budget and trade deficits, which is unsustainable in the long run. Productivity growth, in turn, is driven largely by innovation. We shall briefly explore each link in this chain in turn.

Productivity Growth

MIT Professor Robert Solow (1957), preceded by the Dutch economist Jan Tinbergen, have showed that between half and two-thirds of productivity growth, or more, stems from "total factor productivity (TFP) growth", meaning, better, smarter, more creative use of resources (with the remaining part explained by growth in capital per worker).

A modest paper written by Tinbergen, published in 1942, revealed why innovation is so crucial to our wellbeing. Tinbergen was determined to maintain his research in Holland despite the Nazi occupation. He published an article almost nobody read at the time, in a German journal, *Weltwirtschaftliches Archiv* (Tinbergen, 1942). His paper has a fundamental equation, written as:

$$t = y - 2/3\ N - 1/3\ K \qquad (1)$$

where "y" is the year-to-year change in gross domestic product (GDP), or output, "N" is the year-to-year change in labor input (FTE, or man-years), "K" is the year-to-year change in invested capital; and "t" is free lunch productivity growth – the growth in GDP that cannot be explained by, or attributed to, growth in the basic factors of production, labor and capital, but rather is caused by better, smarter, more productive use of existing resources. (The weights, 1/3 and 2/3, reflect in turn the relative contribution of capital and labor to national income and output.)

The Tinbergen equation has undergone many transformations over the years, and Tinbergen's "t" has been given various names: Total Factor Productivity (TFP, used in the US), Multi-Factor Productivity (MFP, commonly used in Britain), or, as it is sometimes called, Free Lunch Productivity (FLP). This equation has been revived and reframed by MIT Professor Robert Solow, who simplified the equation by adding and subtracting "N" from the right-hand side, to get:

$$t = y - N - 2/3\ N - 1/3\ K + N = y - 1/3\ (K - N) \qquad (2)$$
$$(3)\ t = (y - N) - 1/3\ (K - N)$$

This simplified version says that TFP or total factor productivity growth is the residual, or what is left over, after the contribution of the growth in capital per worker $(K - N)$ is subtracted from overall growth in GDP per worker. Put another way: $(y - N)$ is the growth of gross labor productivity (the percent change in GDP per worker), and $1/3\ (K - N)$ is the part of that gross labor productivity growth driven by higher capital intensity (higher capital per worker). What is left, then, must be the part of gross labor productivity growth caused by factors other than higher capital investment.

Tinbergen's equation has found wide use at the national level, in measuring (TFP). Solow's seminal 1957 paper reveals that for the US, for the period 1900–49, "Gross output per man hour doubled over the interval, with 87.5 percent of the increase attributable to technical change (i.e. TFP) and the remaining 12.5 percent to increased use of capital." (p. 320). This finding has since been replicated for many advanced nations. For 2005, a year chosen because it preceded the 2007–12 global economic downturn, TFP growth accounted for between 55 percent and 72 percent of overall growth in GDP per worker in the USA, India, China, Japan and UK (Cahill and Maital, 2012, p. 22). The inescapable conclusion is that overall growth in output per worker or per hour is driven not mainly by capital deepening (i.e. providing more equipment, machines, computers, etc. to workers), but by gains in knowledge, creativity, innovation and the cleverness with which we employ existing labor and capital.

TFP Growth

But what drives TFP growth? TFP growth, in turn, is driven largely by a combination of improvements in human capital and the creativity and innovation that human capital applies to its resources. Human capital and innovation are almost inextricable. People who are better educated, more skilled and more knowledgeable are by definition more able to do things differently, uniquely better, rather than do them as they always have been done.

Therefore, the teleology of economic progress in economic society is captured by a simple sentence:

> Innovation and human capital drive productivity growth, which drives growth in output and consumption per capita and leads to improved economic wellbeing.

The first crucial link in this chain is therefore innovation. Hence, the growing importance both scholars and policymakers attach to their nations' innovativeness.

IS THERE A STRUCTURAL (PERMANENT) DECLINE IN INNOVATION?

Strong evidence exists that the 2007–12 global economic and financial crisis may not be just another business cycle, albeit a very deep and difficult one, but may in fact reflect deep underlying structural problems, reflecting a secular (permanent) drop in productivity growth, in turn driven by declining TFP growth and declining innovation.

In his widely-discussed 2012 paper, and forthcoming book, Robert J. Gordon (2012) argues alarmingly that "future growth in consumption per capita" (for 99 percent of the US population) could fall below 0.5 percent a year for an extended period of decades" (p. 1). He cites six headwinds that afflict the USA (and, by extension, many other Western economies): "demography (aging populations), education (declines in the quality and quantity of human capital), inequality in the distribution of wealth and income, globalization, energy/environment and the overhang of consumer and government debt." These "headwinds" are in fact global in nature, as shown by the 2013 World Economic Forum Global Risk Report. Gordon claims that ". . . the rapid [economic] progress made over the past 250 years could well turn out to be a unique episode in human history. . . . Growth in the frontier [the technology-leading country – UK until 1906, USA afterwards] accelerated after 1750, reached a peak in the middle of the 20th century and has been slowing down since." Gordon explains that the Third Industrial Revolution, 1960 to the present, featuring computers, the web, mobile phones, created only a "short lived growth revival between 1996 and 2004", and was weak compared with the First (steam, railroads) and Second (electricity, internal combustion engines, communications, chemicals) Industrial Revolutions. Underlying this bleak picture is the secular decline of innovation – new products and services that change and enrich our lives.

Gordon's arguments are summarized in Figure I.1. He is supported by the findings of Professor Tyler Cowen (2011), who argues that the global financial crisis is making a deeper and more disturbing "Great Stagnation"; as *The Economist* summarizes, "for all its flat-screen dazzle and high-bandwidth pizzazz, it seemed that the world had run out of ideas".[2]

Declining Innovation

Underlying Gordon's worrisome research finding is evidence that the pace of innovation has slowed, perhaps permanently. Pierre Azoulay and Benjamin Jones (2006) have found that "The average R&D worker [in the US] adds only 15 percent as much to TFP in 2000 as the average R&D worker did in 1950. Why?" If the productivity of innovation investment itself has declined drastically, and is now 1/7 what it was two generations ago, it is inevitable that the innovation of productivity too will be dismal. Azoulay and Jones note that the share of resources allocated to R&D has risen by a third, since 1975, in the USA, to almost three percent of GDP, yet the results have met sharply diminishing returns. Many nations seek to expand R&D investment; yet if that investment itself is becom-

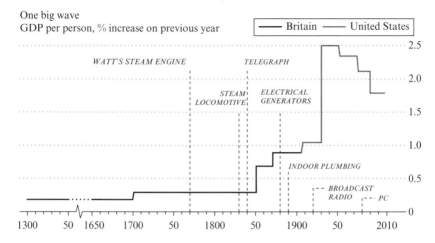

One big wave
GDP per person, % increase on previous year

Britain ——— United States

Source: Robert Gordon, "Is US Economic Growth Over?", NBER Working Paper, 2012,
The Economist.

Figure I.1 Growth in GDP per capita, 1300–2012, in the US and Britain

ing less productive, the result will not be the desired increase in fruitful innovation.

We can confront these research findings with our own pragmatic observations. The speed of traffic has barely increased in the past 60 years, and in city centers, it has greatly slowed. Supersonic air travel no longer exists. Life expectancy soared, as medical innovations prolonged life, but in the USA life expectancy of 78.4 years is just slightly above what it was in 1980. As a founder of PayPal once observed, instead of having flying cars, we have 140 characters (Twitter). And studies of individual self-assessed happiness show that happiness, if anything, has declined over the past decades (see White, 2007). Our own perception of wellbeing supports the claim that the fundamental drivers of wellbeing have stagnated.

The Theory of Stagnating Innovation

To this point, we have offered mainly empirical evidence supporting the concern that productivity growth, and the innovation that drives it, has declined structurally, not just cyclically, as a result of the 2008–12 global downturn. But is there solid economic theory that can explain this hypothesis?

According to Paul Romer (1987), in an influential paper published a generation ago, the decline in productivity growth is caused, perhaps, by Western companies offshoring their production to Asia. Once, rising wages forced companies to innovate, seeking labor-saving innovations to boost productivity and offset higher labor costs. But when inexpensive nearly-inexhaustible labor is available abroad, this incentive disappears. This theory was proposed long before offshoring became predominant. As Romer summarizes his theory, "an increase in the rate of growth of labor will be accompanied by a fall in the rate of growth of labor productivity" (Romer, 1987, p. 198). This may be true, even if the expanded labor supply is in another nation with which a country trades.

A related theory was put forward by MIT Professor Paul Samuelson, in 2004. Samuelson's paper showed that technical progress in a developing country such as China had the potential to reduce welfare in the US. Samuelson's model refutes the universal principle of comparative advantage, which states that all nations gain from free trade. He does this by creating a dynamic model in which China, say, specializes in an industry characterized by rapid productivity gains, and exports the fruits to, say, the USA; China thus captures the benefits of productivity growth, at America's expense. This in part is precisely what has happened. In a sense, at least theoretically, America has exported its productivity gains, and the underlying innovation in production systems driving it, to China. Gordon (2012, p. 15) shows that USA output per hour of $53.70 in 2012 (in 2005 prices) was 60 percent lower than it would have been (i.e. $83.30), had the growth rate of productivity (output per hour) for 1948–72 prevailed in the period 1972–2012, in place of the much lower actual growth rate.

Some economists have argued that in the long run, this negative impact on productivity will be self-correcting, as wages rise in the offshore low-skill producing countries and makes innovation at home more attractive (see Acemoglu, Gancia and Zilibotti, 2012). There is some evidence that this is indeed occurring in China, where wages are indeed rising. But the result has not been to stimulate innovation in the West. Instead, other developing countries (Vietnam, Thailand, Burma, Sri Lanka) have taken China's place at the bottom of the low-wage, low-skill value chain. There is an enormous amount of low-skilled labor that can be exploited in the emerging market nations, before Western countries and companies are pressed to the wall and forced to again seek labor-saving productivity-generating innovations.

Another secular cause of declining innovation, often cited, is that of the changing role of government and globalization. Globalization, and the accompanying rapid expansion of trade between East and West, created a massive imbalance, in which high-saving developing nations exported to low-saving Western nations, creating massive trade deficits in the US in particular, and then lent their savings to the West to enable them to continue to purchase their goods, thus sustaining and deepening the trade deficits. This imbalance ultimately collapsed, in the 2008–12 crisis, as it inevitably had to. It has led to a demand for "rebalancing", which will require a shift in emerging market nations in Asia from saving to consumption, to replace some of their exports, with a proportional and similar shift in the West from consumption to saving, to reduce their borrowing needs from Asia. Since a major source of dissaving in the West lies in government deficits, any rebalancing will require a major shrinkage in the amounts of demand injected by government budgets and a corresponding reduction in the role of government. Some see this as another cause of declining innovation. The stirring address of President John F. Kennedy, in 1962, at Rice University, announcing that "[America] will go to the moon" inspired a generation of young people to study science and engineering. In an age of austerity and shrinking government budgets, we are unlikely to see any similar project like Apollo, which led to a wave of innovation driven by those inspired by it.

CONCLUSION

Economists are notoriously poor at predicting the future. It may well be that the theory and evidence marshaled by some of this generation's leading economists, suggesting that innovation and the resulting growth in productivity may be in permanent long-term structural decline, is completely wrong. But the theory and the empirical evidence are sufficiently reasonable and strong to cause major concern.

The world's innovation machine, which drove three industrial revolutions and generated unprecedented increases in per capita income and consumption, first in Western nations and later and more recently, in emerging market developing countries, may be broken. It is no longer generating the breakthrough change-the-world innovations that it once did.

If the innovation is broken, it needs to be repaired. But how? Repairing a machine requires first that we understand fully how it works. The starting point, then, must be to take a fresh look at the innovation process, by defining and mapping national innovation ecosystems. In Chapter 1, we turn to defining and describing what we mean by innovation ecosystems, and then, in Chapter 2, we show how to visually create and map them.

NOTES

1. A.C. Pigou, *The Economics of Welfare* (4th edition, 1932) online, Library of Economics, accessed 19 February 2014 at http://en.wikiquote.org/wiki/Arthur_Cecil_Pigou: "When a man sets out upon any course of inquiry, the object of his search may be either light or fruit – either knowledge for its own sake or knowledge for the sake of good things to which it leads", p. 3.
2. "Has the Ideas Machine Broken Down?", *The Economist*, 12 January 2013, accessed 19 February 2014 at www.economist.com/news/briefing/21569381-idea-innovation-and-new-technology-have-stopped-driving-growth-getting-increasing.

1. Towards a national innovation system

We concluded the Preface with the rather sweeping statement that according to many experts, the world innovation system is broken. To deepen our understanding of this crucial issue, it is necessary to explore national innovation systems, since it is at the national level that the most important pro-innovation policies are shaped. But what *is* a national innovation ecosystem?

We begin by defining the general term "ecosystem", and then proceed to examine the special case of national *innovation* ecosystems. We shall review the research literature, stressing research that takes a systems approach to innovation.

ECOSYSTEM: ORIGIN AND DEFINITION

The term "ecosystem" was championed by a British botanist, Arthur Tansley, who later became interested in the psychological theories of Sigmund Freud, seeing strong resemblance between the ecosystems of nature and the brain itself. Systems thinking then moved in two directions. The science of cybernetics, or self-regulating systems, was developed by Norbert Wiener (1961), and became the forerunner of modern computer science. The science of system dynamics was developed by MIT Electrical Engineer Jay Forrester (1958), who perceived that businesses, economies, even the whole world, are all systems of feedback loops that can be modeled and understood as analogous to electrical diagrams with feedback loops. System dynamics was used by Meadows et al. (1972) in the book *The Limits to Growth*, to show why unrestrained economic growth in the world economy could not be sustained.

In his comprehensive textbook *Business Dynamics*, Sterman (2000) shows how complex businesses can be fruitfully modeled as a system of interdependent feedback loops. Countries, too, are businesses, and the innovation aspects of national business systems can also be fruitfully modeled using system dynamics (see *Systems of Innovation: Technologies, Institutions and Organizations*, Edquist (1997)).

In its 1997 report on "National Innovation Systems", the OECD (Organisation for Economic Co-operation and Development) notes:

> The national innovation systems approach stresses that the flows of technology and information among people, enterprises and institutions are key to the innovative process. Innovation and technology development are the result of a complex set of relationships among actors in the system, which includes enterprises, universities and government research institutes. For policy-makers, *an understanding of the national innovation system can help identify leverage points for enhancing innovative performance and overall competitiveness.* It can assist in pinpointing mismatches within the system, both among institutions and in relation to government policies, which can thwart technology development and innovation. Policies which seek to improve networking among the actors and institutions in the system and which aim at enhancing the innovative capacity of firms, particularly their ability to identify and absorb technologies, are most valuable in this context. (Executive summary, p. 1)

Innovation policy often focuses single-mindedly on supply-side elements – changes in the supply of innovation infrastructure, resources and capabilities. This can easily lead to neglect of key demand-side and demand-driven innovation. At the extreme, massive supply-side intervention can be inimical to open-market demand-driven innovation. Any innovation ecosystem must take this into account. Maital and Seshadri (2012) observe that successful innovation is not, as is commonly assumed, primarily a matter of creative ideas and inventions, but is principally a result of effective operational implementation of those ideas, using creative business designs. A key part of such implementation is the focus on identifying market needs and wants, and listening to marketplace preferences throughout the innovation process.

Bottazzi and Peri (1999) and Edler and Georghiou (2007) note rightly that demand-side aspects of innovation have been somewhat neglected. Etzkowitz and Leydesdorff (2000) show the importance of innovation dynamics. Kuhlmann (2001) and Jänicke and Jacob (2004) examine the key role of governments in innovation policy and examine how this role is rapidly changing in Europe. These studies provide a strong basis for further research on demand-driven innovation policies, based on a clear visual map of innovation dynamics for each country under study.

There have been several strong efforts to define and model national innovation ecosystems. One definition of "national innovation system" is that of Freeman (1987, Box 1, p. 1): ". . . the network of institutions in the public and private sectors whose activities and interactions initiate, import, modify and diffuse new technologies." An alternate definition is given by Metcalfe (1995, cited in UNCTAD, 2008, p. 3): ". . . that set of distinct institutions which jointly and individually contribute to the development and diffusion of new technologies and which provides the framework within which governments form and implement policies to influence the innovation process. As such it is a system of interconnected institutions to create, store and transfer the knowledge, skills and artifacts which define new technologies."

Niosi et al. in 1993, made a strong effort to provide "semantic content, theoretical basis and methodological dimensions" to the notion of a national innovation system (NIS). Their study is one of the earliest to attempt to define "national innovation systems" operationally. A NIS is defined as a complex network of institutions, in which the output of one institution serves as inputs for another, and is comprised of a series of sub-systems. It is a national system in which private firms and government bodies interact and cooperate, to fund and encourage research and innovative technology and products. Niosi et al. recognize that focusing on NISs, in the age of globalization, may introduce a too-narrow perspective. A major strength of this article is the list of operational measures for quantifying national systems. They show how we might measure the number and size and centralization of innovation intuitions, along with the flows of finance, technology, knowledge, and commercial and political relations among them. A creative part of the essay is the section showing how a variety of disciplines might be employed in studying NISs, including thermodynamics, and organizational theory.

Deborah J. Jackson (undated), a National Science Foundation (NSF) researcher wrote an early paper for the NSF, defining an "innovation ecosystem". In her working paper on NISs she identifies a fundamental paradox in innovation. The paradox is this: innovation is the result of the complex interaction among a large number of separate elements, involving industry, government and academe; successful innovation that generates income, wealth, exports and jobs depends on how well the system as a whole functions, and how well each individual element in the ecosystem supports the other elements. At the same time, it is vitally important that what Jackson calls "the research economy", driven in large part by academic research and by industry-academe cooperation, should be sufficiently independent from the "commercial economy" to retain autonomy and the freedom to explore research questions that do not necessarily emerge directly and immediately from marketplace needs.

In other words, the generally short-run driven commercial economy must be tightly linked to the long-run-driven research economy, yet at the same time insulated from it, to prevent short-term profit considerations from harming long-run research. We view this as one of several fundamental dilemmas characterizing supply-side and demand-side innovation.

A biological ecosystem is a complex set of relationships among living people and animals, habitat and resources, whose functional goal is to maintain an equilibrium sustaining state. An innovation ecosystem similarly reflects the relationships among firms, government bodies, universities, researchers, consumers, owners of capital, workers, whose goal is to drive technology development and innovation, with the goal of achieving sustained and sustainable growth and development through innovative products, services and processes (Jackson, p. 2).

An innovation ecosystem generates increased innovative output in two ways: Through an increase in the quantity of *inputs* (capital and labor) in the system, and through an improvement in the efficiency with which existing inputs are used to generate innovation *outputs*. There is evidence, dating from Solow (1957), that in general, nations grow wealthy not through accumulating physical and financial capital, as Marx argued, but through using existing capital with greater wisdom and creativity, as Nobel Laureates Theodore Schultz (University of Chicago), Gary Becker (University of Chicago) and especially Schumpeter (1942) argued. Innovation lives in both worlds; part of the innovation ecosystem requires large capital investments, and another part simply finds creative ways to use existing resources more productively. It will emerge that a crucial aspect of successful innovation ecosystems is not just the magnitude of the inputs and resources devoted to innovation, but the skill and efficiency with which they are used.

An important source of data that helped us greatly to understand the innovation ecosystem maps we and our experts created is that of the Global Innovation Index, compiled yearly for 141 countries by teams from INSEAD (a leading French business school) together with WIPO (World Intellectual Property Organization). This database provides detailed rankings for each country on almost 100 innovation sub-variables, compiled, ranked and weighted. Among the most interesting are weighted averages for "innovation output" and "innovation input". For example, among the innovation inputs are a variety of variables reflecting the amount and quality of human capital, resources for research, infrastructure and market sophistication. Among the innovation outputs are knowledge and technology outputs, such as patents, royalties, computer and service exports, etc. and creative outputs (trademarks, online creativity measured by domains, etc.). The ratio between innovation outputs and innovation inputs is the efficiency – the degree to which innovation inputs are used well to create innovative results. The results of this compilation for the innovation ecosystems we studied are shown below in Table 1.1.

Table 1.1 reveals that countries differ widely in the efficiency with

Table 1.1   Innovation efficiency

Country	Innovation Input	Innovation Output	Efficiency Ratio
Israel	61.5 (#17)	50.5 (#13)	0.8 (#38)
Poland	47.1 (#41)	33.6 (#50)	0.7 (#80)
Germany	58.8 (#23)	53.7 (#7)	0.9 (#110
France	59.1 (#22)	44.4 (#26)	0.8 (#64)
Canada	65.8 (#10)	48.0 (#20)	0.7 (#74)
Spain	56.0 (#26)	38.5 (#35)	0.7 (#87)
Singapore	74.9 (#1)	52.0 (#11)	0.7 (#83)
China	42.7 (#55)	48.1 (#19)	1.1 (#1)

Note: Material originally provided by the World Intellectual Property Organization (WIPO). The secretariat of WIPO assumes no liability or responsibility with regard to the transformation of this data.

Source: Global Innovation Index 2012, Fontainebleu, France: INSEAD, 2013. Innovation Scores (Rank # 141 nations).

which they use innovative inputs, and not only in the quantities of those inputs. China, for instance, ranks only 55th in the world in the quantities of innovation inputs that it invests. However, because China uses those inputs very efficiently, ranking number one in the world in efficiency (110 percent!). Just how and why China is so efficient in employing its innovation resources deserves further study. Consider France and Germany. France leads Germany in "innovation inputs", but trails Germany badly in "innovation output" (Germany ranks seventh, compared with 26th for France). This is clearly reflected in the relative innovative strengths of the two economies. Canada ranks quite high in innovation inputs, 10th, suggesting that its innovation problem is not one of resource scarcity but perhaps that of how it converts the inputs into innovative outputs (ranked 74th). Singapore, a nation with extremely deep pockets, ranks first in the world in innovation inputs but only 11th in innovation outputs. Here again, the data suggest the need to closely examine how innovation investments are made.

INNOVATION AND CAPITAL SHORTAGES

There is growing concern that the world faces a looming global shortage of capital (Dobbs, Lund and Schreiner, 2011). A McKinsey report notes that "Surging [global] demand for capital, led by developing economies, could put upward pressure on interest rates and crowd out some investment"

(Dobbs et al., 2011, p. 2). If this is so, growing importance will attach to those aspects of growth and development that do not require additional capital resources. For this reason alone, innovation policies are of growing importance. It will be vital for nations to use existing "innovation capital" more efficiently, as Table 1.1 suggests. But how?

An initial first step toward focused effective pro-innovation policies, adapted to the new global environment of increasingly-scarce capital and deficit-ridden government budgets, is to model each nation's innovation ecosystem, to fully understand its components and their interaction. The global business environment is characterized by "the dizzying effects of accelerating change" (Sterman, 2000, p. 3). A partial equilibrium approach to innovation policy runs the risk of embracing what appears to be sound logic, in strengthening a key part of the innovation system, resulting in unexpected, possibly disastrous counter-intuitive effects that achieve precisely the opposite, because the interactive feedback effects were ignored. An example could be the following: Universities, strapped for research funds, might rely increasingly on industry funding, which allegedly improves the links between basic research and market demand, but in fact severely damages the quality and quantity of basic research that drives innovative success in the long run.

The theory of demand-driven innovation can be said to date back to Adam Smith's masterpiece *The Wealth of Nations* (1776). In it, Smith made the widely-quoted (and even more widely-misunderstood) observation regarding the so-called "invisible hand" of free-market competition:

> Every individual endeavors to employ his capital so that its produce may be of greatest value. He generally neither intends to promote the public interest, nor knows how much he is promoting it. He intends only his own security, his own gain. And he is in this led by an invisible hand to promote an end which was no part of his intention. By pursuing his own interest he frequently promotes that of society more effectually than when he really intends to promote it. (Book IV, Ch. II, p. 456)

The Smithian dilemma, in the context of pro-innovation policy, is: *How can policy-makers strengthen the innovation ecosystem, and improve its efficiency, without hampering the intellectual freedom so vital for innovators, and so crucial to the smooth workings of the "invisible hand"?* We believe that an accurate innovation ecosystem map can help avoid policy errors, and help identify creative pro-innovation policies that work well both for individual researchers and for society as a whole. A key issue, a very difficult one, is: How can basic research driven by the curiosity of individual researchers be leveraged to build innovations that meet real human needs and wants (demand-side innovation), without restricting it so much that the energy driving such research (curiosity, freedom, initiative) is diminished or destroyed?

CASE STUDIES: CREATING AN INNOVATIVE ECOSYSTEM

Some of the most valuable innovations in creating and harvesting innovations come from industry, where companies live and die by their ability to bring successful novel products and services to market quickly and efficiently.

Procter and Gamble

Procter and Gamble is a multinational manufacturer of product ranges including personal care, household cleaning, laundry detergents, prescription drugs and disposable diapers. Its legendary former CEO Arthur G. Lafley, who retired in 2010, pondered the issue of innovation efficiency in his firm; his research and development (R&D) group employed 7000 scientists and engineers, many with PhDs, more PhDs than several universities combined. Lafley reasoned that for each of his 7000 brilliant scientists, there were at least 1000 other equally-qualified scientists somewhere in the world, in that specific field. Why then harvest ideas from one person when you could, perhaps, harvest ideas from 1000 more? We will henceforth, Lafley announced, abandon "Not Invented Here" (NIH, a destructive part of many companies' cultures, in which anything not dreamed up within the company is prima facie rejected), and replace it with "Proudly Found Elsewhere" (PFE – use the Procter and Gamble (P&G) network to disseminate challenging problems and find solutions anywhere and everywhere). One of the first fruits of this policy was a method for printing on cakes and on Pringles potato chips. The cake-printing method was found in Italy; an Italian scientist had as a hobby developed a method for printing on cakes. Someone at P&G had the idea of printing cartoons and puzzles on potato chips; but how – potato chips are notoriously delicate. The solution was quickly found elsewhere, saving P&G money and more important, a great deal of time. Lafley had created a new innovation ecosystem for P&G, one that utilized networking, creating a far more powerful and efficient R&D system for the company.[1]

Eli Lilly

Eli Lilly is a global pharmaceutical company. In the late 1990s, Lilly's business was booming. But Alpheus Bingham, a vice president, was worried. The company was making large profits from its blockbuster drug Prozac, but huge investments in innovation, to find the next blockbuster drug, were yielding nothing. The Lilly R&D ecosystem was becoming increasingly inefficient. What was worse was the system's unpredictability. Bingham could not manage the system because he had no idea when solutions would be found to pressing challenges. Nor could anyone tell him. Bingham did not know if he was assigning the right person to work on given problems. He reached a radical conclusion: Ask everyone the question – not only within the company, but outside it. Make the challenges public! For a drug company accustomed to super-secrecy, this was a radical innovation indeed. The result was a website called InnoCentive, launched in June 2001. Eli Lilly posted its hardest scientific problems online and attached a monetary reward to each problem. The solver got the reward. The initial results were zero. But after a few weeks, solutions began to be submitted. "The creativity was simply astonishing," Bingham noted. After a year of operation, the website had become an essential R&D tool for Eli Lilly. By 2003, it was so successful that the website was spun off from the company and began accepting challenges from other R&D-intensive companies, including General Electric and Procter and Gamble. An example of a solved challenge is one posed by Colgate Palmolive. For years the company had injected fluoride dust into its toothpaste tubes with forced air, which sent plumes of dangerous fluoride into the factory's air. A particle physicist named Ed Melcarek quickly solved the problem, even though it had plagued Colgate for years. He suggested simply that the plastic toothpaste tube be grounded, while the fluoride dust be given an electric charge. The fluoride dust would be attracted directly to the tube, like the plus and minus poles of magnets. (A similar technology is used to paint cars; the car itself is charged, the paint has magnetic particles of an opposite charge, and the paint is magnetically drawn to the car's surface evenly and quickly.)[2]

What these cases show is that innovation ecosystems can indeed be innovated themselves. Of course, doing so for an entire nation is many orders of magnitude more difficult.

INNOVATION AND ABANDONMENT

An additional dilemma, as severe as the freedom versus discipline issue and common to many innovation ecosystems, is what management consultant Peter Drucker, cited in Edersheim (2006), terms "innovation and abandonment", i.e. in order for systems to grow and develop, the processes of birth (of ideas) must be accompanied by a process of abandonment and death (elimination of entities that consume resources without contributing to innovation and wellbeing). An innovation ecosystem must contain elements that show what parts of the system must be abandoned, and not only what parts must be created. Birth without death soon results in ecological disaster through "overcrowding". This key element of innovation was also emphasized in the writings of Schumpeter (1942), who called it "creative destruction".

Valley of Death

A key element of innovation ecosystems involves Type I and Type II errors. In Type II errors, technologies that should rightly "die" in fact are heavily funded, futilely; and in Type I errors, technologies that should develop instead unjustly "die", owing to lack of funds. Jackson terms Type I errors the "Valley of Death" – the gap between basic research funded largely by government and commercial development funded by industry (see Figure 1.1). The ability of an innovation ecosystem to avoid both Type I and Type II errors is crucial. Often, success in navigating through the Valley of Death relates to how supply-side and demand-side innovation is integrated. As Jackson (undated) notes (p. 8):

> In Figure 1, the innovation spectrum shows the distribution of resources invested in activities aimed at discovery, technology demonstration, technology development, and commercialization. At the far left of the spectrum (i.e. where academic research is concentrated), there is a heavy concentration of government investment in fundamental research; while to the far right of the spectrum (i.e. in the commercial marketplace) there is a much higher level of industry investment in direct product development. This gap in resources for technology demonstration and development (TD&D) is colloquially known as the Valley of Death. The actors engaged in moving innovations from discovery through commercialization are academia, small businesses, the investor community, and commercial industry. For these actors, it is within this valley that many potential innovations die for lack of the resources to develop them to a stage where industry or the investor community can recognize their commercial potential and assess the risk associated with bringing them to market.

To address at least some of these key issues and dilemmas, we have developed an empirical evidence-based method that generates a visual tool useful for creating a common foundation for policy debate. Without this foundation, all too often innovation policy discussions become dialogues

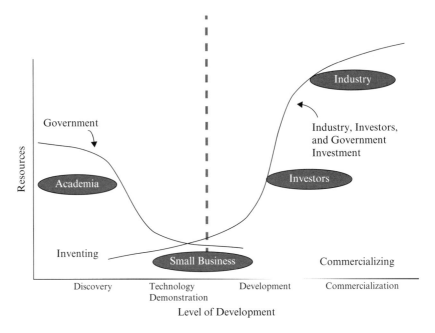

Source: Jackson (undated) based on research by Angus Klingon, Brown University, Providence, Rhode Island, USA.

Figure 1.1   The "Valley of Death" between "discovery" and "invention"

of the deaf, featuring individual agendas and personal interests, with no common agreement on a set of innovation ecosystem facts.

The process of shaping effective policy follows a well-defined pattern. First, analysis – define "what is", by analyzing the existing situation. Second, objectives – define "what ought to be", by setting future objectives. Third, gap analysis – where are there gaps between what is and what will be attained if the current situation continues, and what ought to be, and how can those gaps be closed?

For innovation policy, the process of analyzing "what is" is a highly complex one, because innovation is the result of complex ecosystems involving a wide variety of variables. Yet unless the innovation ecosystem is well understood, effective policy measures cannot be devised. Moreover, such ecosystems have many components, related to history, culture, legal and regulatory frameworks, education, science, and finance, thus are country-specific, in large part unique to national systems. The components are interrelated in complex ways. In most countries, innovation policies are fragmented, driven by individual government ministries and other organizations, each of which are well-meaning, but fail to achieve, and act on, a fundamental integrated big-picture view of the problem.

In this perspective, in applying our methodology to visualizing innovation ecosystems (described in Chapter 2), we identified four key dimensions of innovation that build a generic innovation ecosystem. These are:

- culture;
- markets;
- context (including infrastructure); and
- institutions (including regulations).

We will now turn to describe them in a broader manner and to summarize some of the relevant research literature.[3]

CULTURE DIMENSION

The simplest definition of culture is "shared values", about what a society believes is important and valuable. That definition suggests prima facie that culture is strongly linked with entrepreneurship, partitioning nations between those for whom innovation is important and valued and those for whom it is less so. Guiso et al. (2006, p. 23) defined culture as "those customary beliefs and values that ethnic, religious, and social groups transmit fairly unchanged from generation to generation". This definition reinforces the transmission of entrepreneurship across generations. Kreiser et al. (2010) use data from 1048 firms in six countries to assess the impact of national culture on entrepreneurship, and focus on a key aspect of culture, that of risk-taking among SMEs. In his epic book, Landes (1998), an economic historian, uses culture to explain income differences among nations.

Management guru Peter Drucker once said famously, paraphrasing Charles Darwin, that the organizations that compete best in competitive environments are those that learn the fastest to adapt to changing circumstances (Maital and Seshadri, 2012, p. 345). Lundvall et al. (1994) emphasize the key role of the value of "learning". The ability to learn plays a key role in understanding cultural differences regarding innovation. Scholars who use culture and other factors to explain cross-country differences in high-tech industry include Chen (2008), to explain differences in entrepreneurship, Ardagna et al. (2008) and in adoption of information and computer technology (ICT), Erumban et al. (2006). The latter find (p. 307) "that national culture and ICT adoption rate are closely related". Power distance dimension (refers to the inequality of the distribution of power in a country) and uncertainty avoidance dimensions (the degree to which members of a society feel uncomfortable with uncertainty and ambiguity) are the most significant cultural factors by which some of the differences in ICT adoption rates among countries can be explained. The research on the role of culture (shared values) should be balanced by noting that often, entrepreneurs have unique personality traits that shape how they behave (Nga et al., 2010).

Many multinational firms have R&D centers outside their home country. The impact of different cultures on R&D performance has, according to Ambos and Schlegelmilch (2008), not been sufficiently researched. The authors, in this study, define two types of R&D activities, and link each to culture: (a) capability exploiting; and (b) capability augment. The former is defined as abilities linked to later stages of development, after initial breakthroughs; the latter is defined as capabilities that contribute to breakthrough developments. They link these two R&D activities to five measured and measurable cultural dimensions, derived from Hofstede (1994): power distance, collectivism-individualism, masculinity-femininity, uncertainty avoidance and long-term orientation. The authors conclude that national culture must be taken into account when managing global R&D activities; the interaction between the culture of the home country and the culture of the country in which the R&D center is based cannot be ignored. Within this context a study by Schein (1996) similarly focuses on the clash between three cultures – engineers, managers and operators – which further complicate the organizational difficulty arising from clashes of national cultures.

The pioneering work of Hofstede, built on grounded (field-based) theory, merits further explanation. Hofstede et al. (2010) deepened our understanding of culture and its role in management by quantifying five key cultural dimensions. Individual/collective measures how people live and work in groups or each chooses his or her own path; it measures how and whether individual achievement is highly valued. Masculinity measures masculine traits in the culture, like aggression, competitiveness and materialism. Uncertainty avoidance measures how people react to uncertainty and risk. Long-term/short-term measures whether people focus on immediate, short-term gratification or are patient and seek long-term reward. Finally, power distance measures the extent to which society is rigidly hierarchical, with highly perceived distance between those at the top and at the bottom, or "flat", where people perceive they can interact with and communicate with those in control, no matter where they are in the hierarchy.

Measuring Cultural Dimensions

It is clear just from the description of these key dimensions that they are highly relevant for innovation and innovation policy. For example, Israel has very low power distance. It leads engineers to continually innovate by challenging authority, and often, to start their own business when their ideas are unheeded. Power distance, according to Hofstede, scores only 40 in the USA, and 30 in the UK, compared with 80 in China and 77 in India. This explains in part why America has "garage entrepreneurship", for example in the Silicon Valley, while Asian nations probably need to foster innovation far differently, within the hierarchical organization. Asian cultures score high on long-term orientation (China scores 95; Japan, 80; India, 61; the Asian average is 85; the world average is 48, while the USA scores 30 and Britain and Canada, around 20); this partly explains Asia's high saving rate and indicates why Asian innovators are more patient in working on long-term projects. Impatience may explain entrepreneurial urgency in the West, but failure in longer-term projects. Innovation is risky; we would expect uncertainty avoidance to be closely linked to it. Japan scores 90 on this dimension, indicating one reason why few Japanese take entrepreneurial risk. China scores a low 35, with the world average at 65. The USA is 46, and Britain, 30. Europe has a high average of 74, indicating overall, an aversion to uncertainty (and perhaps the risk attendant on innovation).

It is very important to understand how these findings should be interpreted and applied. Culture is essentially a "given". To some degree, company culture can be shaped, but perhaps less than many companies pretend. Nor should value judgments, "good" and "bad", be attached to cultural dimensions. They are simply there, like body height and eye color. However, in order to "fit" innovation policy to a nation's ecosystem, it is important to understand the nature of a nation's culture and the constraints and opportunities it provides. Some countries have sought to imitate America's Silicon Valley garage entrepreneurship, and utterly failed. These efforts are misguided, because this type of innovation is simply unsuited to countries with high power distance and high uncertainty aversion. There are better and different ways to foster innovation, within a realistic perspective of the nation's culture and its key elements. Singaporean innovative culture, as we will see, thrives in the context of organizations, hierarchy, direction, planning and control. Such a system would probably strangle the entrepreneurial drive in America and in Israel. Of course, the central critique of Hofstede – that not all individuals who belong to a culture are alike – is valid. People in each national culture differ widely. But there still is value in identifying central tendencies and measuring them, even though they vary around the mean. All research contains some short sentences; and, to paraphrase the famed economist Alfred Marshall, "every short sentence on economics is inherently untrue", a dictum that extends well beyond economics.

It will be seen later that one of our main findings is that in every national and regional ecosystem we mapped, the culture dimension plays a key role, but in very different ways. It will emerge later in this book that culture is a highly significant component of every national innovation ecosystem, with cultural forces working both for and against innovation. This is to be expected. In the end, innovation is generated by individuals who take risks, sometimes considerable ones, to create novelty. The culture of risk-taking and creativity, can drive this process forward or hold it back. Culture is often regarded as a given in society; but it can be sometimes shaped and altered, by, for instance, the existence of narratives, or stories, in which people recount how bold innovators tackle major challenges, take large risks and create world-changing value when they succeed.

A key aspect of many national innovation ecosystems is the link between culture and the creation of human capital. In her new book, Jin Li (2012) shows how widely learning and learning models differ across countries (Taiwan, Hong Kong, USA, Israel, Germany), depending on the culture. Again, imitating an educational model successful in the USA may fail when implemented in Asia. Western learning is Socratian. Asian learning is, in some places, Confucian. Li notes that Westerners emphasize the "Aha!" moment of sudden insight (Archimedes shouted, "Eureka!" in his bath, goes the legend, when he saw the Archimedean principle of displacement). The Chinese are far more likely to stress the arduous patient accumulation of learning. Western universities stress pride in achievement; Chinese schools stress humility and modesty. Western students sometimes work harder after praise; Chinese and Asian students, sometimes, work less hard after perceived humiliation. It is true that China has enrolled more than six million university undergraduate students in 2009, more than the EU, USA and Japan combined. They may learn Western science, but probably in different ways than students in the West. For these and many other reasons, China cannot, and is not, imitating the Western style and framework of innovation.

MARKET DIMENSION

This dimension covers aspects of innovation that relate to how the forces of demand interact in the marketplace, including the forces of competition. Research on the market dimension reveals a variety of ways in which innovative businesses and startups can determine the existence of unmet needs and wants, define those wants, and seek ways to satisfy them in a sustained profitable manner. It includes research to help less-developed nations, where market forces are less powerful, strengthen their demand-driven innovation.

Saviotti and Pyka (2011) build a model showing how widening development gaps among countries emerge when countries face entry barriers that hamper efforts to imitate advanced countries' technologies. The role of co-opetition (collaboration with competitors, for instance in R&D) is the topic of another study that found that the more that a technological change makes the capabilities of a firm's suppliers or customers obsolescent, the less well the firm performs (Afuah, 2000). This underscores the importance of using the network as the lens when exploring the impact of a technological change on firm competitive advantage. In that case Afuah concludes: "a firm that is sufficiently short-sighted to emphasize only the effect of technological change on its own abilities can lose a competitive advantage that it gains from its relations with collaborators ('co-opetitors')" (p. 399).

Aghion et al. (2005) find a complex U-shaped relationship between competition and innovation. They have three main findings. First, when product market competition is low, there is what they call an "escape-competition" effect. Second, at higher levels of "neck-and-neck" product market competition, an inverted U-shaped curve exists for industries, which is steeper the higher the level of competition; and third, firms facing the threat of bankruptcy face greater "escape-competition" and hence, on average, are more innovative.

Edler (2007) provides a useful definition of demand-led innovation policy, as a "set of public measures to increase the demand for innovations, to improve the conditions for the uptake of innovations or to improve the articulation of demand in order to spur innovations and the diffusion of innovations" (p. 1). He explains that market failure makes demand-based policy necessary. Such failures include information asymmetries (buyers and sellers have different information), switching costs, and barriers to entry. Based on OECD work from the last ten years, Baland and Francois (1996) relate innovation to monopoly and poverty and provide a broad-brush overview about good policy practices for innovation and highlight recent changes in innovation processes and patterns.

Hansen and Birkinshaw (2006) explore the innovation value chain. They stress that in order to improve innovation, executives need to view the process of transforming ideas into commercial outputs as an integrated flow. They indicate three phases in the chain: generate ideas; convert ideas; or, more specifically, select ideas for funding and developing them into products or practices, and diffuse those products and practices. Mowery and Rosenberg (1979) provide researchers with an invaluable survey of empirical research on the link between market demand and innovation. They recommend that wise policies encourage: (a) interaction, between users and producers; (b) interactive interaction between basic and applied researchers; and (c) focus on provision of information.

Michael Porter's landmark book on competitive strategy (1990) presents his famous five-forces model for market dynamics. Jacob Schmookler (1966) and Joseph Schumpeter (1934) each provide sweeping book-length analyses of the role of inventions, and the role of innovation, respectively, in economic growth. Schumpeter places innovation at the focus of economic change, noting that economic change revolves around innovation, entrepreneurial activities, and market power. Schumpeter argued that innovation-originated market power (restraint of competition, in part through intellectual property) could create more economic value than Smith's "invisible hand" and price competition. According to Schumpeter, technological innovation often creates "temporary monopolies" which permit super-normal profits soon be competed away by rivals and imitators.

INSTITUTION DIMENSION

Institutions are defined as durable systems of established and embedded social rules and conventions that structure social interactions. In other words, institutions are the "rules of the game" that define the context in which innovation occurs. Some institutions are defined precisely, as laws and regulations, while others are unwritten and tacit. Institutions play a key role in the initiation and evolution of innovation.

How can regulation impact the market for innovations? Regulation may be employed to spur technological change for health, safety and environmental purposes as well as to implement a reconfiguration of the industrial process. In addition, regulation crucially shapes new markets for innovative products (Ashford, 1985; Blind, 2004).

The study on "red tape", an enemy of innovation, and its role in delaying entry into a market, defined red tape as the collection or sequence of forms and procedures required to gain bureaucratic approval for something, especially when oppressively complex. The term originates with the red ribbons used by governments to bind documents (Ciccone and Papaioannou, 2007). The study raised the question whether reducing bureaucratic red tape can encourage entrepreneurship and growth? The study examined 45 nations, using as a key independent variable – the time between registering a new company and entry to market, across 28 different industries. Among the main findings, was as expected, red tape in registering startups causing countries to lag in reacting to global trends. The authors suggest that reduction in bureaucratic red tape could possibly come at the expense of workers' rights. They examine this contention and find it has no basis – workers' rights are not enhanced by "red tape" and protection of workers' rights does not slow growth.

Freeman's classic book (1974) provides comprehensive analysis of pro-innovation policies and regulations. Later in 1995, he published an overview on the national system of innovation from a historical perspective and showed that historically there have been major differences between countries in the ways in which they have organized and sustained the development, introduction, improvement and diffusion of new products and processes within their national economies.

The Gallup Organisation (2009) has an "Innobarometer" providing useful survey data on innovation. Its report focuses on innovation spending, on the role of innovation in public procurement tenders, the effects of public policies and private initiatives to boost innovation, and other strategic trends. It provides information on characteristics of innovative enterprises, innovative activities, the role of R&D in innovation, innovation transfer and policy support for innovation. Lichtenthaler (2010) addresses the role of intellectual property, as opposed to open (unpatented) innovation. His results show that the corporate intellectual property portfolio constitutes a major determinant of opening up the innovation process. In 2005, Malerba took an evolutionary perspective in analyzing industrial innovation; evolutionary economics itself evolved from "institutional" economies, which stressed the role of rules, regulations and conventions.

Rosenberg (1969) provides a long historical perspective on "induced innovation". His classic widely-cited paper asks, why do firms and inventors decide to invent what they do? A widely-stated argument repeated for many decades is that firms try to invent technology to save labor when labor is dear, and to save capital when capital is dear. Rosenberg refutes this and provides three ways in which the day-to-day routine at a firm can focus attention on particular problems, thus resolving a firm's indifference about where to direct inventive activity. These ways are compulsion, avoidance of uncertainty/hold-up, and shocks.

Taylor et al. (2005) show how regulation of sulfur dioxide emissions induced technological innovation in the US. They claim that both regulation itself, and even the anticipation of regulation, can spur invention. However, technology-push tools are far less effective at promoting invention than are demand-pull tools. Moreover, tight stringent regulations can guide inventive activity along well-defined technology paths.

Suárez and Utterback (1995) and Utterback and Abernathy (1975) examine the role of innovation in determining which firms live or die, as well as the dynamics of product innovation in fluid uncertain environments. The results show that by employing a design technological evolution model that explicitly includes technology as a dynamic and strategic variable, our understanding of firms' survival potential and success increase, having important implications for the fate of firms entering an industry. Finally, Vossen (1999) links innovation to concentration and market power in industries and came to the conclusion that industrial concentration on R&D is accompanied by a decline in the efficiency, or effectiveness, of R&D spending. In concentrated industries, R&D spending is higher than in less-concentrated industries. However, innovative activity itself in concentrated industries is equal to, or less than those in less-concentrated industries.

CONTEXT DIMENSION

The context dimension refers to the scientific, technological and physical infrastructure in which innovation thrives, with "infrastructure" broadly interpreted to mean any framework that relates to innovative activity. Several studies dealt with this issue. Dumas (2008) examines the link between research and innovation, terming it "alchemy" and stressing the need for "catalytic rather than controlling" government intervention. Feller et al. (2002) survey how engineering research centers (ERC) sited in universities impact industrial innovation. Their study points to problematic continuation of industrial support for ERCs following the ending of NSF funding, when the maximum number of funding years under the program is reached.

Acworth (2008) coins the term "knowledge integration community" (KIC) to describe the interesting ecosystem surrounding the Cambridge University (UK) and Massachusetts Institute of Technology (MIT, in the USA) and concludes "it is something other university, government and industry-based research institutions could embark upon" (p. 1241). Under this approach, the two universities collaborated, through CMI (Cambridge-MIT Institute), to create what it called a KIC "Knowledge Integration Community". This approach arose, when Cambridge University approached MIT and sought to learn why and how MIT has been uniquely successful in collaborating with industry. Starting in 2003, seven such experimental communities were built. These communities involved complex systems for exchange of knowledge between faculty and industry, processes for review of findings, structures for decision-making and management, and mechanisms for supporting joint research activities. The author offers an interesting case study of a project comprising one of the KIC's, on the "Silent Aircraft" (an aircraft with vastly reduced noise levels, to overcome the problem of aircraft noise in urban airports). The conclusion is that the KIC model is one that other universities and countries could well adopt, after suitably adapting it for local conditions.

CONCLUSION: EUROPE AND AMERICA – PARALLEL DECLINES?

We conclude this chapter with an integrative case study of Europe and the European Union (EU) and the efforts of the Directorate-General for Research and Innovation of the European Commission, to spur EU innovation; and with a summary of a bleak report by The Task Force on American Innovation, a coalition of businesses, scientific and university organizations ("American Exceptionalism, American Decline? Research, the Knowledge Economy and the 21st Century Challenge", December 2012).

Europe

As we noted in the Preface, this book was inspired and partially funded by a Seventh Framework EU project and the research that underlies it was a collaborative effort between us, the authors, and research teams across Europe.[4]

A lengthy (765 pages) report titled "Innovation Union Competitiveness Report" was published by the European Commission in 2011. It takes a long hard look at the obstacles and challenges facing the EU in its efforts to spur innovation. In studying this report, we perceive that the overriding challenge for EU innovation policy (reflected in the title, "Innovation Union") is the existence of major differences across EU member countries in their innovation ecosystems and the huge challenge of shaping a common EU policy that works in them all, a "union". This challenge is no different, qualitatively, than similar challenges in creating a common currency union around the euro, a harmonized EU tax system or a harmonized set of labor laws. Here are some examples:

- The Report recognizes that total EU research investment rose by half between 1995 and 2008, but "performance was higher in the rest of the world" (p. 3). In other words, innovation inputs expanded faster abroad. By 2014, China will overtake the EU in intensity of

R&D expenditure, rising 30 times faster in China (9 percent yearly) compared with 0.3 percent in the EU. But even if the EU closed the resource gap, innovation outputs may not respond proportionately.

- More than half of the researchers in the EU work (54 percent) in the public sector, while in the USA China and Japan, a far higher proportion work in the private sector (80 percent, 69 percent and 73 percent, respectively) (p. 4).
- EU researchers generate 29 percent of world peer-reviewed publications, far ahead of the USA's 22 percent; yet a far higher proportion of USA publications are among those most-cited (p. 5), notes the Report.
- European Patent Office (EPO) patents relative to GDP have declined since 2000; and half the EU Member States do not generate high-tech EPO patents at all. The cost of filing an EPO patent is very high, up to 40 times higher than in the USA.
- The EU produces more than twice the number of doctorates than the USA in science and engineering. Yet the USA invests 2.5 times more than the EU (as a proportion of GDP) in higher education. The Report suggests, thus, that the EU may be "sacrificing quality for quantity" in higher education and may not be meeting "the expectations of the business sector" (p. 5). There is a rapid rise in the number of EU citizens gaining doctorates in the USA; many do not return.
- European SMEs invest more in R&D than in the USA but "do not grow sufficiently". Young SMEs are less innovative in the EU than in their USA counterparts.
- While the USA specializes in advanced high technology, the EU focuses on what may be called medium high tech (chemicals, electrical equipment, automobiles and parts), which has less research intensity and perhaps, less innovation. The Report calls for increases in the research intensity of EU industry.
- The EU lags behind the USA in health technologies, lags in the photovoltaic industry behind Asia and the USA, but leads in climate change patents.

What emerges from this exhaustive detailed Report is a highly complex picture, involving the European Commission (and its substantial budget), the EU innovation union, and national innovation ecosystems and innovation policies. It may be that the title of the Report itself is problematic. Is an Innovation Union truly feasible and possible in the EU? Can the diverse innovation ecosystems of the 27 member nations indeed be integrated into an Innovation Union? Is this merely a philosophical dream, or a practical goal? Can the challenges listed above as bullet points indeed be met, on an EU-wide basis?

United States

In 2005, a high-level group drawn from academe, science and industry published a report, titled "The Knowledge Economy: Is the United States Losing Its Competitive Edge?", which found that America's advantage in innovation is "rapidly eroding". A 2006 update expanded the benchmarks and found the erosion was ongoing. In 2012, the same Task Force completed and published a new report. It found that the "difficult economic and fiscal environment" was "challenging our nation's policymakers . . . There are strong indications that the health of the USA innovation system is faltering. . .". Among the key findings:

- First, the stagnation of the American K-12 education system and the inadequate numbers of USA students entering the STEM (science, technology, engineering, and mathematics) disciplines are threatening the nation's ability to recruit, train, and retain the scientists and engineers required to create new products and systems" (p. 2).
- "Years of boom-and-bust cycles of federal funding for scientific research have disrupted the ability of researchers to obtain funding for projects, scared away private sector investments, and sent a chilling signal to young people considering careers in STEM fields" (p. 3).
- "Since the 1960s, when the USA devoted 17 percent of the federal budget to R&D for agencies like NASA and DARPA, outlays have fallen to around nine percent of the discretionary budget" (p. 3).
- "The USA share of worldwide scientific publications and citations has declined. Europe has surpassed the USA in science and engineering publications, and Asia is rapidly catching up – Utility patents (issued for the invention of a new and useful process, machine, manufacture, or composition of matter, or a new and useful improvement) of foreign origin have surpassed patents of USA origin" (p. 3).
- "In 2009, the USA ranked 27th among developed nations in the proportion of college students receiving undergraduate degrees in science or engineering. China now produces nearly an equal number of natural science and engineering doctoral degrees compared to the USA, having increased from approximately 5000 in 1997 to over 20,000 in 2006. In 2007, China became second only to the USA in the estimated number of people engaged in scientific and engineering R&D" (p. 2).

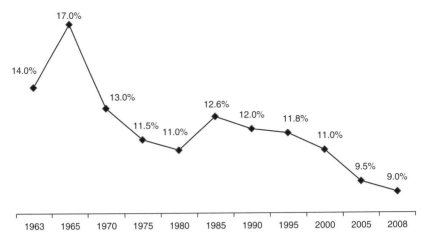

Source: Task Force on American Innovation (2012), p. 8.

Figure 1.2   USA's Federal R&D spending as percent of total discretionary spending 1963–2008

- "This report cites trends in international energy investments which demonstrate that the USA is ceding ground in energy innovation" (p. 3).

The Report notes that the "USA spent up to 17 percent of the national budget on R&D during the space race of the 1960s; in recent years, outlays have fallen to around nine percent of the federal discretionary budget" (p. 8) (see Figure 1.2).

Both the EU and US reports on innovation describe systemic failure. But these reports provide evidence on declining innovation inputs and outputs, without in-depth diagnoses and analyses regarding the innovation systems themselves. Is the problem mainly one of diminishing resources? Lack of interest in science and technology? Moribund educational systems? Are innovation inputs converted into outputs with declining efficiency? Why? What is the underlying source of the systemic failure, if indeed there is such failure?

To answer these questions, we believe it is helpful to visually map the system in which innovation is funded and created in each country, or major region. Such maps show, as the reader will learn, how very challenging the EU's Innovation Union concept is. Some political scientists believe that in a global age, when economic borders have been almost erased, the concept of the nation state is irrelevant. Yet national borders do reflect real borders of language, history and culture, and culture in particular, we found, impacts innovation. As a working hypothesis, it is reasonable to choose the nation state as our unit of analysis for studying innovation ecosystems.

We now proceed in Chapter 2 to describe our methodology.

NOTES

1. Source: S. Maital, D.V.R. Seshadri (2012), *Innovation Management* (2nd edn), Delhi: Sage, p. 477.
2. Source: Jonah Lehrer (2012), *Imagination: How Creativity Works*, New York: Houghton Mifflin, pp. 118–22.
3. For a fuller version, see our forthcoming paper: Amnon Frenkel, Shlomo Maital, Eran Leck and Emil Israel, "Demand-driven innovation: an integrative systems-based review of the literature", *International Journal of Innovation and Technology Management*.
4. The official title of the project is "PICK-ME: Policy Incentives for the Creation of Knowledge: Methods and Evidence (Demand Driven Innovation)". This Project is funded by the European Union under the Seventh Framework Programme.

2. Method for mapping innovation ecosystems

Countries poor at innovation are all unsuccessful, in the same way; countries good at innovation are good, each in its own way. (paraphrase of the opening sentence of Tolstoy, Anna Karenina)

BACKGROUND

William E. Kennard was chairman of America's FCC (Federal Communications Commission) in the late 1990s. He had a front-row seat to the commercialization of the Internet. What led to the birth of the Internet, one of the most important world-changing innovations of the twentieth century? He observes:

> ... DARPA (Defense Advanced Research Projects Agency) played a significant role in the Internet's development by funding initial research. But would the Internet revolution have occurred without a world-class higher-education system and California's networked universities and research institutions? Would the tech revolution have happened in the absence of a culture of risk-taking that fueled venture capital investment in start-up companies?[1]

He continues:

> Other essential ingredients were surely:
> - A telecom regulatory environment of restraint that gave the Internet space to grow;
> - Favorable personal and corporate tax structures, including a moratorium on online transaction sales tax;
> - ... an intellectual property system allowing entrepreneurs to profit from their software and content inventions;
> - ... a fluid labor market and favorable immigration [that] allowed technology companies to tap a global marketplace of talent.

Kennard notes that from 1995–2005, over half of Silicon Valley engineering and technology start-ups had one or more immigrants as key founders.

He concludes:

> Collectively, all these factors created an "innovation ecosystem" that nurtured the Internet's incredible expansion.

Silicon Valley and the Internet are not isolated examples, where an innovation ecosystem has generated world-changing industries and innovation revolutions: "Similar innovation clusters produced Scandinavia's amazing wireless revolution, Spain's burgeoning renewable energy industry, and the remarkable biotech cluster outside Boston." And, Kennard might have added, Israel's "Silicon Wadi" innovation machine that since 1990 has generated a mighty torrent of information and communications technology (ICT) innovations, both in software and in hardware.

What do these innovation ecosystems have in common?

> . . . an integrated well-function innovation ecosystem, where government policy has worked hand-in-hand with the private sector. The lesson is that innovation is a holistic process that cannot be supported by top-down government policies alone, it must also be driven from the bottom up with business and communities leading the way. (Kennard, 2010)

What we learn from Kennard's observations is this: To understand how and why innovation revolutions happen, it is necessary to understand the underlying innovation ecosystem that generated them. These ecosystems have many components, related to history, culture, legal and regulatory frameworks, education, science, and finance. The components are interrelated in complex ways. In most countries, innovation policies are fragmented, driven by individual government ministries and other organizations, each of which are well-meaning, but fail to achieve and act on a fundamental integrated big-picture view of the problem.

The situation recalls the fable of the blind persons and the elephant. Each blind person pictured the elephant differently, depending on the part of the elephant they were able to touch. None were able to envision the elephant as a whole. This, we believe, reflects current policy discussions on innovation, as Kennard suggests. To shape effective innovation policy, suitably tailored for each country's unique innovation ecosystem, it is vital first to understand and map that system.

Some of the components of the innovation system are vital to the smooth functioning of the system – their presence and functioning are "necessary conditions". Other components are "nice to have", but not essential. For every nation, it is crucial to understand how its innovation ecosystem works, what the components are, and how they interact, as a first step to analyzing how to make the system work much better through policy change. Preferably, this innovation ecosystem should be a "visual innovation map", to facilitate reaching a common understanding among all the key players who seek to reinvent and modernize the system, in light of rapid changes occurring in global markets, in technology and in society. What is needed is a powerful methodology that will reveal the underlying dynamics of innovation, in the context of a national ecosystem, simplify it and organize it, and present it visually, so that there will be a common basis of understanding for effective policy discussions and debate. Accordingly we developed a method of mapping innovation ecosystems that enable us to compare and contrast innovation systems, at once tailoring a policy to individual nations' needs and at the same time adapting suitable, proven effective innovation policies from one nation and implementing them, with changes, in another.

The fundamental axiom on which our methodology is based is this: In innovation, particularly in demand-driven innovation, one size never fits all. Innovation is driven, or hampered, by underlying cultural factors, and these factors differ widely across countries. Many countries, in pursuing innovation policies, have in the past sought to import other nations' eco-systems, for instance, Silicon Valley (USA). Indeed, some continue to do this. This has proved ineffective. It is time to treat innovation as a finger-print, unique to each nation, and not as a one-size fits all approach.

Some, All, None

> Innovation ecosystems for a country are like no other country, like some other countries, and like all other countries.

This quote is a paraphrase of a famous saying by an anthropologist, Clyde Kluckhohn: "Each person is like all other persons, some other persons, and no other person."[2]

This provides another, alternate way to look at the issue of innovation ecosystems (see Figure 2.1).

Every country has a given number of innovation "drivers" – processes and capabilities that underlie its innovation success. Some of those drivers are unique to this country, and are shared with no other country. Some of them are shared with some other countries. And some are common to all countries engaged in innovation.

In order to fully understand the innovation ecosystem of a group of countries, to compare and contrast them, with a view to shaping effective innovation policies, it is important to understand what each country's innovation drivers are, and which of them are shared with other nations.

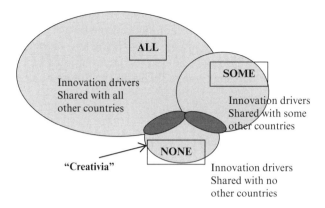

Figure 2.1   Innovation drivers for country "Creativia"

We can then compare and contract innovation ecosystem maps, as a tool for effective differential best-practice benchmarking: What does Country X excel at in innovation that other nations can adapt? What does Country X not excel at in innovation that needs strengthening and perhaps can be helped by studying other countries' innovation ecosystems?

For this purpose we have developed an innovative methodology to create "visual innovation ecosystem maps", applicable to any country and region, to facilitate cross-country/region comparisons. It distinguishes between innovation drivers based mainly on the demand (marketplace) side, and those based mainly on the supply (policy and infrastructure) side.

THE INNOVATION ECOSYSTEM VISUALIZATION MAP METHODOLOGY

This section describes a process for collaborative discussion among experts from various realms and disciplines, in order to "map" the innovation ecosystem. Our goal is to employ this map to guide policy decisions that are system-wide and exploit synergies, to achieve agreed goals and to implement a common vision. This systemic approach stands in contrast to partial approaches, in which emphasis is placed on specific aspects of the innovation ecosystem, without properly mapping or understanding the system as a whole and how its various parts interact with one another. The objective of the process described here is to achieve a visual representation of the innovation ecosystem, simple enough to grasp easily, but complex enough to capture the key elements, as a common foundation or "language" for enlightened discussion of policy. We seek to define a process that can be used in each nation or region, on the assumption that innovation ecosystems have common elements across countries and regions, but some very different elements specific to each place.

The process for gathering basic data on each nation's innovation ecosystem, and then analyzing them, adhered to the following steps.

A.   Experts Workshop

The objective of the Experts Workshop is to identify fundamental "anchors" and "processes" that comprise the main elements of a country/ region's innovation ecosystem. Here are the definitions of these two key concepts:

- "Quality anchors": these are strengths, or core competencies, of the nation/ region, on which innovation can be built, for example: the existence of a high level of human capital or the existence of strong world-class scientific and technological infrastructure.
- "Processes and trends": these are processes that can enable countries/ regions to overcome strategic innovation weaknesses, or constraints, that hamper innovative initiatives and policies, for example: vocational training programs, tax incentives, research and development (R&D) funding, etc.

Identifying the anchors and processes is done in the Experts Workshop and is based on deep intimate knowledge of the experts and their familiarity with all aspects of the innovation ecosystem, including informal and ill-defined ones. Some 15–30 experts should take part, in each workshop in the participant countries or regions, representing all key sectors and disciplines relevant to innovation: stakeholders, policymakers, researchers from the academia, mangers from the industry etc. The objective of the workshop is to formulate a creative systematic and inclusive list of key innovation variables that can be transformed into a visual innovation ecosystem map.

The Workshop is conducted through brainstorming and nominal group technique (Osborn, 1963). During the workshop, each expert is asked, in turn, to propose one anchor (which will be added to the list of "anchors" without discussion or controversy) and it is immediately entered into an Excel file and projected on a screen. After a first round of this process, there are additional rounds, until no more anchors remain to be listed. After the list of "anchors" is completed, to the satisfaction of the experts, a similar process is employed to list comprehensively the "processes and trends". In addition, each expert is asked, in turn, to indicate whether the suggested process belongs to the "demand-driven" or to the "supply-side" of innovation or both. Based on the brainstorming method, it is important to note that during these stages, experts are NOT asked to justify or explain their anchors or processes, but simply list them, nor is there criticism or debate.

The end result of this workshop therefore includes a comprehensive crude list of anchors and processes that reflect the views and insights of experts. The research team will then take this list and process it, refine it, organize it and compile a final, refined list. In this refining process, the final list of anchors and processes is organized, to distinguish between "demand-driven" and "supply-side" innovation. This analysis enables us to show visually and clearly the key elements of demand-side innovation drivers, including consumers, businesses, labor markets, global markets and other channels, and indicate how these demand-side aspects of innovation interact with supply-side elements. Our focus is on identifying "gaps" – crucial market needs that have not been fully met, such that innovative technologies can be leveraged to match supply with demand and create business opportunities. At the same time, we seek to identify supply-driven processes reflecting innovation driven by supply (incentives, funding, etc.), through which resources are directed toward specific markets and products, "pushed" by supply factors rather than "pulled" by demand factors.

B.   Linking Anchors and Processes

This stage involves two complementary analyses. The first comprises "cross impact" analysis where the research teams evaluate the relationship between the anchors and the processes that were identified in the earlier stage on a bipolar five-point Likert scale ranging from strong negative link (1) to strong positive link (5).

The matrices developed (see example in Figure 2.2) processed through exploratory factor analysis – EFA (data reduction technique), a statistical tool whose purpose is to reduce a large number of variables into a smaller, more compact set (Kim and Mueller, 1978; Hair, et al., 1998). In the analysis the anchors serve as observations in order to group the processes into major factors according to the similarities in their linkages with the anchors.

The next step includes classification of processes and anchors into groups. The processes were grouped according to the results of the factor analysis; while the classification of anchors into clusters did not involve a similar mathematical procedure and was based on logic (see example in Figure 2.2).

Cluster	List of Anchors	Factor A — process 1	process 2	process 3	process 4	Factor B — process 5	process 6	process 7	Factor C — process 8	process 9	process 9	Factor D — process 10	process 11	
Cluster A	Anchor 1	4	4	4	5	5	4	3	4	4	5	4	5	·
	Anchor 2	5	3	5	3	3	2	3	3	3	4	3	3	·
	Anchor 3	3	3	3	4	3	3	5	4	4	3	5	5	·
	Anchor 4	3	3	3	5	5	4	5	5	5	5	4	5	·
	Anchor 5	3	3	5	4	3	3	3	4	3	5	5	5	·
Cluster B	Anchor 6	3	3	5	5	5	3	4	4	4	5	4	4	·
	Anchor 7	5	4	5	5	5	2	4	4	5	4	5	5	·
	Anchor 8	2	2	1	2	4	4	4	2	3	1	3	4	·
	Anchor 9	2	2	1	2	4	4	4	4	3	1	3	4	·
	Anchor 10	3	4	3	4	4	4	3	4	3	3	4	4	·
Cluster C	Anchor 11	4	4	3	5	4	5	3	3	4	3	4	4	·
	Anchor 12	3	3	4	4	4	1	3	3	3	4	3	4	·
	Anchor 13	3	3	3	4	3	2	3	3	3	4	3	3	·
	Anchor 14	4	4	4	5	4	5	3	3	4	4	4	5	·
Cluster D	Anchor 15	3	4	5	5	5	5	4	4	4	1	4	5	·
	Anchor 16	1	2	2	5	5	4	4	5	5	5	4	5	·
	Anchor 17	1	2	2	4	5	5	5	4	5	5	4	5	·
	Anchor 18	3	3	3	4	4	3	3	4	3	3	3	3	·
Cluster E	Anchor 19	4	4	3	4	5	5	5	3	3	2	3	5	·
	Anchor 20	1	4	5	5	5	5	5	3	4	2	5	5	·
·	·	·	·	·	·	·	·	·	·	·	·	·	·	·

Key:

Old value	New value
1	1
2	2
3	n/a
4	3
5	4

Weighted Linkage Indicator:

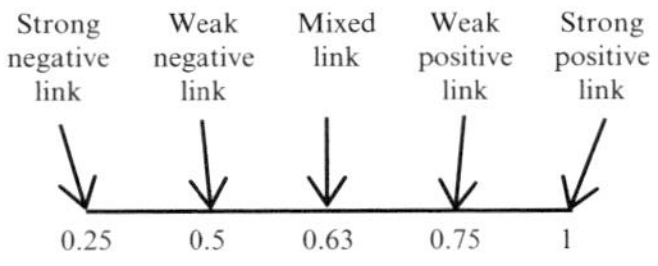

Strong negative link	Weak negative link	Mixed link	Weak positive link	Strong positive link
0.25	0.5	0.63	0.75	1

Legend: 1 = strong negative link; 2 = weak negative link; 3 = no link; 4 = weak positive link; 5 = strong positive link.

Figure 2.2   Example of linkages matrix of the cross-impact results between anchors and processes

In order to compute the major linkages between each process factors and anchor clusters a mathematical procedure was employed. First, the cells in Figure 2.2 were transformed using the key shown beside Figure 2.2.

Second, two indicators were computed for each cluster-factor aggregation. The first is a weighted linkage indicator which is: (the sum of values in aggregation)/(number of non n/a cells in aggregation) x 4. The outcome received a value ranging from 0.25 to 1 (see Figure 2.2).

The second indicator is the neutral linkage indicator, which is: (the number of n/a cells in aggregation)/(total number of cells in aggregation).

Third, the decision rule was determined: if the number of n/a cells (no link) in a particular factor (processes) – cluster (anchors) aggregation is greater than 50 percent, than there is no linkage (NL) between the factor and the cluster; if else the weighted linkage indicator is used to determine the direction and strength of the linkage. The midpoint between each pair of values (0.25 and 0.5, 0.5 and 0.63, 0.63 and 0.75 and 0.75 and 1) used as a basis for calculating the minimum and maximum threshold, i.e. 0.82–1: strong positive linkage (++); 0.62–0.81: weak positive linkage (+); 0.37–0.61: mixed linkage (+/−); 0.29–0.36: weak negative linkage (–); 0.25–0.28: strong negative linkage (−−) as presented in Figure 2.3.

The result that came out from these analyses produces a matrix in which major linkages were identified between process factors and anchor clusters. Based on this matrix the research team prepared a clear visual map of the nation's innovation ecosystem, showing key "anchor" and "process" elements and feedback among them (see illustration in Figure 2.4).

The interactions between the group of anchors (clusters) and the group of processes is shown in the ecosystem map (Figure 2.4) For example cluster A has a strong positive association with three factors: Factor A presents both the supply and demand side of innovation; Factor C presents the supply side of innovation and factor D presents the demand side of innovation. Cluster B has weaker linkages with factors: B, C and D and mixed link ties exist between this cluster and Factor A.

Cluster C has weak positive interactions with all the four factors, while cluster D has a strong positive association with factors B and D and weaker relations with factors A and B. At last cluster E has strong linkages with factors B and D, weaker ties with Factor A and mixed relations with factor C.

We believe this method will also facilitate cross-country comparisons, useful for best-practice benchmarking (transferring, while adapting, proven innovation policies from one country to another).

The developed method presented in this chapter was employed in eight international case studies and will be introduced in the following chapters

Cluster	List of Anchors	Factor A (process 1, process 2, process 3, process 4)	Factor B (process 5, process 6, process 7)	Factor C (process 8, process 9, process 9)	Factor D (process 10, process 11)	
Cluster A	Anchor 1, Anchor 2, Anchor 3, Anchor 4, Anchor 5	++	NL	++	++	.
Cluster B	Anchor 6, Anchor 7, Anchor 8, Anchor 9, Anchor 10	+/-	+	+	+	.
Cluster C	Anchor 11, Anchor 12, Anchor 13, Anchor 14	+	+	+	+	.
Cluster D	Anchor 15, Anchor 16, Anchor 17, Anchor 18	+	++	+	++	.
Cluster E	Anchor 19, Anchor 20	+	++	+/-	++	.
.						.

Legend: Strong positive linkage (++); weak positive linkage (+); mixed linkage (+/–); weak negative linkage (–); strong negative linkage (– –).

Figure 2.3   Decision rule for determining linkage between factors and clusters

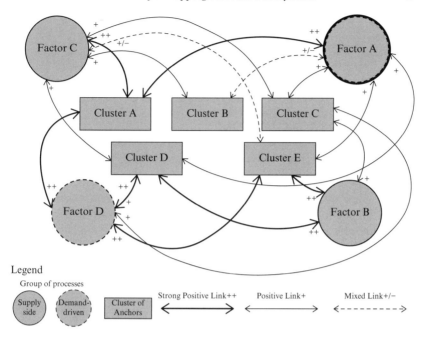

Figure 2.4   Example of innovation ecosystem map

with the addition of a comparative analysis based on these case studies. It demonstrates the strengths and importance of this method in identify the pillars on which the innovation system stands.

NOTES

1. W. Kennard (2010), "Partnership for Innovation", New York Times, 14 December 2010.
2. Henry A. Murray and Clyde Kluckhohn (1953), *Personality in Nature, Society, and Culture*, Oxford: Alfred A. Knopf.

3. The Israeli national innovation ecosystem*

INTRODUCTION

In this chapter, we describe Israel's innovation ecosystem. As a country widely described as the "start-up nation" (Senor and Singer, 2011), there is considerable interest in the system and forces that drive Israel's vigorous entrepreneurship. We begin by presenting some background, describing Israel's economy, society and competitiveness. Next we present the key anchors and processes of Israeli innovation that emerged from the Experts Workshop, along with the cross-impact analysis showing how they are inter-related. To concretize this analysis, we describe in detail some of the main programs in the innovation ecosystem. Finally, the visualization of Israel's innovation ecosystem is presented and discussed.

BACKGROUND

Israel is a small Middle Eastern nation, with a population of 8 million and land area of 22,100 sq km (within the so-called Green Line 1967 borders). Its gross domestic product (GDP) is $242.9 billion (2012); per capita GDP measured in terms of purchasing power parity is $30 500. Its GDP growth rate was 3.1 percent in 2012, down from 4.6 percent in 2011 and five percent in 2010. Reflecting the global economic and financial crisis, Israel's unemployment rate rose to 8 percent in November 2009, fell persistently to a low of 5.4 percent in January 2012, and then rose to 6.7 percent at the close of 2012. In recent years, inflation (annual percent change in the consumer price index) peaked at 4.3 percent in April 2011, declined to only 1 percent in July 2012, and closed at 1.4 percent in December 2012. Israel is an open economy, with exports ($82 billion in 2012) comprising one third of its GDP. As a result of the global slowdown, the annual rate of growth in exports fell from 19 percent in 2010, to 11 percent in 2011 and zero in 2012. A high fraction of exports are comprised of technology-intensive goods and services. The current account of the balance of payments was in balance in 2012, after a decade of current account surpluses, while foreign direct investment amounted to 4.7 percent of GDP.

ISRAEL'S CAPABILITIES IN THE FREE MARKET COMPETITION

In this section we present four economic indices: global competitiveness, economic freedom, ease of doing business and innovation and entrepreneurship with regard to Israel's capabilities to cope with its challenges.

Global Competitiveness

According to the *World Competitiveness Yearbook*, published annually by the Swiss business school International Institute for Management Development (IMD), Israel ranked nineteenth in the world in competitiveness, down two places from 2010 and 2011 (seventeenth). The "competitiveness landscape" diagram (see Figure 3.1) shows the breakdown of overall competitiveness, in terms of four dimensions (economy, government, business and infrastructure). Israel's economic performance ranks only 36th; government efficiency, 21st; business efficiency, 18th; and infrastructure, 13th. An exceedingly poor ranking in basic infrastructure (roads, transportation, communication) of 48th is offset by high rankings in technological and scientific infrastructure (5th, and 4th, respectively).

According to the *World Competitiveness Yearbook*, the five key factors that make Israel's economy attractive are a strong research and development (R&D) culture, skilled workforce, high educational level, dynamism of the economy and open and positive attitudes. All five are closely related to Israel's dynamic start-up culture and its thriving high-tech industry. Among the main challenges facing Israel are reducing bureaucracy, investing in periphery infrastructure, increasing the current low rate of labor force participation, and decreasing the large economic gaps between rich and poor, among the highest in the Organisation for Economic Co-operation and Development (OECD) nations.

Economic Freedom

For over a decade, a think tank called The Heritage Foundation has measured an index of economic freedom for each of 184 countries. The index measures each of five dimensions: size of government, legal system and property rights, sound money, freedom to trade internationally and regulation. Each of the freedoms within these five categories is individually

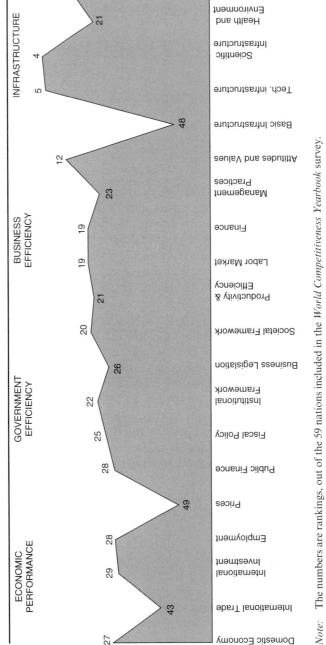

Note: The numbers are rankings, out of the 59 nations included in the *World Competitiveness Yearbook* survey.

Source: IMD, *World Competitiveness Yearbook 2012.*

Figure 3.1 Israel's competitiveness landscape

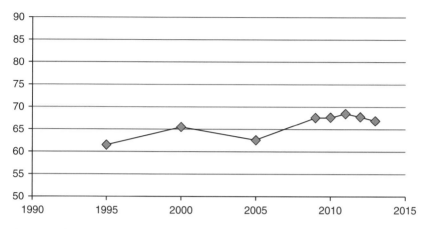

Source:　The Heritage Foundation, Index of Economic Freedom 2013, see www.heritage. org/index/.

Figure 3.2　Israel: Economic freedom score, 1995–2013

scored on a scale of 0 to 10. A country's overall economic freedom score is a simple average of its scores.

Israel's economy has been transformed from one directed and controlled by the government in 1980, to a more open, free and less-regulated economy in 2013 (see Figure 3.2). Its summary "economic freedom" score has risen from 3.48 (and a rank of 95th) in 1980 to a score of 7.25 (and a rank of 43rd) in 2010 (latest year available). The overall score of 7.25 reflects a very high variance, ranging from a low 4.64 and rank of 109th (legal system and property rights) to a high of 8.88 for sound money and 8.41 for freedom to trade internationally. The low score for the legal system reflects a very low score on "legal enforcement of contracts" and a low score on "military interference in rule of law and politics". Against that, the score for "judicial independence" is a high 8.63.

Ease of Doing Business

A key aspect of innovation is the climate in which innovators and entrepreneurs operate. The World Bank conducts carefully crafted measures of the extent to which it is easy to start and run a business, in each of some 185 countries, annually.[1] This index measures 10 key operations involved in starting and running businesses, and World Bank experts actually perform these tasks in each country yearly. Israel's overall rank in this measure, as well as five of the ten selected indicators, are shown in Figure 3.3.

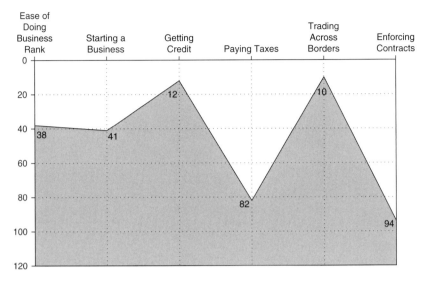

Note: See www.doingbusiness.org/rankings.

Source: Doing Business Project – The World Bank, 2012.

Figure 3.3   Israel: Ease of doing business, 2012

According to the World Bank, in 2012, Israel ranked 38th overall in ease of doing business. While investors are well protected (ranked 5th in the world), and while getting credit is relatively easy (ranked 12th), registering property and dealing with construction permits are very difficult (ranked 147th and 137th, respectively), as is enforcing contracts (94th), resolving insolvency (45th), paying taxes (82nd) and starting a business (41st). In contrast, trading across borders is quite easy (rank of 10).

Innovation and Entrepreneurship

As part of its *World Competitiveness Yearbook*, IMD measures "innovative capacity"; a panel of experts rates countries' "Innovative capacity of firms (to generate new products, processes and/or services)". In 2012, Israel ranked second out of 59 globally-competitive countries, scoring 8.10 out of 10, just behind Switzerland (8.26) and ahead of Germany (8.00) and USA (7.96). Expert respondents also score countries according to whether "entrepreneurship of managers is widespread in business", on a scale of one to ten. In 2012, Israel ranked second (7.44) behind Taiwan (7.67) and ahead of Hong Kong and Lithuania.

The Israeli economy is characterized by a pervasive drive among young people to launch start-ups,[2] supported by strong research universities, hampered somewhat by bureaucracy and poor physical infrastructure, and an inability to trade within its region for political reasons.

INNOVATION ECOSYSTEM

Data Analysis

Anchors and processes
This section provides a summary of raw inputs collected at the Israeli Experts Workshops (see Chapter 2), conducted by the Samuel Neaman Institute (SNI). Table 3.1 lists 53 main anchors which were identified by the Israeli experts as the pillars of their innovation system. Table 3.2 presents a list of 26 processes which were recognized by the experts as key elements driving and fostering innovation. It will be recalled that "anchors" are essentially similar to what economists call "stocks", or fixed assets, while processes are similar to what economists call "flows" (changes related to various anchors or stocks). The processes were ranked by the experts by their importance and classified according to which side of the market (supply or demand) they are assigned to.

Interaction among anchors and processes
The essence of an ecosystem is the interaction among its various components. We used data on "cross-impact analysis" (the perceived links between various anchors and processes) to create a bipolar five-point Likert scale (ranging from a strong negative link, score 1, to a strong positive link, score 5, for each cell in a 26x53 cross-impact matrix.

Analysis of the Cross-Impact Results

Factor analysis was employed on the list of processes (variables). The anchors serve as observations in order to group the processes into major factors according to the similarities in their linkages with the anchors. Tests of sample adequacy constituted the necessary preliminary conditions for conducting factor analysis and obtaining meaningful results. The Spearman correlation matrix among the processes provided the input for both the tests and the factor analysis. The linkage-pattern items obtained in the Israeli workshop demonstrate good sampling adequacy, both at the overall (KMO > 0.74) and at the single item level (KMO = 0.413 – 0.907). The Spearman correlation matrix contains correlations with absolute

Table 3.1   List of Israeli innovation anchors

Number	Cluster Name
1	Existence of high-quality human capital
2	Belief in "beating the system" and making significant changes
3	Passion to innovate
4	Self-confidence
5	Creativity
6	Business-centered entrepreneurship
7	Reject "impossible"
8	Empowerment, achievement
9	High-tech as key success path
10	Pervasive success stories
11	Small country
12	Proximity to US
13	Infrastructure supporting ideas
14	Economic, political democracy
15	Low cost of R&D
16	Immigration from ex-USSR
17	Multi-lingual
18	Diverse population
19	Quality of life
20	Need to export
21	Religious compromise
22	Leadership
23	Trade agreements
24	Perception of Israeli innovation abroad
25	Education creating global perspective
26	Social tolerance
27	Youth entrepreneurship activity
28	Lack of natural resources
29	Survivor mentality
30	Immigrant society
31	Frankness
32	Centrality of high-tech
33	Local stock exchange, NASDAQ
34	Public sector jobs unattractive
35	High percent of scientists
36	National survivor instinct
37	Entrepreneurial finance
38	Low government regulation
39	Impudence
40	Improvisation
41	Low power distance

Table 3.1   (continued)

Number	Cluster Name
42	Ethical flexibility
43	Rejection of authority
44	Lack of conservatism
45	Maturity, responsibility
46	Work ethic
47	Strong university infrastructure
48	High-level medical infrastructure
49	Availability of long-term capital
50	Geopolitical instability spurs creativity
51	Defense industries
52	Large defense R&D budgets
53	Human capital formed by military

Table 3.2   *List of identified processes fostering Israeli innovation, ranked by importance and classified by market side (supply, demand, or both)*

Ranked Number (by importance)	Process Name	Demand side (D), Supply side (S) or both (D S)
1	Chief Scientist programs for supporting technological innovation	S
2	Constant government investment in basic research	S
3	The new Council for Higher Education model for the creation of human capital	S
4	Private initiative programs for supporting innovation	D
5	Incentives for supporting foreign R&D centers of MNCs in Israel	S
6	Creation of capital and infrastructure in 1990s	S
7	Ministry of Defense programs for supporting technological innovation (TALPIOT, MAFAT)	S
8	International cooperation in business as a way of life	D
9	Globalization	D S
10	Technological incubators	S

Table 3.2   (continued)

Ranked Number (by importance)	Process Name	Demand side (D), Supply side (S) or both (D S)
11	Interdisciplinary programs in universities	D
12	Nanotechnology – targeted research that supports cooperation	S
13	Independent financial infrastructure	S
14	Dialogue and ties between industry and government	D
15	Programs for incorporating the ultra-orthodox and Arab populations in the workforce	S
16	Increasing demand for technological development in biomedicine and biotechnology	D
17	Weakened public sector	D
18	Technology transfer companies in universities & technology transfer between the Academe and industry	D
19	Government support for colleges in the periphery that creates human capital infrastructure	S
20	Synergy between military and civilian R&D	D
21	Israeli Industry Center for R&D (MATIMOP) and the Israel Export Institute	S
22	Government and international funds for research	S
23	Government programs for strengthening scientific and technological education	S
24	Local policy for supporting entrepreneurship	D
25	Conducting research and implementing new methodologies in innovation	D
26	Supporting R&D and innovation in traditional industries	S

values between 0.002–0.686, and the value of its determinant is 0.001, hence the existence of correlations without multi-collinearity is established. The result of the Bartlett's sphericity test rejects the null hypothesis that the correlation matrix is an identity matrix ($p = 0.000$).

Exploratory principal axis factor analysis with subsequent orthogonal rotation (Varimax rotation with Kaiser normalization) produced six factors, that together explain 73.4 percent of the variance. The factor loadings are presented in Table 3.3. In order to facilitate factor labeling, the dominant items, marked in bold in Table 3.3, were defined as those with an absolute value of the loading greater than 0.46. Through the factor analysis we distilled the existing innovation process drivers down to six key factors. They are:

1. *Government programs for supporting innovation*: constant government investment in basic research; Ministry of Defense programs for supporting technological innovation (TALPIOT, MAFAT); dialogue and ties between industry and government; globalization; interdisciplinary programs in universities; nanotechnology – targeted research that supports cooperation; the new Council for Higher Education model for the creation of human capital.
2. *Private and public sector activities for supporting innovation*: private initiative programs for supporting innovation; international cooperation in business as a way of life; independent financial infrastructure, Israeli Industry Center for R&D (MATIMOP) and the Israel Export Institute.
3. *Cooperation between the private and public sector in supporting technological innovation*: Chief Scientist programs for supporting technological innovation; incentives for supporting foreign R&D centers of multination corporations (MNCs) in Israel; technological incubators; local policy for supporting entrepreneurship; conducting research and implementing new methodologies in innovation.
4. *Government investments for the creation of human capital*: programs for incorporating the ultra-orthodox and Arab populations in the workforce; creation of capital and infrastructure in the 1990s; government support for colleges in the periphery that creates human capital infrastructure.
5. *Creating demand in the private sector*: increasing demand for technological development in biomedicine and biotechnology; weakening public sector.
6. *National and international research funds*: government and international funds for research.

The second and third factors are both supply and demand driven, focusing on government and public policy measures, private sector activities and private-public initiatives for supporting innovation. The first, fourth and sixth factors are mainly supply, concentrating on government investments and expenses on human capital and research. The fifth factor is demand driven.

Table 3.3 *Factor analysis results for the Israeli innovation ecosystem*

Factor Name	Items (Processes)	Factor					
		1	2	3	4	5	6
Government programs for supporting innovation	Nanotechnology – targeted research that supports cooperation	**0.838**	0.159	0.097	0.072	0.162	0.149
	Interdisciplinary programs in universities	**0.814**	-0.018	0.086	0.009	0.217	0.212
	Constant government investment in basic research	**0.752**	-0.058	0.332	0.385	-0.141	0.206
	Dialogue and ties between industry and government	**0.742**	0.263	0.268	0.247	0.183	-0.116
	Synergy between military and civilian R&D	**0.699**	0.395	0.045	0.155	0.019	-0.036
	Ministry of Defense programs for supporting technological innovation (TALPIOT, MAFAT)	**0.573**	0.201	0.259	0.351	-0.316	0.179
	The new Council for Higher Education model for the creation of human capital	**0.546**	-0.227	0.415	0.121	-0.005	0.333
	Supporting R&D and innovation in traditional industries	**0.488**	0.251	0.202	0.478	-0.013	-0.167
	Globalization	**0.445**	0.436	0.263	-0.131	0.083	0.353
Private and public sector activities for supporting innovation	International cooperation in business as a way of life	0.163	**0.828**	-0.098	0.097	0.208	-0.066
	Independent financial infrastructure	0.003	**0.821**	0.244	0.050	0.069	-0.215
	Israeli Industry Center for R&D (MATIMOP) and the Israel Export Institute	0.241	**0.694**	0.337	0.244	-0.066	0.186

Category	Item						
	Private initiative programs for supporting innovation	0.010	**0.691**	0.025	0.066	0.356	0.423
Cooperation between the private and public sector in supporting technological innovation	Conducting research and implementing new methodologies in innovation	0.406	0.098	**0.807**	-0.088	0.035	0.131
	Local policy for supporting entrepreneurship	-0.070	0.105	**0.666**	0.453	0.307	-0.179
	Technology transfer companies in universities and technology transfer between the academe and industry	0.335	0.452	**0.604**	0.136	-0.054	0.144
	Incentives for supporting foreign R&D centers of MNCs in Israel	0.155	0.398	**0.573**	0.304	0.286	0.232
	Technological incubators	0.184	0.065	**0.565**	0.414	0.119	0.197
	Chief Scientist programs for supporting technological innovation	0.394	0.149	**0.503**	0.437	-0.084	0.232
Government investments for the creation of human capital	Government support for colleges in the periphery that creates human capital infrastructure	0.404	-0.046	0.060	**0.735**	-0.018	-0.029
	Programs for incorporating the ultra-orthodox and Arab populations in the workforce	-0.055	0.130	0.085	**0.714**	0.067	0.094
	Government programs for strengthening scientific and technological education	0.548	0.044	0.314	**0.564**	0.094	0.059
	Creation of capital and infrastructure in 1990s	0.400	0.370	0.205	**0.516**	-0.039	0.157
Creating demand in the private sector	Weakened public sector	0.053	0.245	0.211	-0.089	**0.838**	-0.061
	increasing demand for technological development in biomedicine and biotechnology	0.309	0.126	0.001	0.270	**0.753**	0.348

Table 3.3 (continued)

Factor Name	Items (Processes)	Factor					
National and international research funds	Government and international funds for research	0.197	0.006	0.212	0.106	0.079	**0.862**
Percent of variance		20.7	13.7	12.8	12.0	7.3	7.0
Cumulative percent		20.7	34.4	47.2	59.2	66.5	73.4

KMO* = 0.748
Cronbach's Alpha = 0.935

Major Programs in the Israeli Innovation System

Of the existing government programs and organizations that foster innovation and entrepreneurship, many are specific and unique to Israel. For instance, military support of R&D, including military intelligence and its investment in high technology. An example for this type of organization is MAFAT (Hebrew acronym for the Administration for the Development of Weapons and Technological Infrastructure), a governmental agency aimed at coordinating between the Ministry of Defense, the Israel Defense Forces (IDF), Israel Military Industries, Israel Aerospace Industries, Rafael Advanced Defense Systems, the Institute for Biological Research and the Space Agency.

Close synergy exists between military and civilian R&D in Israel. Israeli defense industries have traditionally focused on components, electronics, avionics and other systems. The development of these auxiliary systems has also given Israeli high-tech industries an edge in civilian spin-offs in security, electronics, computers, software and the internet sectors. Civilian applications of these skills in software, communications, imaging, process control, etc., derived from military industries, have become increasingly important. For example, the need for better night-vision equipment led to local engineers becoming trained in the field of image processing.

Another program connected to military R&D is TALPIOT – an elite IDF training program for young people (high school graduates) who have demonstrated outstanding academic ability in the sciences, physics and mathematics. Graduates of the TALPIOT program pursue higher education while serving in the army, and then utilize their expertise in IDF's R&D projects. During their military service, these very young people develop considerable entrepreneurship skills and gain substantial work experience in a highly competitive and high-pressure environment. After the completion of their military service, TALPIOT graduates easily assimilate into the Israeli labor market and occupy senior positions in the Israeli high-tech industry. Many of the start-ups established in Israel since the early 1990s were launched by TALPIOT graduates. The TALPIOT program is a particularly good example of how a supply-side government program can have significant spillover effects on demand-driven innovation (for example, start-ups) in the long-run, through human capital investments with an emphasis on the teaching and development of entrepreneurial and applied technological skills. Mandatory military service in Israel equips its young people with the connections, management skills and action-oriented entrepreneurial mindset critical for technological development.

An additional supply-side process, connected to government programs for supporting innovation, is the new allocation model of the Council for Higher Education (CHE). The CHE is a supervisory body for universities and colleges in Israel. The most important body of the Council is the Planning and Budgeting Committee (PBC), which deals with the division of funding between the various universities and colleges. The total budget of the CHE for the 2011 academic year (funded by the government) was 7.4 billion NIS (1.5 billion euros).[3] The new budget allocation model places much higher emphasis on research excellence (especially on winning competitive foreign or bi-national research grants such as the EU framework program, BSF, NIH, GIF and others) in its budget allocation considerations. Research excellence strengthens the human capital factor, thus contributing to innovation and entrepreneurship (for example, technology transfer, university incubators etc.).

One of the key private-public sector cooperation frameworks identified by Israeli experts as a factor in driving innovation is the Chief Scientist programs. The Office of the Chief Scientist (OCS) at the Ministry of Economy is responsible for carrying out government policy concerning support for industrial R&D. Firms submit proposals for R&D projects, which the OCS reviews according to set of criteria that include technological and commercial feasibility, merit and risks, as well as estimation of the extent to which these projects can be expected to generate spillovers (Getz and Segal, 2008). The OCS supports and administers a wide range of programs, among them MAGNET, MAGNETON, NOFAR and the technological incubators program.

The MAGNET program involves pre-competitive R&D within a consortium that includes a number of commercial companies together with research personnel from at least one academic or research institution. The R&D focuses on new generic technologies that will lead to the generation of new and advanced products. The industrial partners enjoy a grant amounting to 66 percent of approved R&D costs, whereas the academic partner will receive 80 percent of said costs. A foreign company may be included in the consortium if it can bring a unique contribution to the relationship.

The aim of the Magneton program is to further support an already existing relationship between a single industrial partner and an academic institution. The grant in this case amount to 66 percent of the approved R&D costs.

The NOFAR program is a pure academic research program for basic and applied research in the areas of bio and nano technologies. The goal is to achieve a milestone to allow encouragement of an industrial company access to enough information for investing in further R&D steps. The aim is to support advanced stages of applied academic research, not yet oriented towards a specific product, but already of interest to a business partner, and to bring the research to a maturity phase, enabling an Israeli business partner to invest in it in the future. A minimal requirement of this program is for a company or an incubator to invest 10 percent of the development costs, at this stage, complementing the 90 percent grant given by the government (Getz and Segal, 2008).

The Public Technological Incubator Program (PTIP) was initiated by the OCS in Israel's Ministry of Economy (the former Ministry of Industry and Trade) in the early 1990s in the wake of the large influx of immigrants from the former USSR, many of whom were scientists and engineers. Technological incubators are support organizations that give inexperienced entrepreneurs an opportunity to develop their innovative technological ideas and set up new businesses in order to commercialize them. The goal of the incubators is to support novice entrepreneurs at the earliest stage of technological entrepreneurship, and help them implement their ideas and form new business ventures. Each incubator is structured so as to handle 10–15 projects simultaneously, and provides assistance in the following areas: determining the technological and marketing applicability of the idea, drawing up an R&D plan and organizing the R&D team, raising capital and preparing for marketing, provision of secretarial and administrative service, maintenance, procurements, accounting and legal advice (Frenkel et al., 2008). Other private-public sector cooperation schemes include government incentives for supporting foreign MNCs in Israel. Over the past two decades the Israeli government has provided substantial tax benefits for multinational firms for basing their R&D activities in Israel (for example, the R&D centers of Intel, HP Motorola and Microsoft).

An additional type of public-private cooperation is the technology transfer from academia to industry. Frenkel and Shefer (2012) present basic concepts of a technology-transfer production-function model in which human capital, investment capital, and Technology Transfer Office (TTO) staff interact to produce innovations or patent registration. Universities supply the most important players for the production and diffusion of knowledge and invention promoting economic growth. Universities constitute the major source of technological progress for industry (Henderson et al., 1998; Mowery and Shane, 2002; Bercovitz and Feldman, 2006).

A notable example (one of many successful partnerships) for this type of cooperation is the collaboration between the Weizmann Institute of Science and Teva Pharmaceutical Industries in the discovering and development of the Copaxone drug for the treatment of multiple sclerosis. Copaxone is Teva's largest selling drug, with 1.86 billion dollars in sales in the first half of 2011. Since 2001, the Weizmann Institute of Science, through its commercialization arm Yeda Research and Development Company Ltd, has earned more than one billion NIS in royalties from the commercialization of its IP. Weizmann Institute's Yeda has been named the world's third most profitable technology transfer organization.[4]

In recent years, increasing demand in the private sector, especially in the fields of pharma, biomedicine and biotechnology, has significantly contributed to the strengthening of innovation and entrepreneurship. The pace of innovation, development and growth in Israel's biotechnology sector is unparalleled. Israel's biotech industry (consisting of 180 biotech companies) is the one of the most aggressive in the world, with more start-ups per capita than in any other country. Notable pharmaceutical, biotechnological and biomedical firms are Teva, Compugen, Gamida Cell, D-Pharm, Given Imaging and many others. The increased demand in the private sector for high-quality human capital is directly related to Israel's shrinking public sector. Government-financed GERD (gross expenditure on R&D) as a percentage of GDP (not including defense expenditures) fell from 0.85 percent in 1991 to 0.67 percent in 2008, as the business sector expenditure on R&D (BERD) as a percentage of GDP rose from 1.3 percent to 3.8 percent in this time period (Getz et al., 2010).

Support for private sector activities for supporting innovation is given by two public agencies: the Israeli Industry Center for R&D (MATIMOP) and the Israel Export Institute. MATIMOP, the executive agency of the OCS of MOIT, is the official national agency for industrial R&D cooperation charged with promoting highly supportive policies to build Israel's industrial infrastructure, and nurturing industrial innovation and entrepreneurship. This agency generates and implements international cooperative industrial R&D programs between Israeli and foreign enterprises. The Israel Export Institute is an Israeli governmental agency which operates under the Ministry of Economy to facilitate trade opportunities, joint ventures, and strategic alliances between international businesses and Israeli companies.

Targeted government investments for the creation of human capital were also identified by the experts as a potential for driving innovation and entrepreneurship. A great emphasis is placed in recent years in incorporating the ultra-orthodox (especially men) and Arab (especially women) populations in the workforce. These two populations possess low or irrelevant education (religious education in the case of the ultra-orthodox population) and are characterized by traditionally low participation rates in the Israeli workforce. A notable example for such targeted government investment is MAHAT (Government Institution for Technological and Scientific Training). Approximately 20 percent of the 600 employees in

Intel's Jerusalem branch are ultra-orthodox graduates of the MAHAT institute.[5]

Construction of a National Innovation Ecosystem Map For Israel

The next methodological step included the classification of processes and anchors into groups. The processes were grouped according to the results of the factor analysis. The classification of anchors into clusters did not involve a similar statistical procedure and was based on logic. The anchors were grouped into seven clusters: entrepreneurship; scientific and educational infrastructure; culture of empowerment; competitive structure; culture diversity; economic institutions; "out-of-the-box thinking".

In the final step of this methodological exercise, innovation maps were produced for the Israeli ecosystem. Most interactions between the anchor clusters and the process factors proved to be significant and positive describing the linkages between the two groups. Figure 3.4 presents the overall national innovation ecosystem map for Israel.

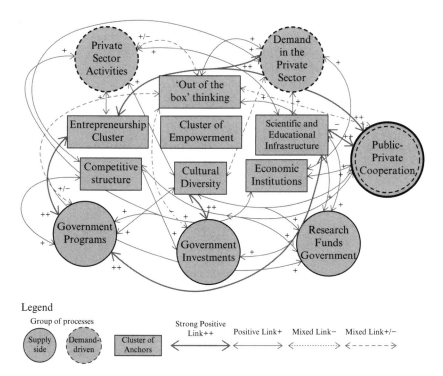

Figure 3.4   Israeli innovation ecosystem

The interactions between the group of anchors (clusters) and the group of processes were computed-based on a mathematical procedure for determining and weighting the direction and strength of link between the factors and clusters (see in Chapter 2). The results show that the entrepreneurship cluster has a strong positive association with three factors: government programs, private-public sector cooperation and the creation of demand in the private sector. Weaker positive ties exist between this cluster and additional three factors: private and public sector activities for supporting innovation, government investments for the creation of human capital and national and international research funds.

The scientific and educational infrastructure cluster has strong positive interactions with two factors: government programs and private-public sector cooperation. The strong association between the scientific and educational infrastructure cluster and these two factors is mainly due to the contribution of Israel's seven main research universities. These research institutions receive substantial government funding for conducting basic research and they are highly involved in Chief Scientist Programs (MAGNET, NOFAR, MAGNETON), aimed at establishing partnerships and technology transfer between the academe and industry. Weak positive ties exist between this cluster and four other factors: private and public sector activities for supporting innovation, government investments for the creation of human capital, creation of demand in the private sector and national and international research funds.

The culture of empowerment cluster has an especially strong positive interaction with government programs. Weaker interactions exist between this cluster and five factors: private sector activities for supporting innovation, private-public sector cooperation, government investments for the creation of human capital, creation of demand in the private sector and national and international research funds. The unique leadership qualities (cultural aspects such as self-confidence, reject "impossible", lack of conservatism) that characterize the Israeli entrepreneur and the high-technology sector are especially important factors in the successes of government (Chief Scientist) programs, in establishing successful private-public partnerships and in promoting the activities of the private sector.

The competitive structure cluster has weak positive ties with all of the six factors. This is highly significant and should not be overlooked. Israel's economy is characterized by the dominance of some 20 families who control both financial and industrial companies and by large companies that dominate such industries as food and banking. A recent task force on the subject has led to draft legislation, the Anti-Concentration Act, now under discussion in Israel's Parliament, the Knesset. While Israeli start-ups compete globally in fiercely competitive world markets from day one, and almost always focus on world markets, the lack of a highly open domestic market may be a drawback. This explains the weak ties.

The diversity cluster has strong positive linkage to the government investments for the creation of human capital factor. Weaker positive linkages exist between this cluster and four other factors: government programs, private sector activities for supporting innovation, private-public sector cooperation and international research funds. Israel is a multi-lingual immigrant society. Studies show that cultural diversity has a significant and positive impact on innovative activity. The differences in knowledge and capabilities of workers from diverse and heterogeneous cultural backgrounds enhance the performance of R&D activity. This is due to the fact that the nature of R&D activity calls for interaction between different workers and a pooling of different ideas and abilities. Diversity among highly qualified employees has the strongest impact on innovation output (Niebuhr, 2010; Alesina and La Ferrara, 2005; Fujita and Weber, 2004; Berliant and Fujita, 2008). Mixed linkages exist between the diversity cluster and the creation of demand in the private sector.

The economic institutions cluster has weak positive interactions with four factors: government programs, private and public sector activities for supporting innovation, private-public sector cooperation and the creation of demand in the private sector. No (neutral) linkages exist between this cluster and the government investments for the creation of human capital and the national and international funds factors. A possible explanation for the weak and neutral associations between this cluster and the various factor groups is that the economic institution cluster is mostly made up from pure demand-driven anchors (low cost of R&D, need to export, trade agreements, local stock exchange, public sector jobs unattractive, low government regulation, availability of long-term capital, entrepreneurial finance), whereas factor groups are mostly made up from supply-driven processes.

The "out-of-the-box thinking" cluster has a weak positive association with the creation of demand in the private sector and with the national and international research funds factors (academic sector). These two sectors often use bold and unconventional methods to solve problems and promote innovative solutions. Weaker negative ties exist between this sector and the private-public sector cooperation and the government investments for the creation of human capital clusters.

Mixed ties exist between the "out-of-the-box thinking" cluster and the government program and private and public sector activities for supporting innovation factors. Government programs and private sector activities supported by public agencies (for example, MATIMOP and Israel Export Institution processes) are much less likely to adopt "outside-the-box" thinking methods due to the conservative and bureaucratic nature of government agencies.

SUMMARY

In the course of the research, an innovation ecosystem map was constructed for Israel, based on the identified (and country-specific) linkages between key anchors and processes. The findings obtained from the analysis show that the Israeli ecosystem is a highly complex and interlinked network, exhibiting strong and significant linkages between its various components.

The results of the study reaffirm the important role of cultural characteristics and assets in driving and nurturing Israeli innovation. Evidence shows that strong ties exist between cultural anchors and supply- and demand-driven processes. Pure supply-side processes such as government support for the defense industries and the establishment of military R&D programs (for example, TALPIOT) were found to exert significant spillover effects on innovation infrastructure (for example, entrepreneurial and applied technological skills). The existence of strong scientific and technological base (for example, research universities) and solid entrepreneurial infrastructure (for example, emphasis on the teaching and development of entrepreneurial and applied technological skills at a young age) seems to be one of the key drivers of the Israeli innovation ecosystem. Israel's high ranking in "technological infrastructure" and in "scientific infrastructure", fifth and fourth in the world, respectively, as shown in the "Background" section above (competitiveness landscape), is reflected in the innovation ecosystem map; it contrasts sharply with Israel's low ranking (48th) in "basic infrastructure" (which includes roads, communications, etc.), which is notably lacking in the ecosystem map.

The negative link between the private and public sectors should not be overlooked. While government bureaucracy and red tape have vastly improved since the days when Israel was a government-dominated planned economy, it is still hard to do business in Israel; in the start-up nation, it is even hard to start a business (as we observed above, in the "Background" section).

The strongest catalysts of the Israeli innovation ecosystem are the joint demand and supply processes, focusing on government and public policy measures, private sector activities and dual private-public initiatives. Notable examples are the Chief Scientist programs (for example, MAGNET, NOFAR, MAGNETON), aimed at establishing cooperation and technology transfer between industry and the academia, and the support given by public sector agencies to private firms (MATIMOP and the Israel Export Institute). Empirical support for these findings is provided by a recent study conducted by Applied Economics Ltd (Lach et al., 2008). The research showed that Chief Scientist programs have two main effects on the Israeli economy: they create additional investment in R&D from the part of the firms (creation of new R&D that would not have been created without the support of the government) and they encourage technological spillovers between firms and industries (create additional GDP). The estimates show that a one million NIS government (Chief Scientist) grant in industry leads to an additional 1.28 million NIS investment by the firms in R&D. For every additional 100,000 NIS government investment in R&D, there is 157,000–224000 NIS growth in GDP.

The most important conclusion emerging from Israel's innovation ecosystem map is that the three core anchors in its center – "out-of-the-box" thinking, culture of empowerment and cultural diversity – are in many ways unique to Israel's history and culture. At independence, on 15 May 1948, Israel's population was only 800000 and GDP per capita was a minimal $1500. As a poor country, Israel developed a culture of improvisation and 'make-do'; facing military threat, Israel developed a culture of empowerment that stressed leadership and individual initiative, as well as a democratic environment in which everyone's views should be heard; and as a nation whose existence was based on providing a homeland for Jewish people persecuted abroad, Israel absorbed twice its initial population in immigrants in its first five years of existence, becoming a culture of diversity. These elements combine to generate unique chemistry that has led to enormous entrepreneurial energy. Other nations can of course study and learn from Israel's innovation ecosystem; but they are urged to adapt the lessons learned from their own history and culture, and to shape their own innovation ecosystems around their unique cultures, as Israel has done.

NOTES

*   With the assistance of Dr Eran Leck, Dr Daphne Getz and Vered Segal, our colleagues at the Samuel Neaman Institute for Advanced Studies in Science and Technology, Technion, Haifa, Israel.
1. World Bank Ease of Doing Business (www.doingbusiness.org, accessed 19 February 2014).
2. See Senor and Singer (2011).
3. See www.che.org.il, accessed 19 February 2014.
4. See www.ishitech.co.il/0904ar5.htm, accessed 19 February 2014.
5. See www.charedicts.org.il/en/about/, accessed 19 February 2014.

4. The Polish national innovation ecosystem*

INTRODUCTION

This chapter presents Poland's innovation ecosystem map. Poland is particularly interesting, in view of its relatively large population and economy (sixth largest in the EU), and its role as a path-breaker in the transition from a planned to market-based economy. We first describe the basics of Poland's economy and dramatic recent history. Next we present several indicators that benchmark Poland's global competitiveness and economic freedom, relative to other nations. We then proceed to map Poland's innovation ecosystem, first identifying key anchors and processes as revealed in the Experts Workshop, then linking the anchors and processes through cross-impact analysis. Finally, we present the innovation ecosystem visualization itself and the implications drawn from it, along with several illustrative case studies.

BACKGROUND

This large country of 38 million people and a land area of 313 000 sq km, had gross domestic product (GDP) growth of 4.3 percent in 2011, faster than nearly all other EU nations – though GDP growth inevitably slowed to 2.1 percent in 2012. Its unemployment rate in 2011 was lower than the EU rate (9.7 percent), though the slowdown in growth has caused unemployment to rise to 12.9 percent in November 2012. Poland attracted massive foreign direct investment in 2011 (2.8 percent of GDP), much of it from Germany. Poland's GDP per capita is a surprising 20 731 dollars (2011). Its currency, the zloty, is about three per dollar, which means it is much like the Chinese yuan, undervalued, giving Polish exports a boost.

According to Marcin Piątkowski, a World Bank Senior Economist, Poland has made effective use of some 10 billion euros of EU funds. Most of it was spent on low-tech, not high-tech, and the result was to make Poland part of Germany's wider industrial ecosystem, with Polish factories and workers providing low-cost manufacturing, buttressed by the undervalued currency. This is almost a Chinese model. It stands in stark contrast to, for instance, Hungary, which had a property bubble and which is mired in debt, much of it euro and dollar debt that both businesses and governments struggle to pay back.

Poland has found a pragmatic competitive strategy. To simplify: "If you have a big neighbor, find how you can hitch a ride on its economy, find what it needs, make it efficiently and at low cost, and you can do well." The big neighbor, of course, is Germany. Germany's economy has done relatively well during the EU/euro crisis. It has used neighboring Poland as an offshore site for lower-cost manufacturing and Poland has willingly and happily cooperated to implement this strategy.

Poland's national innovation ecosystem is particularly interesting for several reasons. First, Poland began the process of transition from a centrally-planned to open market-based economy in 1989. This is only 24 years ago. Unlike its Central European neighbors, Poland maintained its private agricultural sector, not allowing the Soviet Union to convert them to collective farms, and this has given Poland an unbroken history of having at least one major sector with first-hand knowledge of markets. Second, Poland is making strenuous efforts to foster innovation and entrepreneurship, and in some ways is breaking trail for other transition economies. Third, Poland is a large nation, sixth largest in the 27-nation EU bloc, after Germany (81 million), France (65 million), UK (62 million), Italy (60 million) and Spain (47 million). Its economy is relatively important in the Single Market.

According to a study of Poland's transition (Muczyk, undated, p. 4):

> Surprisingly, Poland chose [a] politically more risky strategy – that of converting to capitalism rapidly (known in the popular press as "shock therapy"); and several governments did, in fact, fall as the result of the hardships that much of the citizenry was forced to endure. In the euphoria that followed the demise of communism, politicians from the Solidarity movement lost sight of the actual difficulty associated with the conversion to a free market economy. Otherwise, they probably would have opted for the slower approach, as the Communist Party redux under a different label subsequently did. We must not forget that the leaders of the "Solidarity" movement, until they unexpectedly captured power through the ballot box, only had experience criticizing the old order and protesting, not running a nation; and there is a big difference.

Poland's experience with "shock therapy" was dramatic. American economist Jeffrey Sachs implemented the policy to help end Bolivia's disastrous hyperinflation, and constructed a similar program in Poland. The essence of shock therapy is to shift to a market economy rapidly and abruptly, slashing subsidies and above all ending the massive creation of money.[1] This caused great suffering in Poland; the rationale was that to implement a slow transition would allow the conservative reactionary forces of Communism to organize and oppose it. At the time there was deep concern that the USSR would intervene to end the experiment in free market economics, and social unrest during the early stages of the transition was very pronounced. In the end, Poland's farmers saved the day, as rising prices of eggs brought an increased supply, food prices began to decline; and the USSR leadership chose not to intervene.

POLAND'S CAPABILITIES IN THE FREE MARKET COMPETITION

In the following paragraphs we will present several economic indexes showing Poland's capabilities in coping with its transition challenges.

Global Competitiveness

Poland was 34th in global competitiveness in 2012, up from 44th in 2008. (A major jump occurred in 2010, from 44th to 32nd, a rise of 12 places.) According to the International Institute for Management Development (IMD) *World Competitiveness Yearbook*, Poland has a dynamic economy, predictable policy, a skilled workforce, competitive costs, good education, good labor relations, access to financing; and, of course, a big neighbor, Germany, that likes to invest in Poland because of its proximity.

Figure 4.1 shows Poland's competitiveness landscape. For most nations, the landscape graph resembles the Alps, with peaks and valleys, but for Poland, the rankings are remarkably consistent. Perhaps this in itself is a competitive advantage, with consistent (though mediocre) achievements across the key dimensions of competitiveness. The only real "peak" for Poland, among the sub-factors, is that of education, the very last one in Figure 4.1. Like nearly all post-Socialist nations, Poland has a truly excellent educational system, which it can leverage to achieve strong results in innovation.

Poland's competitiveness ranking reflects an unusual balance among the four dimensions that drive its ranking: Economic performance (30th), government efficiency (36th), business efficiency (39th), and infrastructure (36th). The sub-factors comprising each of the four dimensions are also highly consistent in their ranking, ranging from about 28th through to 39th. According to the IMD Yearbook, Poland's main strengths are: in economic performance, its exchange rate (10th), doggedly held to about 3 zlotys per dollar, in advance of embracing the euro; in government policy, its low corporate tax rate on profits (11th); in business efficiency, in entrepreneurship (6th) and unit labor costs in manufacturing (7th); and in

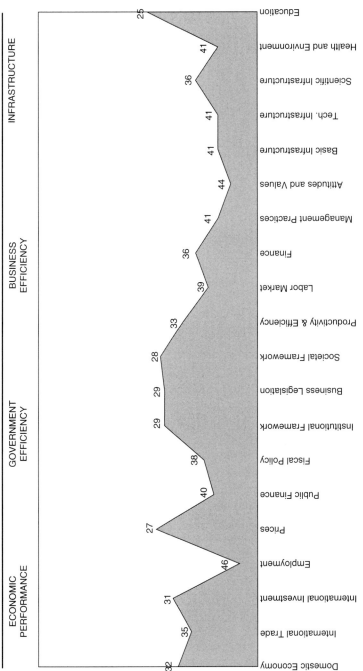

Note: The numbers are rankings, out of the 59 nations included in the *World Competitiveness Yearbook* survey.

Source: IMD, *World Competitiveness Yearbook 2012.*

Figure 4.1 Poland's competitiveness landscape

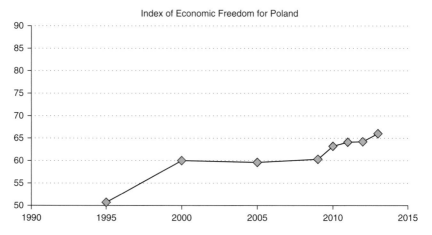

Source: *The Heritage Foundation*, Index of Economic Freedom 2013, see www.heritage.
org/index.

Figure 4.2   Poland: Economic freedom score, 1995–2013

infrastructure, in a low pupil-teacher ratio in primary schools (2nd), a low
dependency ratio, and high secondary school enrollment.

Economic Freedom

Poland first entered the Economic Freedom tabulation in 1985. As
a centrally-planned economy, its score was only 3.46 in 1985, and its
rank, 101st. Since 1990, Poland's economic freedom ranking has risen
rapidly, from 87th to 41st (7.29) in 2010. (See Figure 4.2, Economic
Freedom Index.) This transition has contributed significantly to Poland's
global competitiveness. Among aspects of government efficiency that are
counted among Poland's strengths are: low spending on subsidies, low-
tariff barriers, exchange rate stability, low state ownership of enterprises,
and excellence in central bank policy. It is interesting that Poland ranks
first among 59 countries in "redundancy costs" (that is, the cost of firing
unnecessary workers).

Ease of Doing Business

In practical terms, the climate in which innovators and entrepreneurs
operate depends on a series of 11 actions all business perform (paying
taxes, getting credit, etc.). For Poland, in 2012 the World Bank's ease of
doing business index ranks Poland at a relatively low overall 55th in the

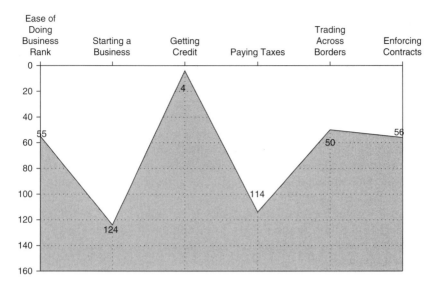

Source: Doing Business Project – The World Bank, 2012. See www.doingbusiness.org/ rankings.

Figure 4.3   Poland: Ease of doing business, 2012

world. Some business procedures are especially (and needlessly) complicated and costly in Poland: starting a business (ranked 124th, incongruous
for a nation striving to foster innovation); getting a construction permit
(ranked 160th), paying taxes (ranked 114th). Other business activities
are still needlessly tedious, but somewhat better: trading across borders
(50th), getting credit (4th), and enforcing contracts (56th).

Innovation and Entrepreneurship

In IMD's *World Competitiveness Yearbook* compilation, Poland ranked
very high in experts' responses to "entrepreneurship of managers is widespread in business", at 6th out of 59 countries, scoring 6.98 out of 10, just
behind Taiwan (7.67), Israel (7.44), Hong Kong (7.39), Lithuania (7.21)
and Malaysia (7.06). It is significant that Poland ranked higher in this variable than any other nation.

However, in "innovative capacity", a sub-factor within the dimension
scientific infrastructure ("innovative capacity of firms to generate new
products, services and/or services in your economy is high"), Poland
scored very low, ranking only 41st out of 59 nations, below most other
European countries. Few nations have such a large disparity between their

ranking on "entrepreneurship" and their ranking on "innovative capacity". We believe this is explained by Poland's competitive strategy, which prefers to subvent its industry to that of Germany, rather than at this stage drive manufacturing through research and development (R&D) and self-generated innovation.

To summarize, Poland has shown major, in some cases dramatic, improvement in its global competitiveness and economic freedom. Poland's competitiveness landscape is remarkably consistent, with rankings around 30th to 40th (of the 59 nations in the IMD sample) in most of the indicators; while the average ranking itself may not be impressive, there is considerable value in Poland's consistency across the four competitiveness dimensions (economy, business, government and infrastructure). In contrast, doing business in Poland ranges from exceptionally easy ("getting credit", ranked 4th in the world), to exceptionally difficult (124th in the world in "starting a business"). These indicators suggest that as in many transition nations, the vestiges of red tape and bureaucracy lingering from the old planning regimes linger long after the transition. This is apparently true for other Central European nations as well. Perhaps the most effective help for Polish innovation could be unrelated to innovation itself – simply removing the bureaucratic obstacles to starting and running businesses.

INNOVATION ECOSYSTEM

In this section, we present the results of the Experts Workshop, which generated a list of Poland's key innovation anchors and processes, in turn leading to the visualization of Poland's innovation ecosystem map.

Data Analysis

Anchors and processes
This section provides a summary of the raw inputs collected at the Polish Experts Workshop (see Chapter 2) conducted by CASE (Centrum Analiz Spoleczno-Ekonomicznych- Fundacja Naukowa). Table 4.1 lists 24 main anchors which were identified by the Polish experts as the pillars of their innovation system. Table 4.2 presents a list of 18 processes which were recognized by the experts as key elements driving and fostering innovation. It will be recalled that "anchors" are essentially similar to what economists call "stocks", or fixed assets, while processes are similar to what economists call "flows" (changes related to various anchors or stocks). The processes were ranked by the experts by their importance and classified according to which side of the market (supply or demand) they belong to.

Table 4.1   List of Polish innovation anchors

Number	Anchor Name
1	Tendency to tinker with things
2	High quality of human capital
3	Desire for success
4	Willingness to work hard
5	Education that fosters open minds
6	Constructive greed
7	Natural-born entrepreneurs
8	Large number of young, educated people
9	Creativity of the Polish society
10	Independence of thinking and acting
11	Selection of innovative people
12	General economic background and conditions
13	National pride (in high achievers)
14	Tendency to go against patterns
15	Broad scope of curriculum (historically)
16	Courage to take risks
17	Growing appreciation of innovation
18	Responsibility for the country at this historic moment
19	Six good regional innovation systems
20	Ample funds for innovation programs – opportunities
21	Historical opportunity for Poland because of EU funds
22	EU membership that forced authorities to think about innovation
23	Pool of people employed by MNCs for 10–15 years (currently being laid off)
24	International experience gained during emigration

Interaction among anchors and processes

The essence of an ecosystem is the interaction among its various components. The data generated in the Polish brainstorming workshop was used as inputs for further and more elaborate analysis. A "cross-impact analysis" (the perceived links between various anchors and processes) was employed to create a bipolar five-point Likert scale (ranging from a strong negative link, score 1, to a strong positive link, score 5, for each cell in a 24x18 cross-impact matrix).

Analysis of the Cross-Impact Results

Factor analysis was employed on the list of processes (variables). The anchors serve as observations in order to group the processes into major

Table 4.2   List of identified processes fostering Polish innovation, ranked by importance and classified by market side (supply, demand, or both)

Ranked Number (by importance)	Process Name	Demand side (D), Supply side (S) or both (D S)
1	Success stories of innovation businesses	D
2	EU money for innovation processes	S
3	Science system reform and the new law on science	S
4	Mobility of researchers – comeback from abroad	D
5	Growing number of researchers who think of commercialization	D
6	Easy ways of making money in Poland are over	D
7	Growing conscience that things depend on us	D
8	Changes in the assessment of scientists	S
9	Policy to attract foreign students to Poland	S
10	Growing awareness of innovation	D S
11	Departments for innovations at public administration	S
12	KFK – National Capital Fund	S
13	Creation of technology park as incubators	D
14	International discussion on innovation	S
15	Evolution of the Higher Education system	D
16	Decision-making process "kills" innovation efficiency	S
17	Public discussion about innovation	D S
18	Inferiority of the innovation system (rent of inferiority)	D S

factors according to the similarities in their linkages with the anchors. Tests of sample adequacy constituted the necessary preliminary conditions for conducting factor analysis and obtaining meaningful results. The Spearman correlation matrix among the processes provided the input for both the tests and the factor analysis. The linkage-pattern items obtained in the Polish workshop demonstrate good sampling adequacy, both at the overall (KMO > 0.514) and at the single item level (KMO $= 0.217 - 0.722$). The Spearman correlation matrix contains correlations with absolute values between 0.002–0.784, and the value of its determinant is 0.001, hence the existence of correlations without multi-collinearity is established. The result of the Bartlett's sphericity test rejects the null hypothesis that the correlation matrix is an identity matrix ($p = 0.000$).

Exploratory principal axis factor analysis with subsequent orthogonal rotation (Varimax rotation with Kaiser Normalization) produced five factors, that together explain 84.0 percent of the variance. The factor loadings are presented in Table 4.3. In order to facilitate factor labeling, the dominant items, marked in bold in Table 4.3, were defined as those with an absolute value of the loading greater than 0.46.

Through the factor analysis we distilled the existing innovation process drivers down to five key factors. They are:

1. *Increased awareness of innovation in public discourse*: public discussion about innovation; international discussion on innovation; growing awareness of innovation; departments for innovation at public administration; success stories of innovation; how business and decision-making process "kills" innovation efficiency. This factor explains 25.5 percent of the variance.

2. *Government policies to encourage innovation implementation*: science system reform and the new law on science; evolution of the higher-education system; changes in the assessment of scientists and policy to attract foreign students to Poland. This factor adds 19 percent to the explanation of the variance.

3. *Government programs*: KFK – National Capital Fund and creation of technology parks as incubators. This factor adds 13.9 percent to the explanation of the variance.

4. *Private sector attractiveness*: growing number of researchers who think of commercialization and mobility of researchers – comeback from abroad. This factor adds 13.2 percent to the explanation of the variance.

5. *Encouragement of technological independence*: growing conscience that things depend on us and easy ways of making money in Poland are over. This factor adds 12.3 percent to the explanation of the variance.

The first, second and third factors are supply-driven, focusing on government and public policy measures, the fourth and fifth factors are mainly demand-driven.

Table 4.3   *Factor analysis results for the Polish innovation ecosystem*

Factor Name	Items (Processes)	Factor				
		1	2	3	4	5
Increased awareness of innovation in public discourse	Public discussion about innovation	**0.896**	0.013	0.059	0.160	0.249
	International discussion on innovation	**0.896**	0.013	0.059	0.160	0.249
	Growing awareness of innovation	**0.784**	0.387	0.303	-0.236	0.074
	Departments for innovations at public administration	**0.784**	0.387	0.303	-0.236	0.074
	EU money for innovation processes	**0.706**	0.230	0.309	-0.245	-0.035
	Success stories of innovation businesses	**-0.619**	0.009	-0.208	0.501	0.180
	Decision making process "kills" innovation efficiency	**-0.445**	0.419	0.191	-0.442	-0.037
Government policies to encourage innovation implementation	Science system reform and the new law on science	0.083	**0.939**	-0.068	-0.002	0.182
	Evolution of the Higher Education system	0.083	**0.939**	-0.068	-0.002	0.182
	Changes in the assessment of scientists	0.184	**0.776**	0.315	0.108	-0.005
	Policy to attract foreign students to Poland	0.223	**0.507**	0.174	0.059	-0.413
Government programs	KFK – National Capital Fund	0.219	0.068	**0.949**	0.107	-0.028
	Creation of technology park as incubators	0.219	0.068	**0.949**	0.107	-0.028
Private sector attractiveness	Growing number of researchers who think of commercialization	0.137	0.109	0.171	**0.896**	-0.212
	Mobility of researchers – comeback from abroad	-0.377	0.037	0.171	**0.841**	0.096

Factor Name	Items (Processes)	Factor				
Encouragement of technological independence	Growing conscience that things depend on us	0.193	0.218	0.054	0.074	**0.913**
	Easy ways of making money in Poland are over	0.192	0.066	-0.060	-0.116	**0.896**
Percent of variance		25.5	19.0	14.0	13.2	12.3
Cumulative percent		25.5	44.5	58.5	71.6	84.0
KMO* = 0.514						
Cronbach's Alpha = 0.969						

CONSTRUCTION OF A NATIONAL INNOVATION ECOSYSTEM MAP FOR POLAND

The next methodological step included the classification of processes and anchors into groups. The processes were grouped according to the results of the factor analysis. The classification of anchors into clusters did not involve a similar statistical procedure and was based on logic. The anchors were grouped into five clusters as listed in Table 4.4: entrepreneurship; human capital infrastructure; culture of empowerment; financial and regional systems; economic institutions.

In the final step of this methodological exercise, an innovation map was produced for the Polish ecosystem. A large number of interactions between

Table 4.4   List of anchors grouped into major clusters

Name of Cluster	Anchor Name
Entrepreneurship cluster	Tendency to tinker things Willingness to work hard Greed Natural-born entrepreneurs Tendency to go against patterns Courage to take the risk Growing appreciation of innovation
Human capital infrastructure	High quality of human capital Education and open mind Number of young, educated people Creativity of the Polish society Pool of people trained for 10–15 years with MNCs (currently being laid off) International experience gained during emigration
Culture of empowerment	Desire for success Independence of thinking and acting Selecting the innovative people National pride (of achievements of participants)
Financial and regional systems	Broad scope of curriculum (historically) Six good regional innovation systems A lot of money for innovation programs – opportunities Historical change in Poland because of EU funds
Economic institutions	General economic background and conditions Responsibility for the country at this historic moment EU membership that forced authorities to think about innovation

anchor clusters and process factors proved to be insignificant. This can be seen in Figure 4.4, describing the linkages between the two groups, and the overall national innovation ecosystem map for Poland.

The interactions between the group of anchors (clusters) and the group of processes was computer-based on a mathematical procedure for determining and weighting the direction and strength of link between the factors and clusters (see in Chapter 2). The results show that the entrepreneurship cluster has strong positive interaction with only one factor: private sector attractiveness (for example, growing number of researchers who think of commercialization and the return of researchers from abroad). It seems that the experience gained by Polish researchers in domestic and foreign universities is a key catalyst in fostering entrepreneurship in Poland. It is important to note that supply-side innovation "tools" such as government programs and government policies to encourage innovation implementations were found to be unconnected to entrepreneurship.

The first factor (increased awareness of innovation in public discourse) has positive and strong linkage with only one component of the entrepreneurship cluster (growing appreciation of innovation anchor), so does the third factor (government program) that only positively relates to the "tendency to tinker things" anchor within the entrepreneurship cluster.

Supply-side polices and strategies (for example, government programs, private-public partnerships) are key tools used by Western countries for supporting innovation since the 1960s. These policies and strategies continuously improve and evolve over time. The lack of a free market economy in Poland until the early 1990s, has placed Poland in an inferior starting point with regard to supply-side initiatives, as these were primarily targeted at the private market and aimed at spurring economic growth. The fast transition from a centrally planned economy to a free market economy in the 1990s has mainly contributed to the enhancement of demand-side processes and initiatives, where supply-side initiatives in supporting innovation remained lagging and insufficient. The success of implementing demand-driven innovation policies largely depends on improving supply-side initiatives, as these two components are complementary. This step will allow Poland to maximize the potential of its innovation ecosystem.

It can be argued that Poland has one major innovation advantage over other Central European "transition" countries – although it was socialist until the early 1990s, it retained its private farms, which the USSR never succeeded in collectivizing. This tradition of entrepreneurial energy in agriculture can provide a strong cultural base on which to revive and strengthen entrepreneurial innovation. Because Russia collectivized everything in 1917, virtually no one alive today has a personal memory of a

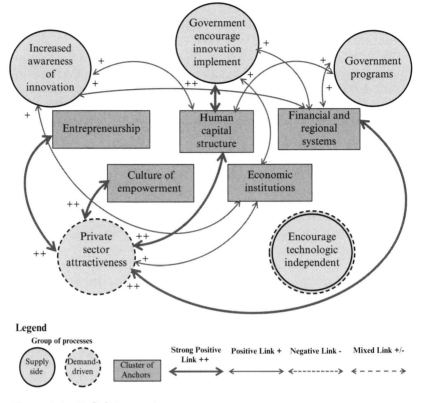

Figure 4.4   Polish innovation ecosystem

free market system; we believe this is a major handicap. However, on the other hand, although the persistence of private farming had an enormous influence on Polish society in general (protecting traditional values from eradication during the Communist era), it cannot be regarded as a true innovation asset in the development of an innovation-driven economy. The ethos of farmers encompasses the virtue of hard work, but at the same time it is characterized by extreme risk aversion, which is anathema to the development of innovative enterprises.

The human capital infrastructure cluster has strong positive ties to two factors (Figure 4.4): government policies to encourage innovation implementation and private sector attractiveness. Weak positive interactions exist between this cluster and two other process factors: increased awareness of innovation in public discourse and government programs. The existence of high-quality human capital is a key component in driving and supporting innovation processes in any country.

The culture of empowerment cluster has strong positive interaction with only one factor: private sector attractiveness. This is not surprising as "empowerment culture" is usually associated with demand-side features. The first, second and third factors (supply-driven) were found to be unconnected to this cluster. It is also important to point out that the last factor (encouragement of technological independence), which belongs to the supply and demand side, was also found to be uncorrelated to the culture of empowerment cluster. Encouragement of technological dependence may not be purely and typically demand side – it reflects a condition specific to Poland and perhaps other transition economies, and is independent of entrepreneurs' strategies and is beyond their control.

The financial and regional systems cluster has especially strong linkage with the private sector attractiveness factor. Weaker positive ties exist between this cluster and three other factors: increased awareness of innovation in public discourse, government policies to encourage innovation implementation and government programs.

The economic institutions cluster has moderate positive ties with three factors: increased awareness of innovation in public discourse, government policies to encourage innovation implementation and private sector attractiveness. Strong economic institutions in Poland are closely related to better-designed and better-informed public policies and also contribute to a stronger private sector. It is noteworthy that the last factor group (encouragement of technological independence) is not connected to any cluster. This emphasizes the weakness of the Polish innovation system.

It is important to stress that the "government policies to encourage innovation implementation" process is in fact strongly related to the science and education sectors, and not directly to technology policy or to innovation implementation. This was clearly the intention of those who participated in the Experts Workshop.

CASE STUDIES

Healthcare

Former socialist countries in Central and Eastern Europe all have one important legacy from the socialist regimes: outstanding educational systems and as a result, superior human capital. This is true of Poland in particular – its educational infrastructure ranks higher than any other variable, in its competitiveness landscape (see "Background" Section). Poland's human capital has helped to generate a vigorous, thriving innovation ecosystem in the area of healthcare. A recent report by the Polish

Academy of Sciences (2012) lists some 100 innovative companies in the healthcare industry, ranked by their innovativeness. The Academy developed its own methodology for this ranking, based on five key variables: market innovation, process innovation, investment in innovation activity, foreign patents and EU contracts.

The second-ranked company, out of the 100, is *Selvita SA*. Selvita leverages research on new chemical entities originating in Polish universities or resulting from Selvita's own discovery programs. The company has expertise in the newest approach to drug discovery, which identifies "target proteins" and identifies "solution proteins" that offset or neutralize the harmful molecule.

Third ranked is *Adamed Sp. Z.o.o.*, founded by Dr Marian Adamkiewicz. Initially the company specialized in manufacturing gynecology products and medical equipment, but is now focused on drug discovery. Its first drug Furaginum, which treats urinary tract infections, was brought to market in 1991 and has since been followed by many new and successful drugs.

The top-ranked firm is *LfC Sp. Z.o.o.* This is the only company that scored four As in the five-variable ranking system. It may well be Poland's most innovative company overall. LfC won a prize in 2007 for the "most innovative product in Poland", and shows the crucial importance of a visionary entrepreneur. Founded by Lechoslaw F. Ciupik some 22 years ago, LfC "creates and produces methods and measures for spine treatment". According to the company founder,[2] "In order to establish and reinforce its position, it had to become competitive on the market. It chose the path of co-creating surgery by contributing the idea, conducting research, implementing bio-engineering high-tech, and introducing new surgical methods. It sold the know-how to the United States, including the patent, and created its own IP management system." Ciupik created a powerful culture in LfC, captured by the mantra he implemented in 1992 (not long after the transition): "If we do it, we do it better [than anyone in the world]." By implementing a system for capturing intellectual property value, Ciupik succeeded in selling his new surgical method for spine treatment to a large American partner, "the first comprehensive IP and patent sale to the U.S. in the post-war history of Poland", he notes, a breakthrough that may blaze a trail for other Polish startups.

Software

Poland has a thriving software industry. A good example is Ivona, which developed text-to-speech technology. Ivona was acquired earlier this year (2013) by Amazon, for use in Amazon's successful consumer product Kindle. Amazon's Vice President, Dave Limp, noted that Ivona's exceptional text-to-speech technology leads the industry in natural voice quality, accuracy and ease of use, and said that Ivona is already instrumental in helping Amazon deliver excellent accessibility features on Kindle Fire, including text-to-speech, voice guide and explore by touch. Co-founder and CEO Lukasz Osowski commented, "For more than ten years, the IVONA team has been focused on creating innovative text-to-speech technologies . . . We are all thrilled that Amazon is supporting our growth so that we can continue to innovate and deliver exceptional voice and language support for our customers."[3] Ivona and LfC both show how Polish entrepreneurs seek alliances and strategic partnerships with large global countries, and how foreign companies seek and value Polish creativity and innovation.

SUMMARY

The Polish innovation ecosystem seems to be in its initial stages of development. This is understandable. As a transition nation, Poland's economy is still a "work in progress", shifting from a planning model to a free market one. (Despite this, there are striking examples of entrepreneurial success, that serve as role models for would-be Polish start-ups.)

As a result, there is low connectivity and loose ties between the various factor and cluster groups. This is probably typical of early-stage innovation ecosystems, which are, in a sense, embryos that are in early stages of development. However, Poland's relative success in innovation may stem in part from the fact that it retained free market structures in its agriculture, which preserved Poland's legacy of enterprise and initiative during the planned economy decades. Poland's agricultural sector was never collectivized under the USSR, in contrast to other Eastern European nations. Thus, Polish farmers have had an unbroken link with the free-enterprise tradition – a fact that played an important role in the difficult early days of Poland's transition to a market-based system. In contrast, Russia's shift to a market system was done with virtually no living Russian having a personal memory of such a system, which disappeared in 1917. However, experts on Poland note rightly that Polish farmers are highly risk averse, like farmers everywhere, and this risk aversion somewhat offsets the culture of enterprise.

The demand-side interactions in the system are much more significant than the supply-side interactions. This conclusion, however, must be qualified by the fact that the demand-side aspect is based on only two true demand-side processes: private sector attractiveness (that is, profitability), and the desire for technological independence, which in turn appears to flow from the ingrained desire of the Polish people to determine their own destiny. While in many nations technological innovation is a path to wealth and value creation, for Poland it also appears to be a source of expression of national pride and sovereignty.

To end on an upbeat note, we believe that the embryonic nature of Poland's innovation ecosystem is a distinct advantage. Poland begins the work of painting its own innovation portrait on a clean canvas. It can benchmark other nations, learn from their experience, and build its own system unencumbered with baggage collected in the past. It can embrace and adapt all the innovation policies that have proved successful in other nations, and reject those that have failed. In this sense, building on a strong human capital base, Poland's innovation ecosystem shows great promise for the future.

NOTES

*   With the assistance of Dr Yitzchak Goldberg and Haik Zakrzewski, CASE, Poland.
1.   See Daniel Yergin and Joseph Stanislow (2002), *The Commanding Heights*, New York: Free Press, ch. 10.
2.   See www.lfc.com.pl/pdf/pm2011.pdf, accessed 19 February 2014.
3.   See www.webpronews.com/amazon-acquires-ivona-makers-of-key-kindle-fire-features-2013-01, accessed 19 February 2014.

5. The German national innovation ecosystem*

INTRODUCTION

Germany has dominated news about the European Union (EU) in recent years, mostly due to its role in supplying emergency financial aid to EU nations and banks in distress. But as Europe's largest economy, and as a technological leader, Germany has another important role – as a driver of innovation. This role has major importance, because when the EU financial crisis is finally resolved, EU nations will then begin to address the key issue, how to restore economic growth. When this issue becomes foremost on the agenda, so will innovation, and Germany's voice will be heard.

This chapter presents Germany's innovation ecosystem. We begin with a short overview of Germany's economy and competitiveness. Next, we examine Germany's global competitiveness, broken down according to the key elements of its "competitiveness landscape", and Germany's economic freedom and ease of doing business, as well as the innovative spirit in its managers. Overall, Germany emerges as a nation with few economic weaknesses, with the possible exception of public debt and labor market rigidity. We then present Germany's key anchors and processes that drive innovation, and how they interact. Finally, we discuss Germany's innovation ecosystem, along with a case study of Berlin's high-energy entrepreneurial activities.

BACKGROUND

Germany's economy is the largest in Europe, and fourth largest in the world, with gross domestic product (GDP) (measured in terms of purchasing power parity (PPP)) of $3.573 trillion (2011). GDP per capita (in terms of PPP) is $38 756 (2011), with a population of 81.3 million. GDP growth slowed from 3 percent in 2011 to only 0.8 percent in 2012, due to the ongoing EU economic and financial crisis. Germany's rate of unemployment, at 6.9 percent of the workforce (November 2012), is significantly lower than that of the EU average (11.7 percent), partly due to Germany's success in maintaining its exports. For the 12-month period up to October 2012, Germany had a staggering current account surplus of $212 billion, larger even than that of China, due in part to German success in exporting to faster-growing Asian economies. German export success is due in part to the fact that for German goods, the external value of the euro is undervalued; this in turn stems from the downward pressure on the euro coming from fiscally-distressed southern European nations (Spain, Greece, Italy). German inflation is about two percent annually, slightly less than the EU average. Germany, as the EU's largest economy, has a very small budget deficit (0.2 percent of GDP), and has been bearing the brunt of financial support for the nations with high deficits, such as Greece, with a deficit of seven percent of GDP.

GERMANY'S COMPETITIVENESS AND ECONOMIC FREEDOM

In the following paragraphs we will introduce several economic benchmarks showing Germany's relative ability to compete in global markets: its global competitiveness rank and a breakdown of its components, the overall freedom to do business in Germany's economy, and the ease of doing business in Germany, measured across ten separate activities that entrepreneurs encounter.

Global Competitiveness

Germany's economy is highly globally competitive, despite its relatively high wages, offset by very high labor productivity. According to the International Institute for Management Development (IMD) *World Competitiveness Yearbook*, Germany ranks ninth in competitiveness, out of 59 globally competing nations. This rank, for 2012, is up from 16th in 2010, and reflects the fact that Germany's economy has fared well, and has been managed well, despite the ongoing euro crisis (See IMD *World Competitiveness Yearbook 2012.*)

Figure 5.1 shows the competitiveness landscape for Germany, across the four dimensions that comprise it. Germany's strength lies in two of the four: in its economic performance (rank of 5), and in its superb infrastructure (rank of 7, including a rank of 3rd in the world in scientific infrastructure, stemming from its great research universities and research and development (R&D) centers, and a rank of seventh in health and environment). In contrast, Germany ranks only 19th in government efficiency and 17th in business efficiency.

The competitiveness landscape reveals some great strengths and glaring

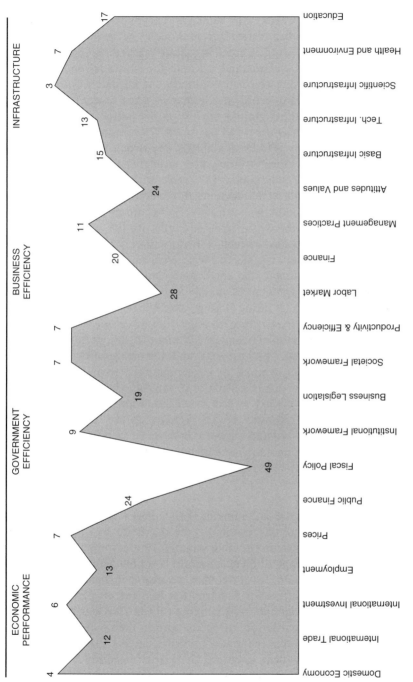

Note: The numbers are rankings, out of the 59 nations included in the *World Competitiveness Yearbook* survey.

Source: IMD, *World Competitiveness Yearbook 2012.*

Figure 5.1 Germany's competitiveness landscape

weaknesses. Germany ranks only 49th in "fiscal policy", reflecting concern over Germany's budget deficit (even though the government budget is essentially balanced). The rank in "labor market" is 28th, reflecting unions, and rigid labor laws, and the rank for "attitudes and values" is 24th, perhaps reflecting Germany's ambivalent attitude toward the EU and the sums needed to rescue it. Germany's great research universities are reflected in its third ranking for "scientific infrastructure", though technological infrastructure ranks only 13th, for reasons that are hard to understand (Germany's R&D capability is very strong, and its Fraunhofer R&D centers are exemplary). Some other strengths are "productivity and efficiency" and "societal framework" (rank of 7 for each), prices (7th, reflecting price stability) and the domestic economy (4th).

What makes Germany attractive? According to the *World Competitiveness Yearbook*, the main strengths are the skilled workforce, stable predictable policy, reliable infrastructure, strong R&D culture, high educational level and effective legal environment. Underlying these is Germany's *mittelstand*, the small and medium-size enterprises that produce precision manufactures, mainly for export.

Among the challenges facing Germany are: the threat of a larger budget deficit, the energy infrastructure (as a decision was made to close nuclear plants), the banking system (which holds unknown amounts of shaky sovereign bonds), barriers to investment, and a shortage of skilled workers as the population ages. Among the key strengths is Germany's diversified economy (ranks first out of all nations), strong exports, strong capital markets, high productivity, protection of intellectual property and high innovative capacity. Among the key weaknesses are Germany's direct investment, both inward and outward; high social security and corporate tax rates, short working hours, and high broadband costs.

Economic Freedom

The Heritage Foundation annually benchmarks leading nations, to measure their "economic freedom" – the degree to which their economies permit unhampered economic initiative and entrepreneurship. This measure combines eight different aspects of "economic freedom": business freedom, trade freedom, fiscal freedom, government spending, monetary freedom, investment freedom, financial freedom and property rights. For 2013, Germany's economic freedom score (out of 100) was 72.8, ranking it 19th freest in the world (out of 177 nations in the rankings). Germany improved in six of ten economic freedoms in 2012, including financial freedom, government spending, and labor freedom. The Heritage Foundation reports that the German economy has demonstrated "impres-

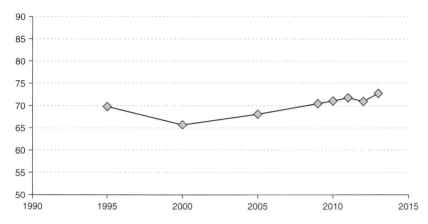

Source: The Heritage Foundation, Index of Economic Freedom 2013, see www.heritage. org/index/.

Figure 5.2   Germany: Economic freedom score, 1995–2013

sive resilience" in withstanding global and European economic instability. Since 2000, Germany has shown small but steady improvements in the economic freedom of its economy (see Figure 5.2).

Germany ranks second in the world in property rights and 14th in "freedom from corruption", giving it a high score in the "rule of law". However, taxes, and regulations give Germany a low ranking in "limited government", with a rank of 159th in fiscal freedom, and a low rank of 148th in government spending. Germany has relative "monetary freedom" and "business freedom", but its labor laws give it a low rank of 149th in "labor freedom".

In terms of markets, German markets are relatively open, with ranks of 11th in "trade freedom", 10th in "investment freedom", and 17th in financial freedom. The major change in 2013 was a substantial improvement in "financial freedom", as regulatory strictures on banks were eased, as the global financial crisis eased somewhat. It is worth noting that the average rate of tariffs in Germany is a low 1.6 percent, with relatively few non-tariff barriers. Goods flow freely across borders, especially, of course, with the EU Single Market. Germany's three-tier system of banks (private, public, and cooperative) is regarded as relatively stable.

Ease of Doing Business

Figure 5.3 shows the results of the World Bank's tabulation of "ease of doing business" for Germany, across its various dimensions.

Overall, Germany ranks 20th in the world in ease of doing business,

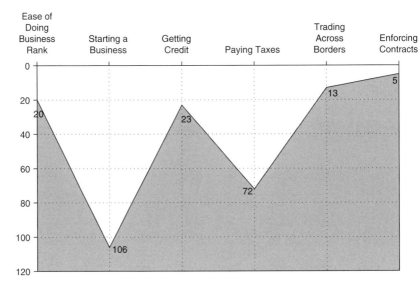

Source: Doing Business Project – The World Bank, 2012, see www.doingbusiness.org/
rankings.

Figure 5.3   Germany: Ease of doing business, 2012

similar to its rank of 19th in economic freedom. Again, typically, there is very high variance. Starting a business is extremely difficult in Germany (rank of 106th). There are nine separate procedures to do (only one in Canada, and three in Singapore), and they take an average of 15 days, compared with three days in Singapore and five days in Canada, and only seven days in France. But getting credit is quite easy (23rd), paying taxes is difficult (rank of 72nd), trading across borders is easy (rank of 13th), and enforcing contracts is very easy (rank of 5th).

Innovation and Entrepreneurship

In the 2012 World Competitiveness rankings, Germany ranks relatively high, 12th out of 59 nations, in "entrepreneurship of managers is widespread in business", according to the experts. In "innovative capacity" (innovative capacity of firms to generate new products, processes and/ or services is high), Germany ranks very high, 3rd out of 59, just behind Switzerland and Israel. Much of this innovative capacity apparently exists in the *mittelstand*, in incremental innovation that constantly seeks to improve existing products and processes, rather than in radical innovation that brings entirely new products to market.

To summarize, overall, the picture that emerges from the above analysis is a German economy that has fundamental strengths in education, science, technology and infrastructure, all of which provide the foundations for innovation. Germany's innovation is mainly incremental, rather than radical, and the result has been perhaps to underestimate the creative skill of German managers and businesspersons, especially since much of this innovation occurs in small and medium-sized businesses that attract little media attention, and involve no highly-publicized exits or financing deals. Germany's innovation is uniquely German, and has yielded strong results despite the ongoing global financial and economic crisis that has afflicted Europe in particular. Its innovation ecosystem has helped make Germany the world's second largest exporter, and one of the few major Western nations able to export significantly to China and the rest of Asia. For these reasons, a deeper understanding of the workings of Germany's innovation ecosystem is worthwhile. We now turn to this subject.

INNOVATION ECOSYSTEM

In this section, we describe the key anchors and processes that drive Germany's innovation ecosystem, as determined in the Experts Workshop, and the interactions among them, as determined by cross-impact analysis. We then show, and discuss, the innovation ecosystem map itself, and provide a case study of entrepreneurship in Berlin. We conclude with some policy implications.

Data Analysis

Anchors and processes
This section provides a summary of the raw inputs collected at the German Experts Workshop (see Chapter 2) conducted by the Stuttgart team from the University Hohenheim, Germany. Table 5.1 lists 31 main anchors which were identified by the German experts as the pillars of their innovation system. Table 5.2 presents a list of 26 processes which were recognized by the experts as key elements driving and fostering innovation. These processes were ranked by the experts by their importance and classified according to which side of the market (supply or demand) they belong to. It will be recalled that "anchors" are essentially similar to what economists call "stocks", or fixed assets, while processes are similar to what economists call "flows" (changes related to various anchors, or stocks).

Table 5.1   List of German innovation anchors

Number	Anchor Name
1	Strong competition encompasses the entire value chain
2	Public-funded basic research
3	Public-funded applied research
4	Diversified education system
5	Diversified technological structure
6	Infrastructure
7	Economic and political federalism
8	Numerous SMEs
9	Big domestic market
10	No tuition fees
11	Efficient patent system
12	Numerous MNEs
13	Decentralized support programs
14	Functioning competition law
15	Human capital
16	Virtues
17	Central location
18	Industry associations
19	Institutional and political stability
20	Technological leadership in numerous industries
21	Middle high-tech
22	Cross-section technologies
23	Joint projects
24	Labor unions
25	Export strengths
26	Good reputation
27	Few natural resources
28	Financial system oriented to SMEs
29	Consumer protection
30	Public test institutions
31	Made in Germany – Reputation

Interaction among anchors and processes

The essence of an ecosystem is the interaction among its various components. The data generated in the German brainstorming workshop was used as inputs for further and more elaborate analysis. First, processes which did not receive any points in the ranking procedure were omitted from the analysis. Second, the original cross-impact analysis key was transformed to a bipolar five-point Likert scale ranging from strongly negative link (1) to strongly positive link (5) for each cell in a 31×17 cross-impact matrix.

Table 5.2 *List of identified processes fostering German innovation,*
ranked by importance and classified by market side (supply,
demand, or both)

Ranked Number (by importance)	Process Name	Demand side (D), Supply side (S) or both (D S)
1	Collective process of innovation	B
2	Tax incentives for R&D expenditures	D
3	Problem-orientation	D
4	Cluster strategies	S
5	Standardization	S
6	Subsidization of environmentally-friendly technology	S
7	Engineering	S
8	Support for SMEs	S
9	Demand-pull strategies of large companies	D
10	"Greening" preferences	B
11	Export orientation	S
12	Vocational training	S
13	Functional optimization	S
14	Maintenance of a strong industrial core	S
15	User-producer relationships	B
16	Public relations	S
17	Funding of so-called MINT subjects: mathematics, information science, natural sciences and technology	S
18	Price subsidies	D
19	Funding of collective research	S
20	Public procurement	D
21	Public foresight	S
22	Technology transfer (public - private)	S
23	Privatization	S
24	Promotion of women	S
25	Cultivating contacts	S
26	Certification	B

Analysis of the Cross-Impact Results

Factor analysis was employed on the list of processes (variables). The anchors serve as observations in order to group the processes into major factors according to the similarities in their linkages with the anchors. Tests of sample adequacy constituted the necessary preliminary conditions for conducting factor analysis and obtaining meaningful results. The Spearman correlation matrix among the processes provided the input for both the tests and the factor analysis. The linkage-pattern items obtained in the German workshop demonstrate good sampling adequacy, both at the overall (KMO > 0.639) and at the single item level (KMO = 0.207 – 0.843). The Spearman correlation matrix contains correlations with absolute value between 0.001–0.699, and the value of its determinant is 0.001, hence the existence of correlations without multi-collinearity is established. The result of the Bartlett's sphericity test rejects the null hypothesis that the correlation matrix is an identity matrix (p = 0.000).

Exploratory principal axis factor analysis with subsequent orthogonal rotation (Varimax rotation with Kaiser normalization) produced five factors, that together explain 70.0 percent of the variance. The factor loadings are presented in Table 5.3. In order to facilitate factor labeling, the dominant items, marked in bold in Table 5.3, were defined as those with an absolute value of the loading greater than 0.49.

Through the factor analysis we distilled the existing innovation process drivers down to five key factors. They are:

1. *Tax and subsidy policies*: problem-orientation; subsidization of environmentally-friendly technology; price subsidies; funding MINT subjects: mathematics, information science, natural sciences and technology; tax incentives for R&D expenditures. This factor explains 21.6 percent of the variance.
2. *Market-driven forces*: demand-pull strategies of large companies; functional optimization; support for SMEs (small and medium enterprises); user-producer relationship. This factor adds 14.8 percent to the explanation of the variance.
3. *Development of key skills*: vocational training; export orientation; maintenance of a strong industrial core; engineering. This factor adds 14.2 percent to the explanation of the variance.
4. *Cluster strategies*: cluster strategies; collective process of innovation. This factor adds 11.5 percent to the explanation of the variance.
5. *Standardization*: standardization. This factor adds 8.0 percent to the explanation of the variance.

The first and third factors are supply-driven, focusing on government and public policy measures, the second, fourth and fifth factors are mostly demand-driven.

Table 5.3 *Factor analysis results for the German innovation ecosystem*

Factor Name	Items (Processes)	Factor				
		1	2	3	4	5
Tax and subsidy policies	Problem-orientation	**0.796**	0.154	0.102	0.093	0.103
	Subsidization of environmentally-friendly technology	**0.725**	0.377	-0.053	-0.069	0.075
	"Greening" preferences	**0.668**	0.153	0.227	0.139	-0.331
	Price subsidies	**0.647**	0.188	0.121	0.377	0.197
	Funding MINT subjects: mathematics, information science, natural sciences and technology	**0.582**	-0.015	0.559	0.061	-0.262
	Tax incentives for R&D expenditures	**0.470**	0.061	-0.092	0.490	-0.012
Market-driven forces	Demand-pull strategies of large companies	0.046	**0.760**	0.203	0.097	0.069
	Functional optimization	0.457	**0.746**	0.254	-0.149	-0.037
	Support for SMEs	0.435	**0.634**	0.012	0.271	-0.075
	User-producer relationships	0.196	**0.571**	0.289	0.440	-0.009
Development of key skills	Vocational training	0.084	0.301	**0.803**	-0.065	-0.174
	Export orientation	-0.147	0.381	**0.661**	0.233	0.253
	Maintenance of a strong industrial core	0.559	-0.033	**0.601**	0.040	0.171
	Engineering	0.535	0.386	**0.560**	0.094	0.189
Cluster strategies	Cluster strategies	0.072	0.021	0.220	**0.769**	-0.257
	Collective process of innovation	0.045	0.176	-0.096	**0.759**	0.355

Table 5.3 (continued)

Factor Name	Items (Processes)	Factor				
		1	2	3	4	5
Standardization	Standardization	0.083	0.011	0.039	0.014	**0.874**
	Percent of variance	21.6	14.8	14.2	11.5	8.0
	Cumulative percent	21.6	36.4	50.6	62.1	70.1

KMO* = 0.639
Cronbach's Alpha = 0.987

CONSTRUCTION OF A NATIONAL INNOVATION ECOSYSTEM MAP FOR GERMANY

BOX 5.1   CASE STUDY: BERLIN AS SILICON "TAL"*

What follows is excerpted from an article in *The New York Times* by Mark Scott (2013): **"Technology Start-Ups Take Root in Berlin: ReadMill, DailyDeal, SoundCloud, RocketInternet, CityDeal, Aupeo, Research Gate, EyeEm, Wooga"**

Near the Rosenthaler Platz subway station here [in Berlin], signs of the city's high-tech future blend seamlessly with its communist past.

Decrepit breweries and stables have been converted to communal offices decked out in colorful Ikea furniture. Achingly cool coffee shops with names like Betahaus and St. Oberholz are packed with programmers in their 20s and 30s hunched over shiny new laptops. And even as the city's unemployment broadly remains high, vintage clothing stores selling patent-leather Dr. Martens boots for 180 euros, or $235, entice technology transplants from across Europe with promotions in English.

"I got sucked into Berlin," said Henrik Berggren, a Swedish college dropout who moved here in 2011 to work on his e-book venture, ReadMill. "It became clear that this was the place to be."

More than two decades after the fall of the Berlin Wall, the German capital has gone from a cold war relic to one of the fastest-growing start-up communities. Engineers and designers have flooded into Berlin in recent years, attracted by the underground music scene, cutting-edge art galleries, stylish bars and low rent.

Hours after landing at Tegel airport, Mr. Berggren, a bearded 33-year-old computer programmer, found an apartment with two 20-something Germans in one of the city's trendiest neighborhoods for just 300 Euros, or $390, a month. A few days later, he secured a cheap office for his four-person team, a space they shared with several other start-ups.

With the new wave of entrepreneurs, Berlin, once viewed as the poor relation to Germany's main business centers, like Frankfurt and Hamburg, is improving its ranking in the country's economic hierarchy.

In March, the country's chancellor, Angela Merkel, toured several local technology firms in a show of support. The city's politicians also are trying to make it easier for international workers to get visas by fast-tracking applications from technology professionals and other workers.

"The scene is very young," said Alex Ljung, the co-founder of SoundCloud, a music Web site backed by the American venture capital giant Kleiner Perkins Caufield & Byers. "Berlin isn't proven yet. It's much like a start-up in that way."

By Silicon Valley standards, Berlin is still a backwater.

Entrepreneurs say high-quality programmers and engineers are hard to find, and a lack of early-stage funding from venture capital firms, particularly those in Europe, has hampered companies' growth. After getting burned by the dot-com bust, German venture capitalists have largely shied away from making big investments, preferring to finance early-stage companies with checks of less than $2 million.

The city also is trying to overcome its reputation for copying American business models rather than developing innovative ideas.

The Samwer brothers, whose Berlin start-up incubator Rocket Internet has completed a series of successful deals, sold German versions of eBay and Groupon to their more famous competitors. The brothers — Alexander, Oliver and Marc — have used the proceeds to invest in companies like Facebook and Zynga. One of their latest projects, a German rival to the online retailer Zappos, is valued at $3.7 billion.

"Previous generations of Berlin start-ups were copycats," said Matt Cohler, a partner at the venture firm Benchmark Capital, who was one of the first employees at both LinkedIn and Facebook, and has invested in a Berlin start-up. "It was the predominant playbook."

More important, there have been few successful exits — sales to larger companies or lucrative initial public offerings — that could cement Berlin's place in the global start-up community. Among those deals, few break the $1 billion mark.

In 2010, Groupon bought the European rival CityDeal for around $260 million. Google acquired DailyDeal, a similar daily deals Web site from Berlin, for a reported $200 million in 2011; earlier this year, the Internet giant sold the start-up back to its founders.

"Many funds got started at the wrong time," said Christophe Maire, an angel investor in Berlin, whose nickname is the Conductor because he has mentored, and invested in, many of the city's new generation of young entrepreneurs.

"There's a reluctance to back innovation."

But as local start-ups gain global audiences — and international backing — entrepreneurs and investors are betting on Berlin.

While venture capital investment in the rest of Europe has remained flat since the financial crisis began, the city attracted 173 million Euros ($226 million) in venture funding last year, a 164 percent increase compared with 2009.

Big technology companies are showing interest, too. Earlier this month, the Japanese technology giant Panasonic bought Aupeo, a local audio streaming service, for an undisclosed amount. Google has invested in a local start-up hub called the Factory that is being built at a site that once was part of the Berlin Wall.

"There are billion-dollar companies just waiting to happen," said Ciaran O'Leary, a partner in the local venture firm Early Bird, in his minimalist office in the center of the city. "Something big is going to happen. It's just a question of time."

Ijad Madisch knows the limits of starting a technology company in Germany.

Mr. Madisch, a Harvard-educated medical doctor, also holds a Ph.D. in virology and has studied computer science. Yet when he started working on Research Gate, a social networking site that allows scientists to share work and collaborate on projects, he faced resistance.

Returning to Hanover to be closer to his family in 2008, Mr. Madisch's college supervisor told him to give up his pet project after he asked to work part time to focus on the start-up.

The next day, Mr. Madisch, 32, quit his job. He soon transferred to Harvard where a former boss was happy to let him work fewer hours while he pursued his business idea. Friends also put him in contact with blue-chip American venture firms, including Benchmark Capital and Accel Partners.

After securing early-stage fund-raising from West Coast backers, Mr. Madisch moved Research Gate from Boston to Berlin in 2011, and has expanded his staff tenfold in less than two years, to 120 employees. The site now connects more than 2.6 million scientists worldwide, and Mr. Madisch plans to make money by selling advertisements for academic conferences and job openings.

In an ironic twist, Mr. Madisch's former boss, who had warned him against starting the company, is now one of the site's most active users.

"I had to leave Germany to get back to Germany," Mr. Madisch said in his three-floor office in central Berlin that has a large game room and sleeping pods to keep programmers fresh. "German venture capitalists had this idea in front of them, and they didn't do anything about it."

For entrepreneurs, Berlin offers the infrastructure, without the costly overhead of Northern California, New York or London. Commercial rents in the once-communist side of the city are about half of that in London, allowing entrepreneurs to stretch their start-up budgets.

Three years ago, the founders of EyeEm, a mobile photo app similar to Instagram, borrowed an art gallery in a chic part of Berlin to start a global online photography competition. The showcase received more than 2000 entries from around the world and formed the basis of their business idea.

EyeEm later replicated the exhibition in SoHo. But costs quickly rose as the founders had to fork over high rent for a trendy gallery, submit multiple forms to receive licensing permits and pay high wages to waiters and security staff.

"The cheap rent Berlin buys you time, and time is everything," said Lorenz Aschoff, a co-founder of EyeEm, in the company's converted loft space. "If we hadn't received the original gallery for free, it would have killed the idea before it took off."

As start-ups in the German capital become more established, entrepreneurs and investors alike are hoping that one of the city's companies will turn the growing interest in Berlin into cash.

Many eyes have focused on Wooga, an online game start-up founded in 2009 that competes with Zynga for users on mobile phones and social networking sites like Facebook.

At a converted bakery colorfully adorned with characters from Wooga's games, the company's 250 employees from more than 35 countries busily plan their next online game.

After raising money from both European and American venture firms, Jens Begemann, Wooga's co-founder and chief executive, said investors are slowly reconsidering untested ideas. He is focused on beefing up its games for smartphones in an effort to diversify away from sites like Facebook.

"Gaming involves combining skilled engineering with a creative atmosphere," said Mr. Begemann, 36, in the start-up's five-story office where programmers share ideas in an open-plan kitchen

that has been designed to look like a leafy forest. "Wooga couldn't exist in any city other than Berlin."
* "Tal" is German for "Valley".

The next methodological step included the classification of processes and anchors into groups. The processes were grouped according to the results of the factor analysis. The classification of anchors into clusters did not involve a similar mathematical procedure and was based on logic. The anchors were grouped into six clusters as listed in Table 5.4: technological capabilities, market structure, pro-innovation culture, availability of human capital, governance and institutional infrastructure and external effect.

In the final step of this methodological exercise, an innovation map was produced for the German ecosystem. Most interactions between the anchor clusters and the process factors proved to be significant and positive. This can be seen in Figure 5.4, describing the main linkages between the two groups and the overall national innovation ecosystem map for Germany.

The interactions between the group of anchors (clusters) and the group of processes was computed-based on a mathematical procedure for determining and weighting the direction and strength of link between the factors and clusters (see in Chapter 2). The results show that the technological capabilities cluster has strong positive interactions with two factors: development of key skills and cluster strategies. Processes extend existing technological capabilities and create new areas of technological leadership; this is an example to the linkage with development of key skills. Another example is the education and research system that allows for continuous integration of new capabilities and technology transfer. In regard to the cluster strategies specialization in clusters (for example, Stuttgart Bosch/ Porsche/ Mercedes), this leads to the combination of complementary capabilities and to the emergence of agglomeration and economies of scale. The technological capabilities cluster also has weak positive ties with three factors: tax and subsidy policies, market-driven forces and standardization. Selective subsidies foster new technologies and build up a unique expertise level (for example, solar panels, electric cars). Strong competition (market-driven forces) in several industries foster innovation processes. Standardization increases the possibilities to exploit technological opportunities on a broader basis and the development of interface capabilities.

The market structure cluster has especially strong positive interaction with the cluster strategies factor. Strong competition (but also cooperation) pushes the competitiveness of local firms and integrates SMEs in larger value chains. Weak positive interactions exist between this cluster

Table 5.4   List of anchors grouped into major clusters

Name of Cluster	Anchor Name
Technological capabilities	Technological leadership in numerous industries Cross-section technologies Diversified technological structure Joint projects
Market structure	Export strengths Numerous SMEs Middle high-tech Numerous MNEs Big domestic market Financial system oriented to SMEs
Pro-innovation culture	Strong competition encompasses the entire value chain Virtues Good reputation
Availability of human capital	Human capital Public-funded basic research Public-funded applied research
Governance and institutional infrastructure	Industry associations Diversified education system Institutional and political stability Decentralized support programs Labor unions Efficient patent system Public test institutions
External effect	Few natural resources Central location

and three other process factors: tax and subsidy policies, market-driven forces and development of key skills. Large internal markets increase the effectiveness of tax programs which can support both, demand and supply side. An example of the linkage between market structure and market-driven forces is the outsourcing of projects to SMEs by strong multi-national enterprises (MNEs) and the large possibilities for cooperative research. The value chain encompasses research and development as well as production, and includes the linkage with the development of key skills.

Strong positive ties exist between the pro-innovation cluster and the market-driven forces and the development of key skills factors. Cooperation within the value chain strengthens the innovative capability of the whole system. There is a wage premium for the attainment of high educational skills (vocational training, focus on engineering). Weaker positive association exists between the pro-innovation cluster and two

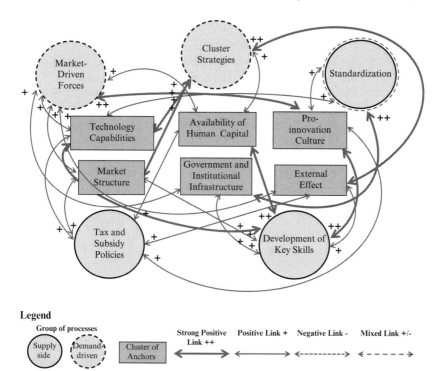

Figure 5.4   Germany's innovation ecosystem

other process factors: tax and subsidy policies and standardization. Government investments into new technologies support the establishment of an innovation-friendly environment. The German system exhibits cooperation for highly-developed standards as well.

The availability of the human capital cluster has strong positive ties with the development of the key skills factor. The development of key skills is advantageous for the transfer of tacit knowledge (for example, master apprentice relation). Weaker positive ties exist between this cluster and three other factors: tax and subsidy policies, market-driven forces and cluster strategies. Tax incentives and targeted subsidies for training and education as well as for new technologies push the accumulation of required human capital. The linkage between market driven forces and the availability of human capital in Germany is expressed by fast, efficient and broad technology transfer between research institutions (for example, Fraunhofer institutes) and the industry. Specialized labor markets and labor agencies expressed the linkage between cluster strategies and the availability of human capital.

A strong positive linkage exists between the governance and institutional infrastructure cluster and the standardization factor (for example, Office for Norms and Standards). Weaker positive links exist between this cluster and two other factors: market driven forces and the development of key skills. The German government fosters innovation by promoting and maintaining market competition by the regulation of anti-competitive behavior (by anti-trust laws). The linkage with development of key skills in Germany is expressed by international relationships with industry and science.

The external effects cluster has strong positive ties with the cluster strategies factor (for example, focus on knowledge creation in clusters). Weaker positive ties exist between this cluster and three factors: tax and subsidy policies (for example, high taxes on energy), market driven forces (good logistics, such as railway, highway, harbor) and development of key skills (for example, social recognition of high education).

SUMMARY

The German innovation ecosystem is highly interconnected, with many strong links between processes and anchors. It is significant that three of the five key processes that drive German innovation are demand-driven. This suggests that for nations interested in strengthening demand-driven innovation, Germany is a country that could and should be benchmarked with useful results.

Germany's relative economic resilience in the face of the global and EU economic crisis, noted earlier, is, we believe, reflected in Germany's highly interconnected innovation ecosystem and in particular in the three demand-driven processes. Market forces appear, in general, to be more agile in adapting to external shocks than forces driven by public policy.

Technological capabilities and the existence of economies of scale (in the market structure cluster) seem to have a profound impact on processes that foster innovation. Cultural ("pro-innovation culture") and public policy anchors (in the availability of capital and government culture clusters) also play a vital role in driving these processes. Labor unions provide a good example. Outside Germany, it is widely thought that the strong labor unions hinder innovation and growth. In fact, they likely contribute, as we see with Germany's innovate *kurzarbeit* policy that kept experienced SME workers in the *mittelstand*. Germany's low ranking for "labor market", in its competitiveness landscape (49th of 59 nations) may reflect some lack of understanding of the role German unions play. In several places in the map (see Tables 5.3 and 5.4), the term "SME" is seen – this reflects the German *mittelstand* SMEs, a rather unique and important feature of German innovation.

One aspect the ecosystem map does not explicitly show, but is strongly present in the background, is Germany's great success in reorienting its export industries. Germany's export is based on high-value-added precision manufacturing, away from Europe, specifically its best export customer France, and toward China, which could possibly one day supplant France as Germany's best customer for exports. Germany's innovation ecosystem is uniquely complementary to that of China and Germany and has wisely positioned itself to join the rapid economic growth of Asian emerging markets, especially China, and away from the slow-growing European economies. The ability of Germany's innovation ecosystem to implement this refocusing, reflects Germany's strategic agility, in turn based on the three market-driven processes. We do not see this capability in other large European nations.

Nor is this government-driven. Germany's government has provided a culture of governmental stability, with crucial interventions, but has allowed market forces to drive innovation that is export-oriented. Basically, China's competitive advantage lies in efficient manufacturing. Germany supplies the innovative machinery and equipment that China vitally needs to sustain this competitive advantage, along with a great many innovative sub-assemblies, around which China assembles the "boxes". This capability is almost totally lacking in, for instance, the United States, which regards itself as highly innovative but which gains little benefit from its innovations, because they are almost entirely produced in China (for example, iPod, iPad and iPhone).

Germany also focuses on "middle high-tech" (moderately innovate technologies) rather than risky break-through technologies. Finally, Germany is very "green", in its culture and politics, perhaps because of the key role played by the "wald" (forests). This aspect of Germany's ecosystem suggests Germany will be among the countries that capitalize on the business opportunities inherent in the new environmental clean-tech industries.

The innovation ecosystem map shows how Germany's discipline and precision, not only in manufacturing but in its regulations (for example, standards) and bureaucracy, can be a double-edged sword. There is no reason why starting a business, or paying taxes, should be so complex. There is no reason why government bureaucracy should be insufferable, while the courts, for instance, are very efficient. On the other hand, entrepreneurs benefit when they cluster close to one another; Berlin shows promise as a potential site for a critical mass of innovative entrepreneurs, as the case study indicates.

NOTE

* With the assistance of Professor Andreas Pyka and Dr Matthias Müller from the University of Hohenheim, Germany.

6. The French national innovation ecosystem*

INTRODUCTION

In this chapter, we describe France's innovation ecosystem. We begin with some background information on the French economy, followed by data on France's global competitiveness, ease of doing business and economic freedom, along with France's global rankings in innovation and entrepreneurship. Next we present the key innovation anchors and processes for France, emerging from the Experts Workshop, and the cross-impact links among them. Finally, we provide France's visual innovation ecosystem map, along with a discussion of its implications and several case studies of innovative French organizations.

BACKGROUND

We found France to be one of the most interesting and complex countries that we researched. French culture and society appear to welcome complexity; France's innovation system is therefore understandably complex, riddled with contradictions.

On the one hand, French inventors and scientists are credited with a very long list of world-changing ideas, including: movies, roulette wheels, discovery of oxygen, hydrogen, chromium, gallium, fluorine, and artificial silk, neon lighting, the calculator, the metric system, Laplace transforms, radioactivity, aspirin, insulin pumps, blood transfusions, telesurgery, identification of HIV, antibiotics, the Concorde, the bicycle, the helicopter, denim, the Bikini, the refrigerator, the bayonet, sonar, the military tank, Minitel (see below), the camera phone, Braille, the dry-cell battery, the triathlon, the ball bearing and many many others.

On the other hand, France today scores low on nearly every indicator that measures entrepreneurial energy and start-up activity.

France is a world leader in engineering education, with its 240 schools known as "Grandes Ecoles d'Ingénieur". French civil engineering, in particular, has long led the world. French engineers designed the Panama

Canal; before that, de Lesseps led the Suez Canal project. French engineers designed and built the Millau Viaduct, in the south of France, the world's longest cable bridge, a work of great beauty.

Conversely, French engineers appear to lack "entrepreneurial spirit"; only some two million people, out of 64 million, were engaged independently in an enterprise at the end of the 1990s. That number has not risen significantly in the past decade.[1]

France and the European Union

France has played a key role in perhaps the greatest "start-up" ever, the European Single Market and European Union (EU), driven by Jean Monnet and later by Jacques Delors. The EU began as a Coal & Steel community (1951), evolved into a European Economic Community (EEC, 1958), and then the EU, under the 1993 Maastricht Treaty. The French vision for the EU was clear from the outset. After three bloody wars between France and Germany, in 1870, 1914–18 and 1939–45, if the French and the Germans did business together and grew wealthy together, the two nations would be unlikely to go to war again. This objective, fully achieved, is sometimes somewhat forgotten. Today, France is Germany's top customer for exports, and the reverse is also true. There is, however, friction between France and Germany, mainly because of differing views regarding fiscal responsibility and austerity; France's Socialist government is far less eager to slash budget deficits than Germany's conservative rulers led by Angela Merkel.

The creation of the single market through a series of standardized laws that apply in all Member States, related to labor, migration, business, money and finance, has proved difficult, especially the monetary union that created the common currency, the euro. Nonetheless, today the EU, with 27 Member States and other states preparing to join (for example Serbia), comprises over 500 million inhabitants, 7.3 percent of world gross domestic product (GDP), or about $16.6 trillion, larger than the USA GDP.

France is the second-largest EU nation, with a population of 63.5 million (second only to Germany). It is the largest EU nation in area (549,200 sq km), ahead of Spain. France's GDP (measured in purchasing power parity (PPP)) was $2.275 trillion in 2012, third largest in the EU, and its per capita GDP (also in PPP) was $35827. France's GDP growth rate for 2012 was essentially zero, though for the latest quarter it rose by 0.4 percent (annual rate). Reflecting the ongoing euro crisis, France's unemployment rate was 10.7 percent of the labor force (November 2012), one percentage point below the EU-wide average of 11.7 percent, though well above that of neighboring Germany (6.9 percent). France had a current account deficit of 2.1 percent of GDP in 2012, up from 1.5 percent in 2011, and a budget deficit of 4.5 percent (about a percentage point above the EU average of 3.3 percent). Inflation in France was 2.2 percent in 2012, but in the latest month available, has slowed to 1.4 percent (November 2012). Paris rivals London as the leading European financial center. In 2012, the French CAC 40 stock price index rose strongly, by 18.2 percent (20.2 percent in terms of the US dollar), reflecting the capital markets' perception that the euro would survive crises in Greece, Ireland, Spain, Portugal and Italy.

FRANCE'S CAPABILITIES IN THE FREE MARKET COMPETITION

In the following paragraphs we describe several economic indexes that benchmark France's capabilities in competing in world markets.

Global Competitiveness

France ranked 29th in 2012 in global competitiveness, out of 59 countries in the survey. Its competitiveness ranking has remained relatively stable since 2008, varying between 25th and 29th. Figure 6.1 shows France's global competitiveness landscape for the four key competitiveness dimensions. The "landscape" reveals wide variation in France's competitiveness, ranging from a rank of 14th in the world in infrastructure (ninth in basic infrastructure, 12th in technological infrastructure, tenth in health and environment), to a low 47th in government efficiency and 45th in business efficiency, along with a ranking of 22nd in its economic performance. The essence of this landscape reveals that France's great strength in its infrastructure is offset largely by a very large and cumbersome government bureaucracy, which hinders its business sector. For this reason, the *World Competitiveness Yearbook* lists among the main challenges facing France: promoting France's business image and attractiveness abroad, prioritizing innovation, reforming enterprise and competitiveness, inducing more flexibility in the labor market, and creating more openness for foreign investment. France's competitiveness landscape (see Figure 6.1) shows greater variation among the four competitiveness dimensions (both among the dimensions and within each) than most other nations in the survey. Its ranks range from 59th (fiscal policy, reflecting the very large amount of public debt, which has shaken confidence in France's banking system) to 9th and 10th in basic infrastructure and health and environment, respectively.

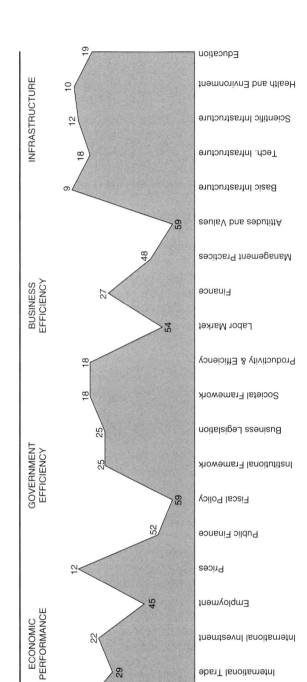

Note: The numbers are rankings, out of the 59 nations included in the *World Competitiveness Yearbook* survey.

Source: IMD, *World Competitiveness Yearbook 2012.*

Figure 6.1   France's competitiveness landscape

Prime Minister Francois Hollande appointed a leading French industrialist Louis Gallois to construct a report of France's competitiveness in July 2012. The report, tabled on 5 November 2012, created shock waves in France.[2] Gallois's report called for a "competitiveness shock" in France, that would "require politicians to curb the 'cult of regulation'" Gallois said was choking business in France. His report noted that France's industrial decline had destroyed 750 000 jobs in a decade, and shrank France's exports to the EU to 9.3 percent of total EU exports from 12.7 percent, during the past decade. Gallois's main recommendation was a major cut in payroll taxes, to reduce labor costs, and in overall business taxation. Recently, the IMF (International Monetary Fund) chimed in, calling for France to cut government spending (which, at 56 percent of GDP is among the highest of any nation in the EU). The IMF added that France's significant loss of competitiveness is the main hurdle to growth and job creation, continuing that these problems would grow if France fails to adapt. Gallois told the *New York Times*, "In France, there is not actually agreement that companies must be competitive to create value. We need to create that consensus first, and after that people can fight over sharing the benefits of competitiveness."

Economic Freedom

France ranked only 62nd in the 2013 Economic Freedom Index. This index (provided by the Heritage Foundation) measures the degree to which economies are "free" or instead are closely regulated and stifled by bureaucracy. In the European region, France ranks 30th out of 43 countries. Since 1995, France's "economic freedom" has changed relatively little, with its score of 64 in 1995 exactly equal to its score in 2013 (64.1) (see Figure 6.2). France's economic freedom score is slightly higher than the world average of 59.6. The relatively low ranking reflects in part the heavy proactive French government and large public debt (86.3 percent of GDP). France scores relatively high in the "rule of law" (21st in property rights, 25th in freedom from corruption); but in fiscal freedom, it scores 53.0, or 168th in the world, and 171st in government spending! While the business start-up process is relatively smooth (23rd ranking for "business freedom"), labor freedom ranks only 181st in the world, because of moribund labor laws. Trade and investment freedom rank only 58th and 56th, respectively, owing to many barriers. France has essentially remained as it was in 1995 in "economic freedom", while other nations have considerably eased the free market climate, leaving France trailing in competitiveness and in attractiveness for foreign investment.

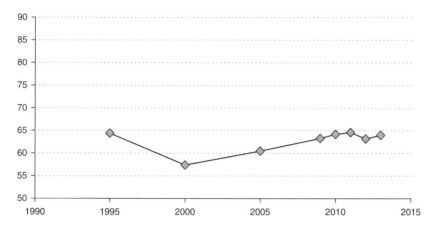

Source: The Heritage Foundation, Index of Economic Freedom 2013, see www.heritage. org/index/.

Figure 6.2   France: Economic freedom score, 1995–2013

Ease of Doing Business

France ranked a low 34th in ease of doing business in 2012, according to the World Bank. Starting a business in France is relatively easy (rank of 27th), but getting credit and paying taxes are both difficult (53rd and 53rd, respectively). Trading across borders ranks 27th in difficulty, and enforcing contracts has a rank of 8th, reflecting the relative efficiency of France's legal system. Again, overall, France shows wide inconsistency in the actions needed to start and run businesses, ranging from very difficult to very easy (see Figure 6.3).

Innovation and Entrepreneurship

According to the *World Competitiveness Yearbook*, in "entrepreneurship" ("entrepreneurship is widespread in business"), France ranked a very low 53rd, in 2012, out of 59 countries, with a score of 4.94 (out of 10). For "innovative capacity" (innovative capacity of firms to generate new products, processes and/ or services), France's rank in 2012 was ranked 25th (with a score of 6.19 out of 10). From this we conclude that while France's excellence in technological, scientific and basic infrastructure does produce innovative engineers, the complex business climate does not encourage innovation in start-ups. Perhaps, then, France's culture points to emphasis on innovation in large existing organizations.

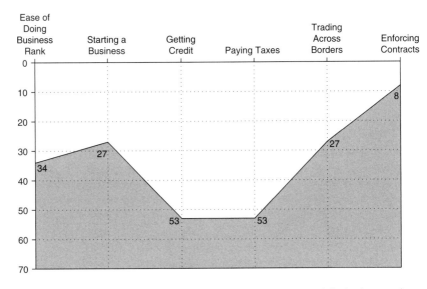

Source: Doing Business Project – The World Bank, 2012, see www.doingbusiness.org/ rankings.

Figure 6.3   France: Ease of doing business, 2012

What emerges from these benchmarks is a rather unusual, perhaps unique, picture. France's "competitiveness landscape" is one of rugged mountain peaks and deep valleys – high excellence in some areas, mainly education and infrastructure, and lack of excellence in its labor market, fiscal management and attitudes and values, reflecting French bureaucracy and lack of entrepreneurial energy. Overall, it is our view that this initial picture of French innovation points to considerable potential for innovation in France, coupled with a distressing lack of vision, ability and desire to exploit that potential. France, with its exceptional human capital, is in innovation a major under-achiever.

We next present our version of France's national innovation ecosystem. It will be followed by several case studies, showing France's unique innovation exists principally in very large organizations, rather than in small start-ups.

INNOVATION ECOSYSTEM

This section describes France's innovation ecosystem. First, we show the results of our Experts Workshop, which listed the key anchors and processes that drive French innovation. We then show the cross-impact analysis linking the anchors and processes, and the innovation map itself. We conclude with case studies that help concretize the map and understand its workings in practice.

Data Analysis

Anchors and processes

This section provides a summary of the raw inputs collected at the France Experts Workshop (see Chapter 2) conducted by the Universite De Nice – Sophia Antipolis. Table 6.1 lists ten main anchors which were identified by the French experts as the pillars of their innovation system. Table 6.2 presents a list of six processes which were recognized by the experts as key elements driving and fostering innovation. It will be recalled that "anchors" are essentially similar to what economists call "stocks", or fixed assets, while processes are similar to what economists call "flows" (changes related to various anchors, or stocks). The processes were ranked by the experts by their importance and classified according to which side of the market (supply or demand) they belong to.

The French experts gave exceedingly high weight to the "public procurement" process. This perhaps reflects the proactive role played by the government in France, the relatively large government budget (as a percentage of GDP) and the belief that the public budget can foster innovation by encouraging innovation and entrepreneurship among those who supply it with goods and services. At first glance this process appears to be both demand side and supply side. After all, public procurement relates to what is purchased (demanded) by the government. But we believe that the

Table 6.1 List of French innovation anchors

Number	Anchor Name
1	Government should assess the rationale and opportunity for policy intervention
2	Characterization of the costs, as well as new business opportunities
3	Characterization of the level of demand measures (firms, sectors, countries)
4	Scale, timing and duration policies
5	Articulation between supply and demand policies and measures
6	Coordination with the different actors
7	Significant potential to boost demand
8	Governance, transparency and accountability
9	Mobilizing public administrations in favor of innovation
10	Consumer policy and education

Table 6.2　List of identified processes fostering French innovation, ranked
by importance and classified by market side (supply, demand,
or both)

Ranked Number (by importance)	Process Name	Demand side (D), Supply side (S) or both (D S)
1	Public procurement	S
2	Innovation-oriented regulations	S
3	Innovation-oriented standards	S
4	Lead markets	D
5	Consumer policies	D
6	Labeling and awareness-raising industries	D, S

process should be placed firmly on the supply side, simply because it is one of a wide variety of policies of government to influence what is produced, and how it is produced. It does not reflect the forces of the marketplace, which is how we traditionally interpret "demand driven". The next two processes, innovation regulations and innovation standards, also reflect the world view that the government in France plays a dominant role in setting the "rules of the game", for the game of innovation.

Interaction among anchors and processes
The essence of an ecosystem is the interaction among its various components. The data generated in the French brainstorming workshop was used as inputs for further and more elaborate analysis. A "cross-impact analysis" (the perceived links between various anchors and processes) was employed to create a bipolar five-point Likert scale (ranging from a strong negative link, score 1, to a strong positive link, score 5, for each cell in a 10x6 cross-impact matrix

CONSTRUCTION OF INNOVATION ECOSYSTEM MAP FOR FRANCE

The next methodological step included the classification of processes and anchors into groups. The classification of anchors into clusters was based on logic. Normally, the list of processes is simplified into a smaller number of groups through the use of factor analysis (see the methodological Chapter 2). However, here, in the case of France, the sparse data did not permit this procedure. We therefore reduced the six processes to four

Table 6.3   Clusters (group of anchors)

Cluster Name	Anchor Number	Anchor Name
1. Public policy, intervention and regulation	1	Government should assess the rationale and opportunity for policy intervention
	4	Scale, timing and duration of policies
	5	Articulation between supply and demand policies and measures
2. Corporate policy	2	Characterization of the costs, as well as new business opportunities
	8	Governance, transparency, and accountability
3. Education, mobilization	10	Consumer policy and education
	9	Mobilizing public administrations in favor of innovation
	6	Coordination with the different actors
4. Demand-side policies	3	Characterization of the level of demand measures (firms, sectors, countries)
	7	Significant potential to boost demand

Table 6.4   Factors (group of processes)

Factor Name	Factor Number	Process Name
1. Public procurement (S)	1	Public procurement
2. Standards and Regulations (S)	2	Innovation-oriented regulations
	3	Innovation-oriented standards
3. Lead markets and Consumer policies (D)	4	Lead markets
	5	Consumer policies
4. Labeling and Awareness-Raising Industries (D S)	6	Labeling and awareness-raising industries

factors through our own judgment. Based on our own understanding of the ten anchors, we grouped them into four key clusters: public policy; intervention and regulation; corporate policy; education, mobilization and demand-side policies (Table 6.3). Similarly we grouped the six processes into four factors: public procurement; standards and regulations; lead markets and consumer policies (Table 6.4).

In the final step of this methodological exercise, an innovation map was produced for the French ecosystem (Figure 6.4), describing the linkages

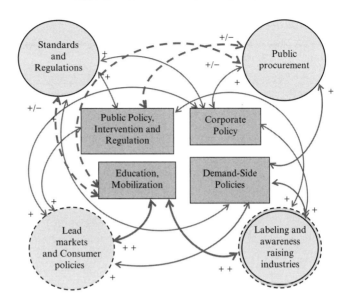

Figure 6.4   France's innovation ecosystem

between the two groups, and the overall national innovation ecosystem
map for France. The interactions between the group of anchors (clusters)
and the group of processes was computed-based on a mathematical procedure for determining and weighting the direction and strength of link
between the factors and clusters (see in Chapter 2). The results show that
the public policy, intervention and regulation cluster has moderate positive interactions with three factors: standards and regulations, markets
and consumer policies, and labeling and awareness-raising industries.
Mixed interaction exists between this cluster and the public procurement
factor.

The education and mobilization cluster has strong positive interaction
with the markets and consumer policies factor and with the labeling and
awareness-raising industries factor. Mixed ties exist between this cluster
and the standards and regulations factor and the public procurement
factor.

The corporate policy and the demand-side policies clusters have moderate positive ties with all four factor groups.

Close inspection of France's innovation ecosystem confirms the dominant role played by the French government, in its budget, policies and regulations. France is one of the few countries we studied where public procurement plays a major role. The major role played by corporate policy confirms the judgment that French innovation is not driven by entrepreneurs but rather by entrepreneurs – innovators within large organizations. Today, with the French economy growing very slowly or not at all, French businesses are reluctant to undertake risky innovation and unwilling to invest significantly in research and development (R&D).

France has not yet been able to shift towards increased entrepreneurial activity, even when the weak job market might be thought to encourage it, due in part to stifling bureaucracy and regulation. Even the single process defined as "demand driven" (lead markets and consumer policies) is in fact strong influenced by central government policies, through policies that define and choose "lead markets" and direct them through regulations that affect market demand and consumers.

In our view, what is remarkable about this map is not just what it reveals, but what it fails to reveal. Indeed, this is a major use of innovation ecosystem mappings – to compare them with those of other nations, in order to reveal key weaknesses and lacunae. Many countries, such as Israel, have innovation systems built crucially around the role of leading world-class science and technology universities, with a network of linkages to and from those institutions. France has such top science and technology universities, e.g., Ecole Polytechnique, ranked higher in the world than, for instance, Technion-Israel Institute of Technology; but Technion has demonstrably generated a torrent of technological breakthroughs and start-ups. In contrast, French engineers and scientists are known worldwide for their excellence and creativity, particularly in civil engineering but increasingly in electronics and in biology. Yet these universities do not appear to play a prominent role in the French innovation ecosystem. We speculate that this is perhaps an extreme case of the "Valley of Death" noted in Chapter 1 – the enormous gap between the production of basic research in science and technology, and the successful rapid and profitable commercial exploitation of such research. For example, an international survey conducted by the Massachusetts Institute of Technology (MIT) (2013) ranked university innovation ecosystems (see Figure 3, p. 9) according to "which universities would you identify as having created/supported the world's most successful technology innovation systems?" Universities from the USA, Israel, UK, Switzerland and Singapore are included, but none from France, even though French engineering universities are recognized as outstanding in academic excellence.

CASE STUDIES

Top 10 Innovators

Forbes magazine regularly chooses the most innovative companies in Europe. For 2012, six of the ten were French, and all the French companies in the ten were very large, global organizations.[3]

The second most innovative company in Europe (and ranked 15th in the world, according to Forbes) was *Pernod Ricard*, a wine and spirits giant. The company has a Breakthrough Innovation group that is said to look like "a Silicon Valley start-up", confirming our view that French innovation is largely within big companies.

The third most innovative company was *Danone*, a food company that has reinvented itself to ride the global trend of healthy eating. Danone has expanded into emerging markets, from which it gains half its revenue today.

Ranked 4th was *Essilor*, a little-known company that serves the 3.5 billion people whose vision needs correction. According to Forbes, Essilor introduced 235 new products in a single year; its products introduced in the past three years generate almost half its total revenue. Its innovations include anti-fog technology and lenses that protect from ultra-violet radiation.

Rounding out the six French organizations, in the top 10 are: L'Oreal (7th), a leading global cosmetics company; ninth is Dassault Systems, whose CAD design software is a market leader used by all the major technology-intensive firms; and 10th is Technip, a project management, engineering and construction company that serves the energy industry. Technip, also relatively little known, operates vessels that lay pipelines under the sea. Technip's innovators and engineers found unique ways to keep oil and gas flowing in undersea pipes by warming the fluids with a pipe-in-pipe invention. With growing amounts of energy coming from offshore and undersea installations, Technip has become a market leader.

All these large French innovators are global in their activities, enabling them to rise above the difficulties of the French economy and regulation, while leveraging successfully France's strong human capital, especially in engineering.

Minitel

Minitel was a remarkable technological breakthrough, led by the predecessor of France Telecom that anticipated today's Internet information and shopping services and preceded them by decades. By rights, France today should be the intellectual parent of the commercial uses of the Internet, rather than the US. Minitel was an online service accessible through telephone lines, through Minitel terminals available throughout France, and was probably the world's most successful pre-World Wide Web online service. It was launched experimentally in Brittany in 1978 (13 years before the World Wide Web), and existed throughout France in 1982, by PTT, which became France Telecom in 1991. From its first days, users of Minitel could make online purchases, reserve train tickets, check stock prices, search a telephone directory, have a mail box, and chat. France Telecom provided millions of Minitel terminals for free to its telephone subscribers. By 1999, Minitel was used by 25 million people (out of France's then 60 million population), providing some 26000 different services offered by over 10000 companies. France Telecom closed the service in 2012 when the Internet made it obsolete. The technological wizardry demonstrated by Minitel was not accompanied by equally innovative business creativity; it appears that Minitel lost money, owing to the high capital investment it required and France Telecom's inability to discover how to make Minitel profitable, and it's failure to leverage Minitel's before-its-time visionary technology on a global basis. Minitel is a powerful example of how France's remarkable technological skills, along with its once deep-pocket organizations funded by government budgets, achieved path-breaking innovations. Those who believe that the commercial services available today over the Internet are innovative are invited to explore the 1978 version of Minitel; 35 years ago; it existed already throughout France.

Perhaps the French people and government today should be doing some soul-searching, asking themselves why France today cannot achieve similar world-changing innovations that it generated for centuries. Why is France's innovation ecosystem shown above no longer producing the remarkable stream of breakthrough inventions that it once did? And why are the few exceptions – the innovative global French companies mentioned above – simply ones that prove the rule?

SUMMARY AND CONCLUSION

The dominant role of public policy and government budgets in France's innovation ecosystem is striking. We are led to wonder whether France can define a new type of pro-innovation policy, in which government procurement policies specifically, clearly and persistently award contracts to smaller innovative businesses and start-ups, in light of the very high weight awarded by the French experts to "public procurement". Such policies have been implemented elsewhere, by governments, to help develop peripheral underdeveloped regions. Why not employ them to strengthen underdeveloped entrepreneurship in France? Alternatively, perhaps the appropriate path in the future is one that builds on existing successes – innovativeness within large French global companies that should be encouraged to create employment and production opportunities within France. Charles de Gaulle rose to political success by promising France he would restore "gloire" (France's onetime historical glory and world leadership). Will France's current leaders build a similar vision, restoring France's remarkable inventiveness that for centuries led the world, and changed it dramatically?

NOTES

*   With the assistance of Professor Jackie Krafft and Professor Francesco Quatraro, Universite De Nice – Sophia Antipolis, France.
1. Source: www.gaebler.com/French-Entrepreneurs.htm, accessed 24 October 2011.
2. Liz Alderman (2012), "Challenging France to Do Business Differently", *New York Times*, 19 December 2012, www.nytimes.com/2012/12/20/business/global/challenging-france-to-do-business-differently.html?pagewanted=all&_r=0, accessed 14 May 2013.
3. Source: www.forbes.com/sites/samanthasharf/2012/09/05/the-ten-most-innovative-comp anies-in-europe/print/ by Samantha Sharf, accessed 14 May 2013.

7. The Spanish national innovation ecosystem*

INTRODUCTION

This chapter presents our view of Spain's national innovation ecosystem. After providing some background information on Spain's economy, competitiveness, business climate and innovativeness, we describe the results of the Experts Workshop, which identified key anchors and processes for Spanish innovation. After analyzing the interactions among these anchors and processes, we show the innovation map itself and discuss its implications. To concretize the map, we describe a wide range of Spanish pro-innovation programs and policies.

We found Spain an exceptionally interesting nation, for three main reasons. First, Spain is in the throes of a deep economic crisis; the rate of unemployment reached a record high of 27.2 percent in the first quarter of 2013. What began as a cyclical crisis, related to the European and global downturn during 2008–13, has now become a structural challenge for Spain, with the need for major reforms in the structure of Spain's capital, labor and goods markets and its public sector. Like other European nations, Spain is seeking practical answers to the questions, what can Spain do better than other nations, and how can Spain stimulate demand through its European and global competitiveness, to reduce severe unemployment, especially among the young? Spanish innovation will help supply at least some of the answers.

Second, Spanish innovation is highly regional in nature. Spain's thirty odd regions differ widely in language, culture and history, and in their innovativeness. The strongly regional flavor of Spanish innovation, and the huge variations in innovation across the regions, led us later to seek to construct a regional innovation ecosystem map for Greater Toronto (see Chapter 8 that follows).

Third, Spanish experts have intensively researched innovation and have even constructed an innovation ecosystem map for Spain (see European Commission, 2012a, 2012b; Munoz, de los Monteros and Diaz, 2000; Ministry of Science and Technology, Government of Spain, 2011). This research is extremely well done and gives us a benchmark against which to compare our own findings and ecosystem map. This research suggests Spain has used EU funds well, mainly for infrastructure, but needs now to leverage that infrastructure to achieve scientific and technological innovation.

BACKGROUND

This section provides some important background facts for Spain that impact its innovation ecosystem. We will discuss first Spanish governance and politics, then its economy, competitiveness and innovativeness.

Governance

Spain is comprised of 17 autonomous communities and two autonomous cities, created by the 1978 Constitution. Spain is not a federation but a decentralized unitary state with considerable authority and independence devolved to the autonomies. There is therefore great importance, and major complexity, in understanding regional differences in innovation and innovation policies across the various autonomies. Spain has five official "protected" languages, of which three dominate: Catalan, Galician, and Basque, together with, of course, Spanish. There are 11 million Catalan speakers, three million Galician speakers and 580 000 Basque speakers.

Economy

Spain is one of the largest countries in Europe, with a land area of 505 400 sq kms and a population of 47 million. Spain's gross domestic product (GDP) (2012), measured in purchasing power parity (PPP), was $1.407 trillion, and per capita GDP (also in PPP) was $30,400.[1] Spain has been one of the EU and euro nations mired in financial and economic crisis, in part because of large budget deficits and public debt. Spain's current budget deficit is 7.4 percent of GDP. This is roughly equal to that of the USA, which in contrast was not facing crises of confidence in its government bonds. Spain's public debt in 2011 was not high, amounting to only 68.5 percent of GDP. But Spain's difficulties relate to its banking system, and deep uncertainty about the amount of their assets that need to be written down, or written off, and the size of the "bailout" that Spain and its banks will require. Unemployment in Spain is very high, at 26.2 percent (October 2012), while GDP growth went from 0.7 percent in 2011 to a negative –1.4 percent in 2012, with little improvement forecasted for 2013. Spain's five-year average GDP growth rate has been only 0.2 percent, indicating the urgent need for restoring higher GDP growth. Youth unemployment is particularly high in Spain. Part of Spain's woes stem from an extreme property bubble, which like that in the USA, when it burst led to mortgage foreclosures and a deep financial crisis in the banking system.

SPAIN'S CAPABILITIES IN GLOBAL FREE MARKET COMPETITION

In this section we present four economic indices: global competitiveness, economic freedom, ease of doing business and innovation and entrepreneurship with regard to Spain's capabilities in coping with its challenges. These indices are shown against a backdrop of the enormous regional variation across Spain, in its competitiveness, and Spain's pronounced weakness in transforming its substantial innovation inputs into innovation outputs, ranking 87th (out of 141 nations) in "innovation efficiency".[2]

In 2000, Munoz, de los Monteros and V. Diaz concluded that "Spain does possess a national system of research, but there is no specific well defined Spanish national system of innovation" (p. 38). They go on to recommend that "the analogy of the 'ecosystem' where hierarchical principles (layers) and adaptation concepts do apply might be useful and give new insights for further analysis" (op. cit.). We happily take up their suggestion, and begin by surveying aspects of Spain's ability to compete in world markets.

Global Competitiveness

Spain suffered a sharp decline in its global competitiveness, according to the International Institute for Management Development (IMD) *World Competitiveness Yearbook* (WCY), from a rank of 33rd (of 59) in 2008 to 39th, improving slightly in 2010 and 2011, and again declining to 39th in 2012. Clearly competitiveness in world markets remains a significant long-term issue in Spain, overshadowed by its financial woes and those of its banking system. Spain's infrastructure ranks 27th, but its economic performance ranks 51st, while government efficiency ranks 40th and business efficiency 46th. Clearly, the weak economy is responsible for a great deal of Spain's low competitiveness ranking. Among the challenges Spain faces in coming years are, according to IMD, streamlining the public sector, restructuring its banks and financial system, ensuring the unity of the nation, improving small and medium-size businesses, and improving the educational system. Spain's economic crisis has required a plan to rescue Spain's failing saving banks (*cajas*), which have been protected from market pressures for years because of their significant strong regional political power. This plan has not been very successful to this point. The "cajas" (boxes, in Spanish, meaning inadequate housing) are now threatening the stability of larger banks, in a domino effect.

Figure 7.1 shows Spain's competitiveness landscape for 2012. It reveals sharp differences in many aspects of Spain's economy. There is much weakness in the labor market (employment, etc.), in management practices, and in the public finances. There is strength in basic infrastructure, health and environment and scientific infrastructure. Spain needs to find ways to leverage its strengths to improve its competitiveness and restore economic growth. Among the aspects of Spain that are regarded as attractive in the WCY are: reliable infrastructure, workforce skills, open attitudes, business-friendly environment and cost competitiveness. In terms of the four sub-dimensions of competitiveness, weak employment impacts the domestic economy dimension strongly; the public finances (budget) drags down the government efficiency ranking; management practices damage business efficiency; while infrastructure components are all relatively strong, with the possible exception of education (rank of 35th).

Economic Freedom

Spain ranks 46th in the world in "economic freedom", which measures the extent to which Spain's markets are open, free and unrestricted (see Figure 7.2). Spain's Economic Freedom Index has declined in the past two years, and according to the Heritage Foundation, "has fallen behind other major European countries and has the status only of 'moderately free'". The decline was attributed to a fall in financial freedom, fiscal freedom and monetary freedom, which outweighed improvements in labor freedom and the control of government spending, in the wake of reforms imposed as a condition for receiving EU financial bailout aid, which totaled 100 billion Euros in June 2012.

The components of Spain's Economic Freedom Index are revealing. In terms of the "rule of law", Spain ranks 26th in property rights, and 31st in freedom of corruption – rankings higher than the overall ranking of economic freedom. But for "limited government", Spain ranks an abysmal 167th in "fiscal freedom" (owing to high tax rates, with a corporate tax rate of 30 percent and personal income tax top rate of 56 percent), and 141st in government spending (equal to 43.6 percent of GDP).

Spain's regulatory environment varies widely. Business freedom ranks 33rd, and monetary freedom, 37th, but labor freedom (owing to a vast array of archaic labor laws) ranks only 117th. For "open markets", Spain scores high, partly owing to its extensive integration in the Single Market:

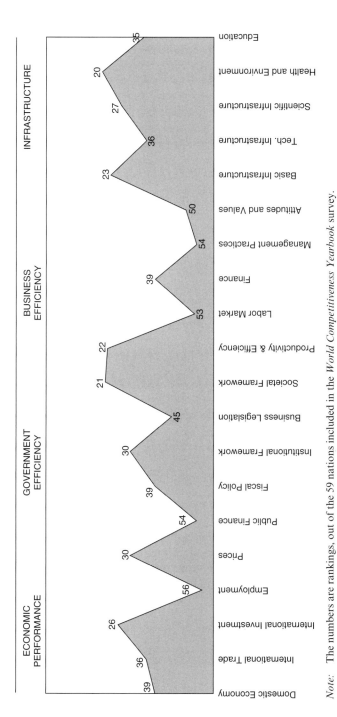

Note: The numbers are rankings, out of the 59 nations included in the *World Competitiveness Yearbook* survey.

Source: IMD, *World Competitiveness Yearbook 2012.*

Figure 7.1   Spain's competitiveness landscape

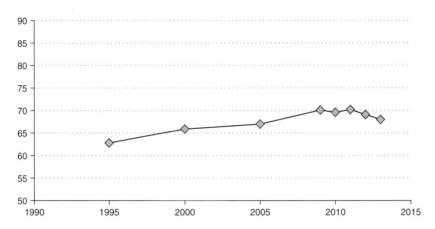

Source: The Heritage Foundation, Index of Economic Freedom 2013, see www.heritage. org/index/.

Figure 7.2   Spain: Economic freedom score, 1995–2013

a rank of 11th in the world in trade freedom (tariffs are essentially zero), 17th in investment freedom, and 17th in financial freedom. Overall, Spain could improve its "economic freedom" ranking with reforms in its labor laws.

Ease of Doing Business

Spain ranks only 44th in the world in ease of doing business, according to the World Bank. Starting a business in Spain takes 28 days, longer than in most countries, and involves ten separate procedures, giving Spain a rank of 136th in the world in this dimension. Getting credit is moderately difficult, but paying taxes and trading across borders are both quite easy. But enforcing a contract is costly, very time consuming (510 days), and involves 40 different procedures, giving Spain a rank of only 64th in the world. Many of the elements that give Spain a low world ranking in ease of doing business could easily be repaired, contributing to a better climate for foreign direct investment.

Innovation and Entrepreneurship

Spain ranks an extraordinarily low 58th out of 59 nations, in entrepreneurship ("entrepreneurship of managers is widespread in business"). Only Croatia ranks lower in this variable. In "innovative capacity" (innovative

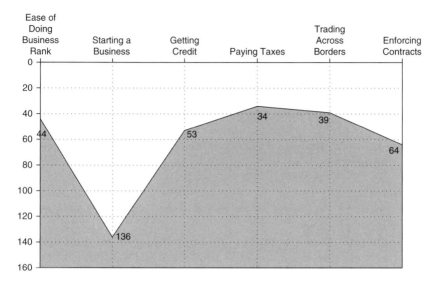

Source: Doing Business Project – The World Bank, 2012, see www.doingbusiness.org/rankings.

Figure 7.3   Spain: Ease of doing business, 2012

capacity of firms to generate new products, processes and/or services in your economy), Spain ranks 44th of 58 nations. Part of Spain's weakness in innovation may stem from the weakness of its small and medium-size enterprises (SMEs). Spain has a large number of such enterprises. Their efficiency rates quite low (Spain ranks 35th out of 59 countries, but in the expert-rated score for small and medium-size enterprises, is efficient by international standards).

What emerges from these competitiveness indicators is this: Spain's serious efforts to foster innovation have so far not yielded major benefits. Part of the reason may be the extraordinary variance in Spanish society, across regions, and across economic variables, with a few regions (for example Catalonia) having high entrepreneurial energy, and others, almost none, and with relative excellence in some variables (health and environment, basic infrastructure) dragged down by poor performance in management, labor market, public finances and attitudes. Above all, the predominance of Spain's fiscal crisis, housing bubble and resulting banking crisis has drained most of the energy and attention of public officials in recent years, leaving little for thinking about how to reinvent Spain and revamp its innovativeness.

INNOVATION ECOSYSTEM

In this section, we describe Spain's national innovation ecosystem. We begin by listing and describing the key anchors and processes that drive innovation, as revealed in the Experts Workshop. After discussing the cross-impact links among these anchors and processes, we show the results of our statistical analysis that groups key processes into clusters. We next present a number of Spanish pro-innovation programs and projects, and finally show the innovation ecosystem map itself, followed by summary and conclusions.

Data Analysis

Anchors and processes

This section provides a summary of the raw inputs collected at the Spanish Experts Workshop (see Chapter 2) conducted by INGENIO. Table 7.1 lists 11 main anchors which were identified by the Spanish experts as the pillars of their innovation system. Table 7.2 presents a list of 17 processes which were recognized by the experts as key elements driving and fostering innovation. It will be recalled that "anchors" are essentially similar to what economists call "stocks", or fixed assets, while processes are similar to what economists call "flows" (changes related to various anchors, or stocks). The processes were ranked by the experts by their importance and classified according to which side of the market (supply or demand) they belong to.

Table 7.1   List of Spanish innovation anchors

Number	Anchor Name
1	Technological infrastructure
2	Human resources competences (public and private sector)
3	Creativity (Mediterranean special features)
4	Entrepreneurship attitude
5	Development potential of Spanish innovation system
6	Positive political attitude towards innovation
7	Strong presence of SMEs stimulate entrepreneurship attitude among young generations
8	Quality of innovation (ratio science/recourses)
9	Valorization of intangible assets
10	Wide range of improvement in the innovation system (R&D investment, patents, etc.)
11	Leading positions of technological sectors

Table 7.2   *List of identified processes fostering Spanish innovation, ranked by importance and classified by market side (supply, demand, or both)*

Ranked Number (by importance)	Process Name	Demand side (D), Supply side (S) or both (D S)
1	Enhancement of firm-oriented technological centers	D
2	Enhancement of third mission of universities and related infrastructure	S
3	Public procurement supporting innovation	S D
4	AVANZA Plan (TICS)	S
5	Multi-level innovation programs. Interaction among EU, central administration and regions, e.g Innoempresas program	S
6	Projects supported by CDTI program. SMEs easy access.	S
7	IDEAS program (university-managed entrepreneurship support program)	S
8	Regional strategic plan (Valencia region)	S
9	CENIT program (leading firms encouraging and attracting SMEs in innovation activities)	D S
10	Support policies for non-technological innovations	S
11	Support to social innovation (Euskadi Region – Agency)	S
12	Quality improvement of human capital (especially service sector)	S
13	Science policy supporting actions (highlighting importance of science in the Spanish innovation system)	S
14	PROFIT (national support program for technological innovation)	S
15	Open software support policy (Andalucía region)	S/D
16	Technological infrastructure support program	S/D
17	Projects supported by GESTA program	S

Interaction among anchors and processes

The essence of an ecosystem is the interaction among its various components. The data generated in the Spanish brainstorming workshop was used as inputs for further and more elaborate analysis. A "cross-impact analysis" (the perceived links between various anchors and processes) was employed to create a bipolar five-point Likert scale ranging from strong negative link, score 1 to strong positive link, score 5 for each cell in a 17 × 11 cross-impact matrix.

Analysis of the Cross-Impact Results

Subsequent exploratory factor analysis established the validity of the developed scales and helped to avoid redundant items and assured the association of each item to a single scale. Factor analysis was employed on the list of processes (variables). The anchors serve as observations in order to group the processes into major factors according to the similarities in their linkages with the anchors.

Exploratory principal axis factor analysis with subsequent orthogonal rotation (Varimax rotation with Kaiser normalization) produced five factors, that together explain 87.6 percent of the variance. The factor loadings are presented in Table 7.3. In order to facilitate factor labeling, the dominant items, marked in bold in Table 7.3, were defined as those with an absolute value of the loading greater than 0.58.

Through the factor analysis we distilled the existing innovation process drivers down to five key factors. They are:

1. *Local and regional incentives supporting innovation*: regional strategic plan; enhancement of third mission of universities and related infrastructure; multi-level innovation programs. This factor explains 20.9 percent of the variance.
2. *Targeted public programs*: public procurement supporting innovation; AVANZA plan (TICS); IDEAS program. This factor adds 19.0 percent to the explanation of the variance.
3. *Joint public-private initiatives for supporting innovation*: science policy supporting actions; CENIT program; technological infrastructure support program; projects supported by CDTI program. This factor adds 18.5 percent to the explanation of the variance.
4. *Public funding of private entities and programs*: PROFIT program; support policies for non-technological innovations; support to social innovation; enhancement of firm-oriented technological centers. This factor adds 17.1 percent to the explanation of the variance.
5. *Development of human capital*: open software support policy; quality improvement of human capital. This factor adds 12.0 percent to the explanation of the variance.

Table 7.3 Factor analysis results for the Spanish innovation ecosystem

Factor Name	Items (Processes)	Factor				
		1	2	3	4	5
Local and regional incentives supporting innovation	Regional strategic plan	**0.956**	−0.076	−0.024	−0.202	−0.107
	Enhancement of third mission of universities and related infrastructure	**0.935**	−0.231	0.052	0.072	−0.060
	Multi-level innovation programs	**0.903**	0.243	0.168	0.136	0.136
Targeted public programs	Public procurement supporting innovation	−0.032	**0.911**	−0.289	−0.118	−0.131
	AVANZA plan (TICS)	−0.082	**−0.750**	−0.031	−0.059	−0.261
	IDEAS program	−0.177	**0.685**	0.471	−0.14	0.340
Joint public-private initiatives for supporting innovation	Science policy supporting actions	−0.242	0.207	**−0.920**	−0.029	−0.071
	CENIT program	−0.47	−0.038	**0.851**	0.061	−0.046
	Technological infrastructure support program	−0.267	0.042	**−0.688**	0.464	−0.457
	Projects supported by CDTI program	0.391	0.339	**0.666**	0.295	−0.094
Public funding of private entities and programs	PROFIT program	−0.006	−0.278	−0.041	**0.919**	−0.019
	Support policies for non-technological innovations	0.082	−0.254	−0.042	**−0.819**	−0.06
	Support to social innovation	−0.099	0.494	−0.168	**−0.639**	0.399
	Enhancement of firm oriented technological centers	0.363	−0.555	0.017	**0.584**	−0.062
Development of human capital	Capital Open software support policy	−0.127	0.067	−0.033	0.067	**0.918**
	Quality improvement of human capital	0.190	0.443	0.317	−0.255	**0.677**

The first, second, and fourth factors are supply-driven, focusing on government and public policy measures; the third and fifth factors belong to both sides (supply and demand), as they focus on joint public-private initiatives.

Major Programs in the Spanish Innovation System

This section provides a brief summary of the main processes identified by the Spanish experts as the main drivers of the Spanish innovation system. These include government or public programs for supporting innovation (for example AVANZA, IDEAS), various local and regional incentives and plans (for example regional plan for Valencia, open software policy – Andalucia), Public funding of private entities (for example PROFIT program) and joint public-private initiatives (CENIT, CDTI).

The AVANZA program involves a set of activities and instruments to support research, development and innovation (R&D&I) activities. The beneficiaries of these programs are private firms and regional and local public institutions. Chronologically, the plan can be divided into Avanza I (2005–09) and Avanza II (2009–15). The main activities of the Avanza I program include:

- Digital citizenship: increase in the share of homes with information and communications technology (ICT) access by providing infrastructure.
- Digital economy: facilitate access to ICT sources for SMEs.[3]
- Digital public services: support initiatives on e-government, citizens' access to public information and ICT-based educational systems.
- Digital contexts: support the development of infrastructure in less populated areas, increase concern with ICT potential.

AVANZA provides a part of the funding for these activities. Complementary funding comes from regional and local government as well as from the private sector. The second part of the plan (Avanza II) retains the focus on supporting the access to ICT resources. Sustainability and energy-efficiency criteria were also incorporated. The main activities of the Avanza II program are:

- Development of ICT sector (663 million Euros in 2009). The program supports firms in the development of new products, processes, applications, services and contents. SMEs are the main focus.

- ICT training (549 million Euros in 2009). Training activities on ICT for firms, their employees as well as target groups such as elderly and disable people.
- Infrastructure (83 million Euros in 2009). Support implementation at the local level of ICT facilities. Introduction of digital TV and e-government instruments.
- Trust and security (11 million Euros in 2009). Increase concern on safety issues in ICT by introducing public policies for security and public access to information.

The CENIT (National Strategic Consortia for Technological Research) program seeks to stimulate collaboration in research and development (R&D) between companies, universities, agencies and public research centers, science and technology parks and technology centers. Approximately 50 percent of the funding for the program comes from the public sector and 50 percent from the private sector. One billion Euros were allocated over a four-year period to finance large industrial lines of research. In the third cycle (April 2007), 16 major strategic industrial research projects were approved. These 16 projects involve 252 companies, of which 59 percent are SMEs (20 percent increase from the previous round) and 261 research organizations (6 percent increase from in the previous round). These projects represent a qualitative leap in R&D cooperation between companies and research organizations. The total budget outsourced to the agencies in this cycle is more than 121 million Euros. The Center for Industrial Technological Development (CDTI) will allocate 180 million Euros in grants to fund the 16 new projects. Since the beginning of the program in 2006, more than 580 million Euros were committed to support the projects.

The CDTI is a public organization, under the Ministry of Science and Innovation (MICINN), whose objective is to help Spanish companies to increase their technological profile. The CDTI is governed by private law in its relations with third parties. This arrangement allows the CDTI to offer swift and flexible support services to Spanish companies for the development of R&D&I business projects and international exploitation of technologies developed by Spanish companies. Its functions are:

- technical-economic evaluation and financing of R&D projects developed by companies;
- management and promotion of the Spanish participation in international technological cooperation;
- promotion of international technology transfer and support services to business technological innovation;
- support for the creation and consolidation of technology companies.

The main objective of the program for the Promotion of Technical Research (PROFIT) is to raise the technological and innovative capacity of enterprises, promote the creation of an innovative business network, contribute to the creation of an enabling environment for investment in R&D&I and to improve the interaction between the public research sector and the business sector. PROFIT is a set of calls for aid, designed to encourage businesses and others to carry out research and technological development. The program fits into the overall objectives of the National Plan for Research, Development and Innovation. PROFIT grant calls for aid for R&D are carried out by companies, technology centers and public research institutions (which include universities). The program's objectives are not bankable projects of basic research, but all projects submitted must be oriented to industrial research or technological development as well as activities to promote technology transfer. Grants are awarded as a kind of subsidy, repayable loans, or a combination of both. These calls are made annually and are divided into thematic areas and strategic actions in a more horizontal manner than previously. Obstacles include: lack of tradition of innovation and poor cooperation between businesses. During 2000–05, the calls have supported 11,950 projects, involving both companies and technology centers in various research themes. The aid amounted to 762.5 million Euros in grants and 2807.6 million Euros in the form of credit. This action has mobilized 30 735 investments worth millions of Euros.

The IDEAS program provides support for the creation of innovative technology base. Its contribution to economic and social development of the region is one of the pillars of the Entrepreneurial University. Therefore, the Polytechnic University of Valencia (UPV) has been committed to this mission since 1992 with the first program to support the entrepreneurship university in Spain – IDEAS Institute for Creation and Enterprise Development. The main activities of the IDEAS program are:

- Entrepreneurial culture dissemination: organizing events to spread the entrepreneurial culture.
- Advice for business creation: advice for start-ups, one-stop shop for creating spin-off UPVs.
- Business development support: specific advice for the development and consolidation of companies, accommodation in the virtual center of innovative companies (innovation parks).
- Training entrepreneurs: training for entrepreneurs and business.
- Training and advice to entrepreneur support institutions: technical consultancy and training institutions.

Regional plans, such as the strategic regional plan for Valencia is designed as a chronologically ordered and sequential process (typical of regional strategic planning) which enhances the principle of participation and public-private consensus in order to facilitate economic implementation and the further involvement of social partners. Activities included are the preparation of the plan, design and organization, diagnosis of the position of economic and social development and building future scenarios and determination of focus and strategic guidelines.

Another regional plan is the open software policy. The program is designed to serve as an instrument capable of making the autonomous Andalusia to be fully incorporated into the information society and knowledge, according to the mandate given to regional government. The main objectives of the program are to:

• achieve and deploy the resources needed to allow all citizens to be informed, enterprising, innovative, participatory and knowledgeable about the benefits and potential associated with the use of information technology;
• reconfigure business processes depending on the available knowledge, using the ICT and investment in R&D&I, as basic mechanisms essential for achieving productivity growth and competitiveness;
• strengthen the Andalusian ICT sector through actions aimed at improving their position in relation to indicators of science, technology and investment. This will allow the development of a solid ICT industry in the region which could compete at the national and international levels.

Table 7.4 shows a comparison of the various programs by main activities and resources. It is important to note that information on budget and performance is only available for national plans. Activities and general objectives are described for programs at regional level.

Construction of a National Innovation Ecosystem Map For Spain

The next methodological step included the classification of processes and anchors into groups. The processes were grouped according to the results of the factor analysis. The classification of anchors into clusters did not involve a similar statistical procedure and was based on logic. The anchors were grouped into three clusters as listed in Table 7.5: technological and entrepreneurial infrastructure; human capital and leadership; pro-innovation culture and attitudes. Figure 7.4 presents the new linkage matrix based on these classifications.

Table 7.4 Comparison of programs by main activities and resources

Program / Activity	National Plans					Regional Level	
	Avanza Plan	CDTI	PROFIT	CENIT	IDEAS	Strategic Regional Plan	Open Software Policy
Regulation and legal advice						X	X
Technical support	X						X
Formation	X	X			X	X	X
Information and dissemination	X	X	X		X	X	X
Consultancy		X			X		
Funding sources:							
1. R&D		X	X	X			
2. Corporate activities		X	X				
3. Public-private activities	X		X	X			
4. Public or non-private organization activities	X		X				

Table 7.5   List of anchors grouped into major clusters

Name of Cluster	Anchor Name
Technological and entrepreneurial infrastructure	Technological infrastructure Valorization of intangible assets Wide range of improvement in the innovation system Strong presence of SMEs stimulate entrepreneurship attitude among young generations
Human capital and leadership	Human resources competences (public and private sector) Development potential of Spanish innovation system Quality of innovation (ratio science/recourses) Leading positions of technological sectors
Pro-innovation culture and attitudes	Creativity (Mediterranean special features) Entrepreneurship attitude Positive political attitude towards innovation

In the final step of this methodological exercise, an innovation map was produced for the Spanish ecosystem. All interactions between the anchor clusters and the process factors proved to be significant and positive. This can be seen in Figure 7.4, describing the linkages between the two groups and the overall national innovation ecosystem map for Spain. The interactions between the group of anchors (clusters) and the group of processes was computer-based on a mathematical procedure for determining and weighting the direction and strength of the link between the factors and clusters (see in Chapter 2). The results show that the technological and entrepreneurial infrastructure cluster has strong positive interactions with two factors: joint public-private initiatives for supporting innovation and public funding of private entities and programs. The improvement of the technological (education spending) and R&D infrastructure (mainly through public investment) in Spain in recent years has enabled the fostering and development of public (for example PROFIT – university-industry technological research program) and joint public-private initiatives for supporting innovation (for example CENIT program, CDTI program). Weaker positive ties exist between this cluster and three other factors: targeted public programs, local and regional incentives supporting innovation, and the development of human capital. It is evident that a significant number of the processes composing the last two factor groups apply to the regional and local levels (for example regional strategic plan for Valencia, open software policy specific to Andalucia, enhancement of third mission). This may explain the weaker ties between these factors and

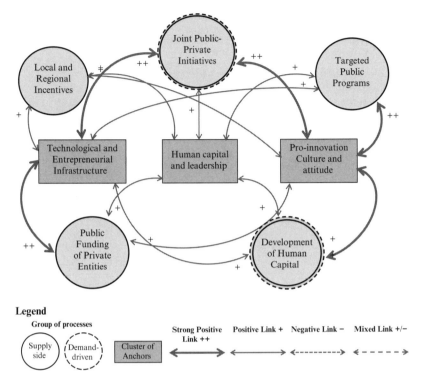

Figure 7.4   Spanish innovation ecosystem

the technological and entrepreneurial infrastructure cluster, which mainly describes national-level anchors.

The human capital and leadership cluster has moderate positive ties with all five factors. The existence of high-quality human capital is a key component in driving and supporting innovation processes in any country. In Spain, the impact of this component on innovation processes is not as predominant as in other Organisation for Economic Co-operation and Development (OECD) countries (for example Finland, Sweden, Germany etc.) Spanish experts recognize significant potential, but in spite of the increasing amount of R&D and education investment, this element is not fully reflected in the national innovation system.

The pro-innovation culture and attitudes cluster has strong positive interaction with three factors: targeted public program, joint public-private initiatives for supporting innovation and the development of the human capital factor. The existence of a pro-innovation culture as a basic anchor in the Spanish society is crucial in inducing initiatives processes both from the public side as well as the market side that have the potential to encourage the development of innovation in the future. The improvement in the quality of the human capital in Spain is a key driver in nurturing innovation culture (for example creativity, entrepreneurship attitudes etc.) Weak positive interactions exist between this cluster and two other process factors: Local and regional incentives supporting innovation, and public funding of private entities and programs.

SUMMARY

The Spanish innovation ecosystem is highly interconnected, and is mainly characterized by moderate positive links between processes and anchors. It is significant that all five key processes that drive Spanish innovation are supply-driven, though two are jointly supply- and demand-driven. This finding accentuates the importance of strengthening targeted demand-driven policies in Spain. What is interesting about the ecosystem map is what is lacking, not just what is present – a strong financial system able and willing to fund start-ups, such as venture capital funds. It is not just outside funding that is lacking, but internal corporate funding. In general, just over half of the total R&D in Spain is funded by companies, compared with nearly two-thirds in the 27 EU nations. In general, R&D funded by companies tends to have higher commercialization success rates than R&D funded by government, though there are major exceptions. Spain's mediocre innovation is not principally because of a lack of resources. As a proportion of GDP, Spain's R&D spending rose from 0.91 percent in 2000 to 1.35 percent in 2008 – though Spain's severe fiscal crisis has recently hurt R&D investment, as it has nearly all government programs.

Munoz et al.'s generic "National Innovation Ecosystem" diagram (Munoz et al, 2000, p.21) presents an inner circle of innovation capabilities (support institutions, public research, scientific systems, firms and network skills) surrounded by an external circle related to "market conditions for products and factors (of production)". Our innovation ecosystem map for Spain, built on the views of Spanish experts, reveals the need for bottom-up market-driven innovation processes as well as the extensive top-down policy-driven innovation programs that now exist. At the same time, Spain should not and must not imitate other nations, even successful ones. It is entirely feasible for Spain to build its own innovation ecosystem, driven by regional variations and led by regional autonomy, and advanced through strong supply-side programs.

We believe that Spanish scholars and officials already understand Spain's innovation system well and have already identified its problems and challenges. The excellent report by the Ministry of Science and Technology (2011) lists these innovation challenges (p. 17):

● economic growth is currently based on low-innovation sectors, e.g. agriculture;
● the Spanish financial sector channels "few resources to innovative companies";
● the educational system and corporate needs have a "lack of coordination";
● massive red tape and bureaucracy.

We began this chapter with some competitiveness indicators. They show that in most areas related to competitiveness and innovation, Spain is neither outstanding nor awful, but occupies middle positions. In some ways, the "middle" is the worst place to be. It is neither good enough to generate competitive advantage, nor bad enough to attract decisive effective action to improve it. Spain's excellence in human capital is placed right in the center of its innovation ecosystem map above. In this, Spain somewhat resembles the transition nations of Eastern Europe (Spain, too, often refers to its own "transition" to democracy). The challenge for Spain is to find effective ways to leverage that human capital – the cleverness, ingenuity and enterprise of the Spanish people – to create a vision for the future of innovation-led growth, one that can replace the current malaise focused solely on deficits, debt, bank failure and financial crisis.

NOTES

*   With the assistance of Dr David Consoli, Dr Pablo D'Este Cukierman, Mr Rodrigo Martinez Novo and Cristian Paulo Matti from the Institute of Innovation and Knowledge Management (INGENIO) Polytechnic University of Valencia (UPV), Spain.
1.   Source: Central Intelligence Agency (CIA) World Factbook 2013.
2.   See Global Innovation Index 2012, p. 293.
3.   In the past year (2012) in Spain, firms with broadband connection increased from 51 percent of all firms to 87 percent.

8. The health industry innovation ecosystem of Ontario, Canada*

INTRODUCTION

In this chapter, we will begin by describing Canada's economy overall, and its competitiveness characteristics. We then zero in on a specific subsystem of Canadian innovation, the Toronto, Ontario, health industry innovation ecosystem. The methodology we developed is aimed in general at mapping national innovation ecosystems. But it can also be adapted to mapping parts of national ecosystems, so we have chosen to study a key part of Canadian innovation, related to health. While the ecosystem itself is primarily cited in Toronto, the capital of the Province of Ontario, it stretches beyond Toronto's borders and embraces much of Ontario, especially since many of the programs described in the ecosystem are province-wide. (Canada has a federal form of government, with ten provinces, each of which has substantial powers and its own Premier.)

BACKGROUND

Canada is a very large country in land mass, (almost 10 million sq km), relatively sparsely populated (about 34 million people), with gross domestic product (GDP) per capita of about USA $40,000. It ranks 6th in the world in overall global competitiveness, according to the International Institute for Management Development (IMD) *World Competitiveness Yearbook*, (and ranks 2nd among nations with a population over 20 million), yet ranks only 14th in GDP per capita. It is a nation with significant resource wealth (oil, gas, minerals, potash, hydropower), strong agriculture, strong human capital and a good track record in innovation. Some experts believe that global warming will make the huge stretches of land in Western Canada even more productive, making Canada the world's breadbasket.

Canada's national economy faces major challenges. While it outperformed its huge neighbor to the south, the USA, during the global economic crisis, IMF (International Monetary Fund) projections show

139

Table 8.1 Percentage change in GDP, 2010–2017, Canada v USA

Country	2010	2011	2012	2013	2014	2015	2016	2017
Canada	3.2	2.4	1.9	2.0	2.4	2.4	2.4	2.3
United States	2.4	1.8	2.2	2.1	2.9	3.4	3.4	3.3

Source: International Monetary Fund, World Economic Outlook, April 2012: "Global Growth Is Picking Up Gradually".

Canada's economy growing significantly more slowly than that of the USA (see Table 8.1); this, despite Canada's abundance of natural and human resources. A main reason for the IMF's pessimistic projections appears to be a forecast of slower export growth, with the percent change in real exports of goods and services slowing from 6.4 percent in 2010 to 3.4 percent in 2013, apparently due to a slowdown in the growth of world trade. Canada consistently allocates a larger fraction of GDP to capital formation than does the USA (22 24 percent, compared with the USA's 15–17 percent). Canada's current account deficit (primarily, the gap between imports and exports) is projected to rise to 3.7 percent of GDP in 2013 and 2014, higher than that of the USA (3.1 percent), in part due to the strong Canadian dollar.

CANADA'S CAPABILITIES IN THE FREE MARKET COMPETITION

In this section we present four economic indices: global competitiveness, economic freedom, ease of doing business and innovation and entrepreneurship with regard to Canada's capabilities to cope with its challenges.

Global Competitiveness

Canada's rank of 6th in overall global competitiveness has risen from 8th in 2009. Canada's economy has performed relatively well during the 2007–11 global crisis, and its financial and banking system has avoided the huge losses, bankruptcies and bailouts that characterized the corresponding American financial sector, largely because Canadian banks eschewed investing in dubious high-risk financial assets and because Canadian financial regulation has always been considerably tighter than that in America.

Canada's Global Competitiveness Landscape (see Figure 8.1) has relatively few "troughs" – among them, "international trade" (reflecting

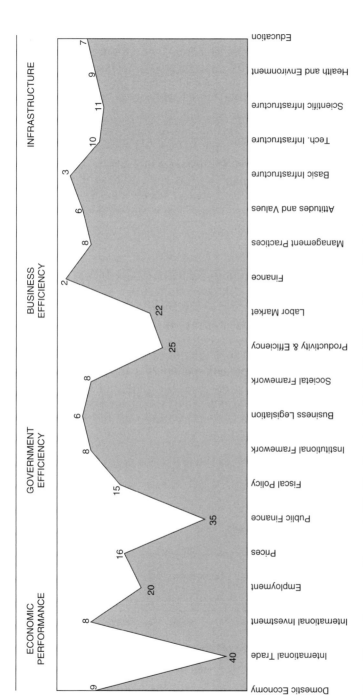

Note: The numbers are rankings, out of the 59 nations included in the *World Competitiveness Yearbook* survey.

Source: IMD, *World Competitiveness Yearbook 2012.*

Figure 8.1 Canada's competitiveness landscape

141

Canada's chronic import surplus), public finance (reflecting budget deficits and relatively high government spending), and productivity and efficiency. Canada scores consistently high in infrastructure, in particular,
ranking from 11th to 3rd (3rd in the world in basic infrastructure), and
in some aspects of business efficiency (2nd in finance, 6th in attitudes and
values).

Canada's key attractiveness indicators are its policy stability and pre-
dictability, reliable infrastucture, high educational level, skilled workforce, effective legal environment, business-friendly environment, access
to financing and economy's dynamism. Later, we will see that some of
these strengths find expression in Toronto's health industry innovation
ecosystem.

Economic Freedom

Figure 8.2 shows that since 1995, the openness and freedom of Canada's
economy have risen steeply, though the main increase occurred between
2000 and 2009; since then, the index has remained stable, at around 80, or
6th in the world. Part of the increase is explained by the electoral victory
of the pro-free-market Conservative Party, led by Stephen Harper,
elected three times since 2006. The overall picture is mixed; Canada has
a relatively large level of government spending, giving it (according to
the Heritage Foundation data) a score of only 44.8, but its regulatory
framework is relatively open (despite what was mentioned above, the
tight regulation of financial markets), with scores of 91.7 (out of 100)

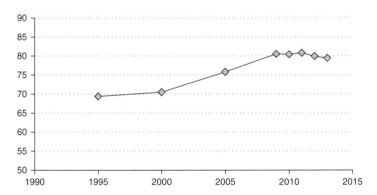

Source: The Heritage Foundation, Index of Economic Freedom 2013, see www.heritage.
org/index/.

Figure 8.2   Canada: Economic freedom score, 1995–2013

for business freedom, 82.3 for "labor freedom" and 76.2 for "monetary freedom". "Trade freedom" (88.2) and "investment freedom" (75.0) also score high.

Ease of Doing Business

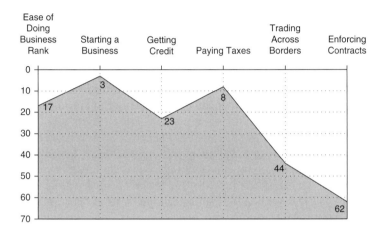

Source: Doing Business Project – The World Bank, 2012, see www.doingbusiness.org/ rankings.

Figure 8.3 Canada: Ease of doing business, 2012

Figure 8.3 shows the World Bank's "ease of doing business" for Canada, relative to 184 other nations. Canada ranks 17th overall. It ranks 3rd, in ease of starting a business, but 69th in ease of getting a construction permit and an abysmal 152nd in getting electricity, and 62nd in enforcing contracts. Canada is troubled by cumbersome inefficiency in some areas, though not in all. Paying taxes is relatively easy, as is getting credit. Cross-border trade and resolving insolvency, are all very easy in Canada.

Innovation and Entrepreneurship

When a panel of world experts rated Canada in terms of "entrepreneurship of managers is widespread", Canada ranked only 26th in the world, surprisingly low relative to its overall 6th place ranking in competitiveness. However, in terms of innovation capacity of firms, experts ranked Canada 14th.

Health Expenditures

Canada ranks 9th in the world in health expenditures as a percentage of GDP (10.9 percent, compared with 16.2 percent in the USA). Despite this very large gap, Canada's life expectancy at birth is higher than that of the USA (81 years, compared with 78.5 in the USA); and Canada's health infrastructure is rated as better equipped to "meet the needs of society" (ranked 16th, compared with only 31st for the USA). In terms of "healthy life expectancy" (years of life in which good health is enjoyed), Canada ranks 15th, at 73.2 years, compared with USA's lowly 29th (70.4 years); and in infant mortality, Canada's rate is six deaths per 1000 live births, compared with America's eight. One wonders why the USA, which struggles with high and soaring health costs, does not benchmark its neighbor to the north. To learn more about Canada's healthcare innovations, and to learn why Canada is able to supply better health services at a lower cost, we now proceed to map the innovation ecosystem prevailing in the Greater Metro Toronto area, in the Province of Ontario. The same methodology is employed, except that it is restricted to the healthcare industry and to the Toronto region.

Toronto has 2.6 million residents, making it the fifth largest city in North America. Metropolitan Toronto (Greater Toronto Area (GTA)) has a population of 6 million. Toronto is one of the world's most diverse cities, with half of the population born outside Canada. Toronto is Canada's financial and commercial capital. It is the capital of the Province of Ontario, and comprises fully half the total population of the province.

INNOVATION ECOSYSTEM

We may now present the regional innovation ecosystem for Greater Toronto and Ontario, with regard to healthcare. We begin by describing the anchors and processes; next, we discuss the interactions among them, and then we present the interactions among the key processes with the aid of factor analysis. To make the analysis more concrete, we describe in detail a number of the most important public programs that support healthcare innovation in the region. This material is then used to prepare the innovation ecosystem map. We conclude with a discussion and summary.

Data Analysis

Anchors and processes
This section provides a summary of raw inputs collected at the Toronto Experts Workshops (see Chapter 2), conducted by the Rotman School

of Management, University of Toronto. Table 8.2 lists 38 main anchors which were identified by the Canadian experts as the pillars of their health industry innovation system. Table 8.3 presents a list of 31 processes which were recognized by the experts as key elements driving and fostering health industry innovation. It will be recalled that "anchors" are essentially similar to what economists call "stocks", or fixed assets, while processes are similar to what economists call "flows" (changes related to various anchors, or stocks). The processes were ranked by the experts according to their importance and classified according to which side of the market (supply or demand) they are assigned to.

A few of these anchors and processes require explanation. Our Workshop experts provided a rather long list of key anchors. Many of those 38 anchors reflect Canada's high ranking in "infrastructure" noted above, in the IMD World Competitiveness database. Some refer to the diversity in Canada's population, reflecting a liberal immigration policy for decades, and the high quality of Canada's human capital.

The list of 31 key processes contains a very large number of acronyms. Perhaps fully a third of the processes are acronym-based, that is, refer to specific government or public-private programs. This reflects Canada's relatively large public sector and relatively high level of government spending and taxation. See below, for an explanation of many of these alphabet-letter acronym programs.

Interaction among anchors and processes
The essence of an ecosystem is the interaction among its various components. The data generated in the Canadian brainstorming workshop were used as inputs for further and more elaborate analysis. A "cross-impact analysis" (the perceived links between various anchors and processes) was employed to create a bipolar five-point Likert scale ranging from strong negative link, score 1, to strong positive link, score 5, for each cell in a 38x31 cross-impact matrix.

Analysis of the Cross-Impact Results

Factor analysis was employed on the list of processes (variables). The anchors serve as observations in order to group the processes into major factors according to the similarities in their linkages with the anchors. Tests of sample adequacy constituted the necessary preliminary conditions for conducting factor analysis and obtaining meaningful results. The Spearman correlation matrix among the processes provided the input for both the tests and the factor analysis. The linkage-pattern items obtained in the Canadian workshop demonstrate good sampling adequacy, both at the

Table 8.2   List of Province of Ontario innovation anchors

Number	Anchor Name
1	The number of clinical innovators in a small geographical area
2	Hospital infrastructure and the amount of equipment and medical devices/technology currently in use
3	New momentum towards innovation and entrepreneurship
4	Potential for $46 billion integrated delivery network
5	High cost of healthcare
6	Canada's most diverse population – 57 percent immigrants – different thinkers
7	Proximity of researchers, clinicians, purchasers and users in the SW Ontario region
8	High number of experienced entrepreneurs
9	Excellent track record of biomedical discovery
10	Highly diverse patient population for studies and trials
11	Number of university-based research and innovation centers
12	Relatively large number of university graduates with higher degrees – human capital infrastructure
13	Wide range of proactive and supportive government programs
14	Close collaboration between universities and hospitals
15	People who are actively looking for cross-disciplinary collaboration
16	Proximity to US market and healthcare systems
17	High-quality linked healthcare data stores (ICES)
18	Large number of non-profit disease associations
19	Proximity to Canada's business capital-financial centers
20	Little willingness for venture capitalists to fund
21	World class institutions and hospitals with key opinion leaders/early stage testing ground
22	Large scale entrepreneurship development programs
23	Rural, urban and remote treatment scenarios/paradigms
24	Clearly centralized government leadership in health and development innovation (MEDI and MOH)
25	Relatively small, cohesive, saleable healthcare systems (petri dish/ pilot)
26	Healthy competition among researchers
27	Number of global connections and collaborators in the region
28	Philanthropy
29	Vertically integrated province-wide translational organizations such as OBI and OICR
30	Very limited integration and support with the industry (e.g. pharma)
31	Moral imperative for academics to think about the latent application of their discoveries
32	Knowledge of many different global markets

Table 8.2 (continued)

Number	Anchor Name
33	Perception that we have a good brand in innovation (global address for innovation)
34	Willingness to collaborate between private/public partners (well accessed – should be accessed by SMEs)
35	Global ambitions, connections (global community) and respect
36	Influence Canadian decisions have on other global markets
37	Landmark success stories that act as beacons, e.g. insulin
38	Perceived economic stability

Table 8.3 *List of identified processes fostering health industry Ontario Province innovation, ranked by importance and classified by market side (supply, demand, or both)*

Number	Process Name	Demand side (D), Supply side (S), Both (D S)
1	Clinically oriented research training program run by hospitals and universities	S
2	Tax credits for R&D (SRED)	S
3	Investment value assessment by private sector	D
4	Industry hospital development partnerships	S/D
5	Intellectual property commercialization protocols	S
6	Industry participation and in public funding and review	S/D
7	Clinical trials in Ontario and cooperative groups/ processes that allow trials at major hospitals	S
8	FedDev Ontario (federal funding programs) and CIHR (grant)	S
9	Proof of principal funding, e.g. OICR, MARS	S
10	Ontario network of excellence (ONE), e.g. MARS, RIC, HTX, OCE training and funding for start-ups	S/D
11	Entrepreneur programs for students	S
12	Innovation showcases for industry	S
13	Pre-market HTA EXCITE program	S
14	MARS innovation program accelerates commercialization of academic intellectual property	S

Table 8.3   (continued)

Number	Process Name	Demand side (D), Supply side (S), Both (D S)
15	CECR programs (federal government funding programs)	S/D
16	Data collection, sharing and reporting (ICES)	S
17	International recruitment programs at university and profile raising	S/D
18	Plethora of funding mechanisms	S
19	Joint training program for medical and science students (science to business)	S
20	Process by which innovation gets on the formulary list	D
21	Provincial healthcare founding allows many clinical anchors to exist	S
22	MITACS program (federal government program funding trainees, internships, professional development, STEM)	S/D
23	Conferences and networking meetings	S/D
24	Joint industry and private sector horizon scanning, e.g. OBI, OICR	S/D
25	Mentorship programs	S
26	International grant review panels bring diversity of view	S
27	Innovation implementation programs, e.g. CAHO, Ivey, HQO	S
28	Mobility of human capital	S/D
29	Health tribe collaboration	S/D
30	SIM-one (simulation training) funded by MOHLTC	S/D
31	Industry innovation awards, GSK, Merck	D

overall (KMO > 0.654). The result of the Bartlett's sphericity test rejects the null hypothesis that the correlation matrix is an identity matrix (p = 0.000).

Exploratory principal axis factor analysis with subsequent orthogonal rotation (Varimax rotation with Kaiser normalization) produced five factors that together explain 75.6 percent of the variance. The factor loadings are presented in Table 8.4. In order to facilitate factor labeling, the dominant items, marked in bold in Table 8.4, were defined as those with an absolute value of the loading greater than 0.49. Through the factor analysis we distilled the existing innovation process drivers down to five key factors. They are:

1. *Specific tailored programs* – specific programs that aimed to support firms in their initial steps: Ontario Network of Excellence (MaRS, RIC, HTX, OCE), pre-market HTA EXCITE program or proof of principal funding (OICR, MaRS); joint program to assist partnership between academia and the industry: MaRS innovation program, CECR programs and MITACS program, industry hospital development partnerships, intellectual property (IP) commercialization protocols; public-private partnerships that include: investment value assessment by private sector and industry participation in public funding and review; investment in creating human capital like entrepreneur programs for students. This factor explains 32.0 percent of the variance.
2. *Human capital clinical training* – international support programs: international grant review panels, international recruitment programs at university; research incentives: simulation research and innovation grant (SIM-one), clinically-oriented research training program, clinical trials, Ontario and cooperative groups at major hospitals, provincial healthcare funding; programs supporting innovation: innovation implementation programs (CAHO, Ivey, HQO), joint industry and private sector horizon scanning (OBI, OICR); formal regulation: process by which innovation gets on the formulary list, data collection sharing and reporting (ICES); training human capital: joint training program for medical and science students, conferences and networking meetings. This factor explains 21.8 percent of the variance.
3. *Awards visibility* – industry innovation awards (GSK, Merck); innovation showcases for industry. This factor explains 9.8 percent of the variance.
4. *Government direct funding* – tax credits for research and development (R&D) (SRED); Ontario federal funding programs and CIHR grant. This factor explains 6.1 percent of the variance.
5. *Mentoring* – mentorship programs. This factor explains 5.1 percent of the variance.

The first, second and third factors are both supply- and demand-driven, focusing on government and public policy measures, private sector activities and private-public initiatives for supporting innovation. The fourth and the fifth factors are mainly supply, concentrating on government direct investment programs and mentorship.

Table 8.4 Factor analysis results for the health industry innovation ecosystem of the Ontario Province, Canada

Factor Name	Items (Processes)	Factors				
		1	2	3	4	5
Specific tailored programs	Ontario network of excellence (ONE), e.g. MARS, RIC, HTX, OCE training and funding for start-ups	**0.843**	0.394	−0.025	0.181	0.096
	Investment value assessment by private sector	**0.835**	0.123	0.018	0.269	−0.177
	Plethora of funding mechanisms	**0.834**	0.304	0.193	0.031	0.045
	Industry participation in public funding and review	**0.805**	0.335	0.166	0.196	−0.083
	Intellectual property commercialization protocols	**0.804**	0.259	0.232	0.125	0.007
	Proof of principal funding, e.g. OICR, MARS	**0.785**	0.353	0.220	0.142	0.156
	Industry hospital development partnerships	**0.781**	0.339	0.257	0.174	−0.047
	MARS innovation program accelerates commercialization of academic intellectual property	**0.759**	0.349	0.330	0.084	0.157
	Mobility of human capital	**0.752**	0.184	0.230	0.076	0.400
	Entrepreneur programs for students	**0.731**	0.035	0.480	−0.016	0.207
	Pre-market HTA EXCITE program	**0.696**	0.359	0.202	0.229	0.268
	MITACS program (federal government program funding trainees, internships, Professional development, STEM)	**0.687**	0.250	0.337	0.250	0.257
	CECR programs (federal government funding programs)	**0.602**	0.311	0.119	0.295	0.153
Human capital clinical training	International grant review panels bring diversity of view	0.176	**0.863**	0.029	0.035	0.162
	SIM-one (simulation training) funded by MOHLTC	0.327	**0.760**	0.151	0.213	0.132
	Clinically-oriented research training program run by hospitals and universities	0.045	**0.715**	−0.108	0.245	0.010
	Clinical trials in Ontario and cooperative groups/processes that allow trials at major hospitals	0.364	**0.706**	0.199	−0.068	0.018

Provincial health care funding allows many clinical anchors to exist	0.508	**0.703**	0.165	−0.054	−0.043
Process by which innovation gets on the formulary list	0.246	**0.637**	0.395	0.181	−0.060
Data collection, sharing and reporting (ICES)	0.319	**0.625**	0.341	0.270	0.019
Joint training program for medical and science students (science to business)	0.400	**0.616**	0.406	0.321	−0.023
Innovation implementation programs, e.g. CAHO, Ivey, HQO	0.503	**0.598**	−0.033	0.031	0.340
Joint industry and private sector horizon scanning, e.g. OBI, OICR	0.522	**0.546**	0.226	0.121	0.113
Conferences and networking meetings	0.364	**0.514**	0.499	−0.219	−0.064
International recruitment programs at university and profile raising	0.411	**0.489**	0.067	0.299	0.220
Awards visibility Industry innovation awards, GSK, Merck	0.220	0.148	**0.905**	0.080	0.030
Innovation showcases for industry	0.355	0.095	**0.678**	0.407	0.157
Government direct funding Tax credits for R&D (SRED)	0.315	0.062	0.121	**0.723**	−0.028
FedDev Ontario (federal government funding programs) and CIHR (grant)	0.156	0.456	0.108	**0.689**	0.190
Mentoring Mentorship programs	0.111	0.090	0.054	0.065	**0.874**
Percent of variance	32.0	21.8	9.8	6.9	5.1
Cumulative percent	32.0	53.8	63.6	70.5	75.6

KMO* = 0.654
Cronbach's Alpha = 0.969

Major Programs in the Health Industry Innovation System

In this section we provide a brief summary of the main projects' processes identified by the Canadian experts that appear in the list of processes as the main drivers of the Ontario health industry innovation system. These include: government or public programs for supporting innovation (Ontario Network of Excellence (ONE), which includes: MaRS, OICR, HTX.ca and OCE for training and funding start-ups); pre-market program (EXCITE); research internship program (Mitacs-Accelerate); federal government funding programs (CECR); human capital clinical training programs (SIM-one, ICES, CAHO, HQO); research institutes (OBI, OICR); awarding visibility companies that foster innovation (GSK, Merk); and government direct funding programs (SRED, CIHR).

The main government or public programs for supporting innovation are as follows.

Ontario Network of Excellence

The Ontario Network of Excellence (ONE) is a collaborative network of a province-wide team of member organizations with commercialization experts that help innovators, technology-based businesses, entrepreneurs, or researchers to commercialize their ideas. They provide services and programs to sharpen the skills of new initiators in order to advance their business goals. They supply expert coaching and mentorship to help penetrate the market and accelerate growth. The network launches programs to support collaboration between business and academia, and directs early stage imitators toward financing programs and opportunities with potential investors. Major programs that belong to this network are as follows.

MaRS   Medical and Related Sciences (MaRS) is a part of a community of organizations that are working to help nurture innovation through new initiatives and a maturing suite of programs and services to support entrepreneurs. MaRS began acting in 2000 with a group of visionary business founders, working with leaders in academe, government and the community. Today, MaRS offers a broad range of support services, from entrepreneurship education and market intelligence, to hands-on mentorship and access to talent, customer and capital networks. These services focus on providing entrepreneurs with the knowledge, talent and tools they need to launch, grow and scale their businesses. MaRS focuses its services on start-ups and emerging companies among others in life sciences and healthcare.

The MaRS Center facilities include lab and office space, event venues and meeting rooms, incubator space and retail services – which support a diverse tenant community that includes start-ups, mid-size companies and multinationals, investors, researchers, community developers, professional service firms and retailers. Today, the MaRS Centre houses more than 120 organizations, bringing almost 2500 innovative people from diverse backgrounds to work in the center every day (MaRS 2011/12 Annual Report). MaRS was named as Toronto's regional innovation center (RIC) and serves as the Ontario government's partner in coordinating the Business Acceleration Program (BAP) to support entrepreneurship education, market research, mentorship (through entrepreneurs-in-residence) and small critical projects (intellectual property strategy, primary market research, etc.) to help strengthen and accelerate the growth of Ontario's innovative startups.

OICR   Within its major facilities in the health industry is the Ontario Institute for Cancer Research (OICR) which is dedicated to research on the prevention, early detection, diagnosis and treatment of cancer. The Institute was established by the Government of Ontario in 2005 to create tangible health benefits for cancer patients worldwide, as well as economic benefits for the people of Ontario. The Institute's research activities build on Ontario's existing global strengths: medical imaging, clinical trials, cancer stem cells and bio-therapeutics. OICR has complemented these strengths with world-leading programs and facilities in genomics, bio-informatics and high-throughput screening. The Institute has an annual budget of more than $150 million. It is led by world-renowned scientists and supports more than 1600 researchers, clinician scientists, research staff and trainees (OICR Annual Report 2011/12, 2013). Another key organization is Public Health Ontario, a central player in public health research and policy, and in infectious disease management.

OCE   The Ontario Centers of Excellence (OCE) is another program within this network established by the Government of Ontario (in 2004) to strengthen research linkages between academia and industry. OCE drives the development of Ontario's economy by helping create new jobs, products, services, technologies and businesses. In partnership with industry and academia, OCE co-invests to commercialize innovation originating in the province's colleges, universities and research hospitals (OCE, 2013).

HTX.ca   The Health Technology Exchange (HTX.ca) is another program within this network, established in 2004, with the support of the Government of Ontario, to accelerate innovation, commercialization and the growth of Ontario's medical and assistive technologies sector. The organization helps Ontario's scientists, engineers, and entrepreneurs commercialize their ideas into innovative medical and assistive technology products. It does this through three main program areas (HTX.ca, 2013):

- The Medical and Assistive Technology R&D Program: provides funding, on a competitive basis and in partnership with other research and commercialization partners, for the development and commercialization of assistive and medical technologies by Ontario researchers.
- The Medical and Assistive Technology Commercialization and Market Development Program: connects and fosters collaborations among researchers, entrepreneurs and start-up companies. It also provides information resources such as technology development roadmaps, market research and intelligence, and seminars to build a vibrant medical and assistive technology innovation sector in Ontario.
- The "HTX.ca" Business-to-Business Web Portal: provides a searchable database on opportunities for innovators and investors; innovative products currently under development or available for licensing or distribution; and information about medical and assistive technology innovators, research institutions, companies, products, professional services and other providers in Ontario and beyond.

The following is an example of a pre-market program.

EXCITE
MaRS Excellence in Clinical Innovation and Technology Evaluation ('EXCITE') launched at the end of 2011 and is a world first partnership between government, the healthcare system, academia, clinicians and industry (both established large firms and emerging Ontario companies). EXCITE harmonizes health technology evaluation into a single, pre-market, evidence-based process that supports regulatory reviews, accelerates reimbursement and strengthens competitive positioning. EXCITE is designed to improve the adoption and uptake for breakthrough health technology innovations, enabling better health technologies to get to market – and to patients – faster for improved health outcomes (EXCITE, 2013).

The following is an example of a research internship program.

Mitacs-Accelerate
Mitacs-Accelerate is Canada's premiere research internship program. It connects companies with over 50 research-based universities through

graduate students and postdoctoral fellows, who apply their specialized expertise to business research challenges. Interns transfer their skills from theory to real-world application; while the companies gain a competitive advantage by accessing high-quality research expertise (Mitacs-Accelerate, 2013).

The following is an example of a federal government funding program.

CECR
The Centers of Excellence for Commercialization and Research (CECR) is a public-private research and commercialization partnership created by a university, college, firm or other interested non-government party that matches clusters of research expertise with the business community. Each Center (of the 22 centers included) shares knowledge, expertise and resources to bring new technologies to market faster.

The major human capital clinical training programs are as follows.

SIM-one
SIM-one is Ontario's healthcare simulation network which represents all healthcare professions across sectors – including colleges/universities and the private sector in the Province of Ontario. As a provincial initiative, SIM-one is dedicated to the expansion and advancement of inter-professional healthcare simulation training and learning in Ontario as this will lead to improvements in the quality of patient care and patient safety. Its members come from various professional backgrounds, including nurses, technologists, physicians, emergency medical services (EMS) and others. SIM-one is a provincial network, supported through the MOHLTC (Ministry of Health and Long-Term Care). SIM-one's educational offerings are designed for all healthcare professionals who are interested in learning more about the healthcare simulation field. These activities have been done through the development of collaborations between multiple sites for faculties and facilities. SIM-one maintains a pool of associate consultants with expertise across all healthcare specialties and all simulation modalities (SIM-one Annual Report 2012, 2013).

ICES
The Institute for Clinical Evaluative Sciences (ICES) (established in 1992) plays a key role in providing unique scientific insights to help policymakers, managers, planners, practitioners and other researchers shape the future direction of the Ontario healthcare system. It provides

evidence-based knowledge and recommendations, profiled in atlases, investigative reports, and peer-reviewed journals, used to guide decision-making and inform changes in healthcare delivery. Its work encompasses the assessment of care delivery, patterns of service utilization, health technologies, drug therapies and treatment modalities (ICES, 2013).

CAHO

The Council of Academic Hospitals of Ontario (CAHO) is a non-profit association of Ontario's 24 academic hospitals and their research institutes. CAHO provides a focal point for strategic initiatives on behalf of these academic hospitals. It seeks to improve lives for a stronger Ontario through the integration of health research, education, and specialized care. CAHO provides a focal point and a voice for strategic initiatives, on behalf of their member hospitals. Its role has evolved to meet the challenges of providing healthcare management and services in the most complex environments (CAHO, 2013).

HQO

Health Quality Ontario (HQO) is an independent government agency, created under the Commitment to the Future of Medicare Act of 12 September 2005. This agency acts as a partner and leader in transforming Ontario's healthcare system in order to deliver a better experience of care and better outcomes for the residences of Ontario Province. HQO's legislated mandate under the Excellent Care for All Act 2010 is to evaluate the effectiveness of new healthcare technologies and services, report to the public on the quality of the healthcare system, support quality improvement activities and make evidence-based recommendations on healthcare funding. HQO is an arms-length agency of the Ontario government (HQO, 2013).

Two institutes in the province were mentioned by the experts who participated in our workshop, as examples of joint industry/private sector collaboration – OBI and OICR.

OBI

The Ontario Brain Institute (OBI) is a government-funded, not-for-profit initiative whose scope spans the entire continuum of brain science and treatment. Its projects and programs are focused on bringing actors and elements together and enabling their interaction. The Institute facilitates the kind of continual interaction and discovery among these players that delivers innovative services and products for brain-related healthcare.

Award visibility, an important component that fosters innovation, is exemplified by the following.

GSK
GlaxoSmithKline Inc. (GSK) a world leading research-based pharmaceutical company devoted to discovering and developing new and innovative medicines and vaccines for Canadians and people around the world. GSK is one of the largest research and development (R&D) investors in the industry, collaborating with academic institutions, governments and other pharmaceutical and biotechnology companies (GSK, 2013).

Merck Animal Health
Merck Animal Health is an industry leader in animal health in Canada. Merck is a global, research-driven company that develops, manufactures and markets a broad range of veterinary medicines and services. The company offers one of the industry's most innovative portfolios, spanning products for the prevention, treatment and control of disease in all major farm and companion animal species.

Finally, there are government direct funding programs to support innovation, as follows.

SR&ED
The Scientific Research and Experimental Development program (SR&ED) is a federal tax incentive program to encourage Canadian businesses of all sizes and in all sectors to conduct R&D in Canada that will lead to new, improved, or technologically advanced products or processes. The program operates under the Ontario Research and Development Tax Credit (ORDTC), a non-refundable tax credit that is available to corporations that carry out scientific research and experimental development that work in Ontario. The Canada Revenue Agency (CRA) administers the program on behalf of Ontario through the federal income tax system. The program through ORDTC provides a 4.5 percent tax credit based on eligible SR&ED expenses carried out in Ontario. The credit may be used to reduce corporate income tax payable (SR&ED, 2013).

CIHR
The Canadian Institutes of Health Research (CIHR) is the Government of Canada's health research investment agency. CIHR is composed of 13 Institutes and provides leadership and support to more than 14 100 health researchers and trainees across Canada. The Institute is giving funds in order to create new scientific knowledge and to enable its translation

into improved health, more effective health services and products, and a strengthened Canadian healthcare system. CIHR provides funding opportunities for four themes of health research: biomedical, clinical, health systems services and social, cultural, environmental and population health (CIHR, 2013).

To summarize: Our factor analysis shows that almost a third of the overall variance in innovation processes is accounted for by the first factor, "specific tailored programs", which apparently are very important. A fifth of the variance is accounted for by the second most important factor, "human capital and clinical training". Together these two factors account for over half of the overall variance. Apparently the interaction of high-quality people, supported by a wide basket of government programs, is the driver of Toronto's healthcare innovation system. We will examine this in more detail below.

CONSTRUCTION OF THE HEALTH INDUSTRY INNOVATION ECOSYSTEM MAP FOR THE PROVINCE OF ONTARIO

The next methodological step included the classification of processes and anchors into groups. The processes were grouped according to the results of the factor analysis. The classification of anchors into clusters did not involve a similar statistical procedure and was based on logic. The anchors were grouped into six clusters as listed in Table 8.5: culture and entrepreneurship, science and technology infrastructure, finance, governmental infrastructure, global and human capital. As with the other national innovation ecosystems we constructed, "culture" here plays a key role. So does finance, infrastructure, and human capital. An interesting group of anchors is that of "global" – Canada's aspiration to have global influence, and its openness to accepting global influences.

In the final step of this methodological exercise, an innovation map was produced for the Ontario Province ecosystem. All interactions between the anchor clusters and the process factors proved to be significant and positive. This can be seen in Figure 8.4, describing the linkages between the two groups and the overall health industry regional innovation ecosystem map for the Province of Ontario. The interactions between the group of anchors (clusters) and the group of processes was computed based on a mathematical procedure for determining and weighting the direction and strength of link between the factors and clusters (see explanation in Chapter 2).

The results of the innovation ecosystem map show that the culture and entrepreneurship cluster has a strong positive association with two factors:

Table 8.5   List of anchors grouped into major clusters

Name of Cluster	Anchor Name
Culture and entrepreneurship	New momentum towards innovation and entrepreneurship Large-scale entrepreneurship development programs Healthy competition among researchers Very limited integration and support with the industry (e.g. pharma) Moral imperative for academics to think about the latent application of their discoveries Knowledge of many different global markets Perception that we have a good brand in innovation (global address for innovation) Willingness to collaborate between private/public partners (well accessed – should be accessed by SMEs) Landmark success stories that act as beacons, e.g. insulin
Science and technology Infrastructure	The number of clinical innovators in a small geographical area Hospital infrastructure and the amount of equipment and medical devices/technology currently in use Potential for $46 billion integrated delivery network Excellent track record of biomedical discovery Highly diverse patient population for studies and trials High-quality linked healthcare data stores (ICES) Rural, urban and remote treatment scenarios/paradigms
Finance	High cost of healthcare Wide range of proactive and supportive government programs Proximity to Canada's business capital-financial centers Little willingness for venture capitalists to fund Clearly centralized government leadership in health and development innovation (MEDI and MOH) Philanthropy Perceived economic stability
Governmental infrastructure	Number of university-based research and innovation centers Close collaboration between universities and hospitals Large number of non-profit disease associations World class institutions and hospitals with key opinion leaders/early stage testing ground Relatively small, cohesive, saleable healthcare systems (petri dish/ pilot)

Table 8.5   (continued)

Name of Cluster	Anchor Name
	Vertically integrated province-wide translational organizations such as OBI and OICR
Global	Canada's most diverse population – 57 percent immigrants – different thinkers Proximity to US market and healthcare systems Number of global connections and collaborators in the region Global ambitions, connections (global community) and respect Influence Canadian decisions have on other global markets
Human capital	Proximity of researchers, clinicians, purchasers and users in the Southwestern Ontario region High number of experienced entrepreneurs Relatively large number of university graduates with higher degrees – human capital infrastructure People who are actively looking for cross-disciplinary collaboration

specific tailored programs and award visibility. Weaker positive ties exist between this cluster and an additional three factors: human capital clinical training, government direct funding and mentorship. The existence of a culture of entrepreneurship is an important component of the system which creates a huge base for launching a large scale of programs with the collaboration between the province government, the academia and the private sectors. This anchor cluster is based among other things on the willingness to collaborate on the part of private and public partners in this region, on new momentum towards innovation, on the existence of competition among researchers, on the belief of academics on the latent application of their discoveries, and finally, on landmark success stories, that push potential partners to collaborate in large-scale diversified networks programs (Ontario Network of Excellence (ONE), MaRS, OCE, HTX.ca, EXCITE, Mitacs-Accelerate and CECR (see details above)).

But culture and entrepreneurship are not sufficient for the creation of such a large scale of network collaborations. The innovation ecosystem obtained from our analysis (Figure 8.4) shows clearly that these collaborations are also strongly supported by the existence of the science and technology infrastructure in the region. This infrastructure is built on a large number of clinical innovators in Ontario and the hospital infrastruc-

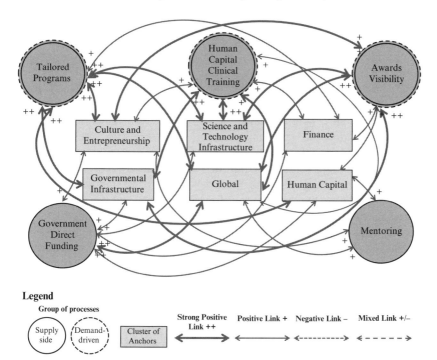

Figure 8.4   The health industry innovation ecosystem of the Ontario Province, Canada

ture, equipment and medical devices. The availability of a large budget for the sake of networking, together with a highly diverse population in the region, creates good platforms for studies and trials, thus encouraging specific tailored programs. These programs are also supported by the human capital cluster which creates a base upon which such networks can flourish. The existence of a large agglomeration of researchers, clinicians, purchasers and users in the Ontario region, together with high number of experienced entrepreneurs and a relatively large number of university graduates with higher degrees, without doubt, are the engines behind the success of these networks.

In addition, the science and technology infrastructure cluster together with the government infrastructure and global clusters are strongly and positively tied to another major processes factor in the innovation ecosystem – the human capital clinical training. These three anchor clusters strongly supported the existence of clinical training programs such as: SIM-one, ICES, CAHO, HQO, OBI and OICR (see details above). In that sense, the aforementioned government infrastructure that contributed to this factor and the clinical training programs, benefit greatly from the neighboring US market, from the existence of large number of connections and collaborations and global community in the region, and largely from the fact that Canada is a country of inward migration that has created a highly diverse society. The human capital/clinical training is positively supported by the governmental infrastructure that provides excellent facilities such as good research universities and innovation centers that collaborate with world class institutions and hospitals and with key opinion leaders in the region. The three anchor clusters mentioned above also have a strong positive association with the award visibility factor.

It is worth noting that the three leading process factors – specific tailored findings, human capital clinical training and award visibility together contribute 65 percent of the variance as obtained from the factor analysis, maximizing the collaboration between private and public sectors characterized the Ontario system. They comprise many joint programs thereby representing both the supply side and demand side of innovation. The two other process factors – government direct finding (tax credits for R&D and federal funding programs) and mentoring, are a pure top-down governmental program, both representing only the supply side of innovation. They are less important, adding only 11 percent to the explanation of the variance, thus stressing again the deceptive role played by both the demand and supply side of innovation that characterizes the health industry innovation ecosystem of the Ontario region.

Surprisingly the finance anchors cluster has only positive but weak ties with the three important processes factors – specific tailored findings, human capital clinical training and award visibility. Therefore the high cost of healthcare, the proximity to Canada's business capital-financial centers, the little willingness for venture capitalists to fund – mean that philanthropy and perceived economic stability contribute to the strength of the innovation system, but to a smaller extent in comparison to other anchors clusters mentioned above.

SUMMARY

In the end, the success of an innovation system is measured by its fruits. Canada's healthcare system appears to yield better health and longer lives for its population, at a substantially lower cost than its southern neighbor, as we noted at the outset of this chapter. At least a part of this success must be attributed to innovation, and Greater Toronto is the main center for such healthcare innovation.

The Greater Toronto healthcare innovation ecosystem shown in

Figure 8.4 appears to have all the elements needed for successful innovation, and reflects Canada's relatively high ranking in innovation indicators described at the beginning of this chapter. Finance, human capital, science and technology infrastructure, the culture of entrepreneurship, government support and a global outlook, all anchor innovation and are supported by the key processes, which integrate both supply-side and demand-side processes and reflect a wide variety of government programs for supporting innovation. We found the alphabet-soup letters of these programs more than a little confusing, but innovators seem capable of sifting through them and exploiting those that meet their needs and which their innovations are suited for.

Canada's "secret sauce", if there is one, appears to be finding a way to create both a free, open and competitive economic system (scoring 80 on the Economic Freedom Index, 6th in the world), and a large, complex variety of public funding programs for innovation, while finding a way to help the wolf of competition lie down with the lamb of regulation and public proactive policy. This easy co-existence was evident to us in the Greater Toronto innovation ecosystem. We also found that the healthcare innovation ecosystem was highly integrated, with close links among human and financial capital, hospitals, universities, entrepreneurs, government, and local and foreign markets.

If there is a major problem with the system, it is probably the one described by one of our Experts Workshop colleagues, who commented that the "Valley of Death" (the crevasse separating basic research findings and commercial success) does exist in healthcare innovation, and that commercialization is difficult. Our critic, who read an earlier draft of this chapter, suggested that commercialization was a challenge especially for the vast array of tailored programs aimed at specific illnesses, projects and institutions, and warned us not to be too praiseful, lest the innovators become complacent.

NOTE

*   With the assistance of Mark Leung, Director of Rotman Design Works, Rotman School of Management, University of Toronto.

9. The innovation ecosystem in Shanghai, China*

INTRODUCTION

In this chapter, we first survey China's surprising rapid economic growth, extending over almost three decades, and examine China's shifting strategy toward innovation and domestic consumption-driven gross domestic product (GDP) growth. After exploring China's global competitiveness and competitiveness landscape, we examine data on innovation and entrepreneurship, economic freedom and ease of doing business. We then present the results of our Experts Workshop held at Zhangjiang Science Park, Shanghai, to better understand the innovation ecosystem at the park and in the Shanghai region. Next, a series of case studies are presented, showcasing Chinese innovation in all its varieties. We conclude by summarizing the results and examining some of the key issues facing China's efforts to re-establish its economy on the basis not just solely on production efficiency, but also creativity and innovativeness.

BACKGROUND

Napoleon's famous quote about China, "Let China sleep, for when she wakes, she will shake the world", is well known. China has awakened and its economy is powerfully influencing the world. Table 9.1 and Figure 9.1 show China's GDP, measured in terms of purchasing power parity ($ billion), for 1990 through to 2017, based on IMF (International Monetary Fund) estimates and forecasts. For this period, China's GDP growth rate averages an unprecedented 12.2 percent annually, for 27 years. At this growth rate, GDP doubles every six years. Thus over the 27-year period, China's GDP will double more than four times, becoming over 16 times larger in 2017 than it was in 1990. The world may not shake, but it is certainly amazed.

China's GDP is now about $12.4 trillion, measured in terms of purchasing power parity (see Table 9.1). This makes China's economy the world's second largest, just ahead of Japan, and rapidly overtaking the leading

Table 9.1 China's GDP ($ billion, PPP) and annual year-to-year GDP growth rates, 1990–2017

Year	GDP ($ billion, PPP)	Annually growth (percent)
1990	910.27	
1991	1029.04	13.0
1992	1203.46	16.9
1993	1401.82	16.5
1994	1618.59	15.5
1995	1832.83	13.2
1996	2054.67	12.1
1997	2285.33	11.2
1998	2492.19	9.1
1999	2721.56	9.2
2000	3014.89	10.8
2001	3338.92	10.7
2002	3701.13	10.8
2003	4157.82	12.3
2004	4697.90	13.0
2005	5364.26	14.2
2006	6239.57	16.3
2007	7329.92	17.5
2008	8214.37	12.1
2009	9049.45	10.2
2010	10128.4	11.9
2011	11299.79	11.6
2012	12382.56	9.6
2013	13580.54	9.7
2014	14947.84	10.1
2015	16492.40	10.3
2016	18233.83	10.6
2017	20198.14	10.8

Source: International Monetary Fund, World Economic Outlook, April 2012: "Global Growth Is Picking Up Gradually". Figures for 2012–17 are forecasts.

economy, the US. But China is still a poor country. Its GDP per capita is about $8242, which places China still among the emerging market nations. China is an enormous country, with a land area of 9.6 million sq kms and a population of about 1.4 billion people. It has a current account surplus of about 5.2 percent of GDP, and attracts massive annual foreign direct investment flows ($300 billion in 2010, about three percent of GDP), while China itself invests massive sums abroad (IMD *World Competitiveness Yearbook*, 2012, "China Mainland").

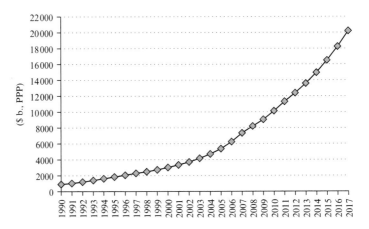

Source: IMF World Economic Outlook 2012. Figures for 2012–17 are forecasts.

Figure 9.1   China's GDP ($ billion, PPP) 1990–2017

China's rising economic influence is reflected in the changing role of its currency, the renminbi (which means "money of the people") or yuan.[1] The yuan is becoming increasingly a global currency. Some 15 percent of the world's money supply is accounted for by the yuan, and one-seventh of China's trade is conducted now in yuan, rather than in dollars or Euros. It is now possible to deposit yuan not only in Hong Kong, but also in Singapore and London, and Taiwan.

A key to understanding China's rapid economic growth is its high rate of domestic saving (see Table 9.2). Since 2006, China has consistently saved half its GDP. This enormous pool of domestic savings provides resources for a high level of gross domestic capital formation, some 43 percent of GDP, and still enables a high export surplus. It also provides a pool of resources available for investment in research and development (R&D) and in innovation.

Yet even as China achieves unprecedented success in economic growth, it is attempting to reinvent its economy and its fundamental competitive strategy. As the former head of the Zhangjiang Science Park once told a group of visiting Israeli managers some years ago: "Today, Made in China. Tomorrow: Invented in China". China is making immense efforts to move up the economic value chain, to produce products and services that are innovated in China, rather than invented and designed elsewhere and sent to a Foxconn plant for manufacture. (Foxconn is a Taiwanese electronics contract manufacturer with enormous plants in China; some deploy 200,000 workers in a single plant,

Table 9.2   Gross national saving, as percentage of GDP, China, 1990–2017

Year	Gross National Saving as percentage of GDP
1990	39.2
1991	39.4
1992	38.8
1993	42.5
1994	43.6
1995	42.1
1996	41.3
1997	41.8
1998	40.2
1999	38.2
2000	36.8
2001	37.6
2002	40.3
2003	44.0
2004	46.8
2005	48.0
2006	51.6
2007	51.9
2008	53.2
2009	53.5
2010	52.2
2011	51.3
2012	50.1
2013	50.0
2014	49.8
2015	49.6
2016	49.4
2017	49.0

Source: International Monetary Fund, World Economic Outlook, April 2012: "Global Growth Is Picking Up Gradually". Figures for 2012–17 are forecasts.

and can reorganize to accommodate almost any product, rapidly and efficiently.) This capability has brought rapid economic growth. Yet China now seeks to build its competitive strategy in its ability to innovate, rather than solely its ability to manufacture. As *The Economist* notes: "The end of cheap China is at hand. China is no longer a place where manufacturers can go to find ultra-cheap hands. China's leaders know this and are pouring billions of dollars into research and development."[2] China's new leadership, President Xi Jinping and Prime

Minister Li Kequiang, have succeeded former President Hu Jintao and Premier Wen Jiabao, who served for a decade, and are committed to major reform, including spurring innovation in China and shifting toward a consumer-demand-driven economy.

For this reason, our efforts to understand China's national innovation ecosystem are to us of great interest. Should China succeed in moving up the value chain, perhaps displacing other major Western nations; the world may indeed shake.

CHINA'S CAPABILITIES IN FREE MARKET COMPETITION

In this section we present four economic indices: global competitiveness, economic freedom, ease of doing business and innovation and entrepreneurship with regard to China capabilities to cope with its challenges.

Global Competitiveness

China (mainland) ranks only 23rd in the world in competitiveness, according to the International Institute for Management Development (IMD) *World Competitiveness Yearbook* (2012). That ranking has declined from 17th in 2008. China's competitiveness landscape (see Figure 9.2) has a great many peaks and valleys. It ranks very high in the size of its massive labor force (1st in the world, or some 734 million workers), and in its labor market (8th), and in basic and scientific infrastructure (10th and 8th, respectively). China scores low in its business legislation (53rd in the world), management practices (45th), and health and environment (51st) and education (45th). Among the challenges facing China, according to the IMD report, are: the need to shift to domestic consumption as the primary engine of economic growth, and away from exports as foreign markets' demand slows; the need to control an ominous real estate bubble; the need to reduce very high disparities in income and wealth distribution; and the need to resolve financing problems of small and medium size enterprises.

China's main "attractiveness" indicators, according to the *World Competitiveness Yearbook*, are the dynamism of the economy and its cost competitiveness; its skilled workforce; stable predictable policy; open attitudes; quality of governance; and effective labor relations. Among China's weaknesses are: a weak social safety net, red tape needed to start a business, pollution problems, and high-energy intensity.

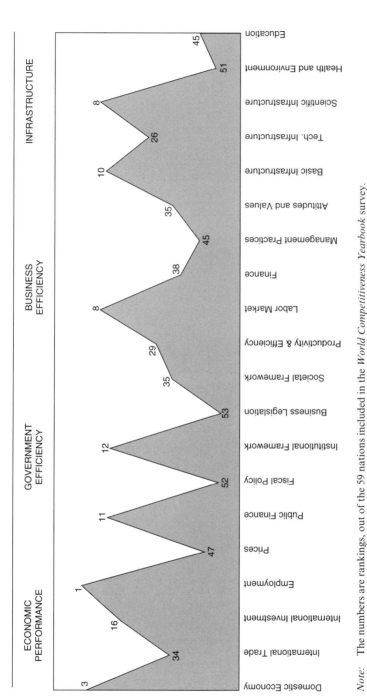

ECONOMIC PERFORMANCE

- Domestic Economy — 3
- International Trade — 34
- International Investment — 16
- Employment — 1

GOVERNMENT EFFICIENCY

- Prices — 47
- Public Finance — 11
- Fiscal Policy — 52
- Institutional Framework — 12
- Business Legislation — 53

BUSINESS EFFICIENCY

- Societal Framework — 35
- Productivity & Efficiency — 29
- Labor Market — 8
- Finance — 38
- Management Practices — 45
- Attitudes and Values — 35

INFRASTRUCTURE

- Basic Infrastructure — 10
- Tech. Infrastructure — 26
- Scientific Infrastructure — 8
- Health and Environment — 51
- Education — 45

Note: The numbers are rankings, out of the 59 nations included in the *World Competitiveness Yearbook* survey.

Source: IMD, *World Competitiveness Yearbook 2012.*

Figure 9.2 China's competitiveness landscape

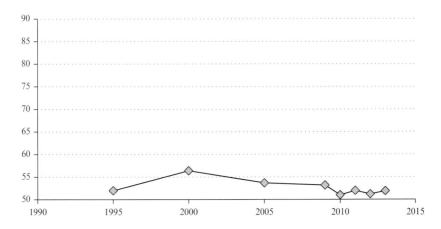

Source: The Heritage Foundation, Index of Economic Freedom 2013, see www.heritage. org/index/.

Figure 9.3   China: Economic freedom score, 1995–2013

Economic Freedom

The Heritage Foundation's Index of Economic Freedom for China has remained essentially unchanged since 1995 (see Figure 9.3). With a score of about 51.9 (out of 100), China ranks 136th in the world in economic freedom. In some ways, this is both a strength and a weakness – a strength, because the tight control of China's authorities over finance and economy enables it to intervene rapidly and massively, for instance, during the global downturn 2008–11, but also stifles free enterprise and individual initiative. The Heritage Foundation classifies China's economy as "mostly unfree" (characterizing those nations in the range of 50–59).

Ease of Doing Business

Doing business in China is not easy, according to the World Bank's annual survey (2012) (see Figure 9.4). Overall, China ranks 91st. Starting a business is hard; China ranks only 151st. Getting credit is somewhat easier (rank of 70th), but paying taxes is complex (rank of 122nd), as is trading across borders (rank of 68th). Only enforcing contracts is relatively simple, ranking 19th.

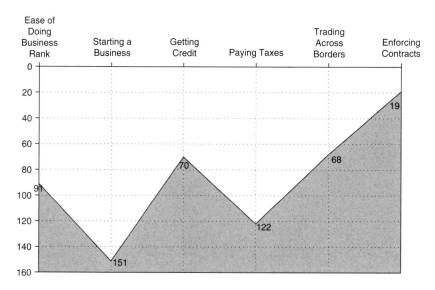

Source: Doing Business Project – The World Bank, 2012, see www.doingbusiness.org/ rankings.

Figure 9.4   China: Ease of doing business, 2012

Innovation and Entrepreneurship

According to the *World Competitiveness Yearbook* database, China main-land ranks fairly low in "innovative capacity", at 46th (Hong Kong, a part of China, is listed separately, and ranks consistently at the top of global competitiveness, innovation and entrepreneurship). China, of course, is aware of this, and is making efforts to improve (see Figure 9.5).

China ranks much higher in entrepreneurship; experts rate China as 15th in the world ("entrepreneurship among managers is widespread"), just after the US. This stems from the view that Chinese managers are indeed entrepreneurial, but not necessarily in terms of conventional product innovation (see Figure 9.6).

According to Gordon Orr and Eric Roth, McKinsey consultants based in Shanghai, "China is innovating".[3] The number of patents granted to Chinese inventors doubled between 2005–11; Chinese companies now play leading roles in wind-power and solar-power industries. China is also pro-gressing in "domestically oriented consumer electronics, instant messaging and online gaming", areas that may be "escaping the notice of executives who aren't on the ground in China", they note. China's advantage, they

INNOVATIVE CAPACITY

2012

Innovative capacity of firms (to generate new products, processes and/or services) is

low in your economy   S UE Y   high in your economy

44	SPAIN		4.63
45	INDONESIA		4.59
46	CHINA MAINLAND		4.57
47	SLOVENIA		4.56
48	MEXICO		4.55
49	ROMANIA		4.52

Source: IMD, *World Competitiveness Yearbook 2012.*

Figure 9.5   Innovative capacity

ENTREPRENEURSHIP

2012

Entrepreneurship of managers

is not widespread in   S UE Y   is widespread in business
business

13	ICELAND		6.61
14	USA		6.58
15	CHINA MAINLAND		6.54
16	KOREA		6.50

Source: IMD, *World Competitiveness Yearbook 2012.*

Figure 9.6   Entrepreneurship

state, in the past has been in "putting a new product or service [developed elsewhere] into the market quickly and improving its performance through subsequent generations" and "products launch in a fraction of the time that it would take in more developed markets". Since time-to-market is often vital in innovation, China offers foreign firms a competitive edge. This capability, too, is innovation – process innovation. China now seeks to complement it with R&D-based product innovation. It is well placed to produce the products that it will innovate.

According to *The Economist*,[4] China has overtaken America in patenting. China's patent office received more applications than any other country, in 2011. The driving force behind this is the rapid rise in patent applications by local citizens (Chinese) themselves, responsible for over three-quarters of the total. In contrast, in America and in Europe, half of patent applications are lodged by foreigners. *The Economist* notes that, according to the World Intellectual Property Office, patents in China are less valuable than those in America or Europe, and fewer than five percent of Chinese inventors seek to patent their ideas abroad (as well as in China). In America, the figure is 27 percent.

INNOVATION ECOSYSTEM

Background

The Zhangjiang High-Tech Park (ZJ Park), or Science Park, is located in Pudong, Shanghai. It specializes in life sciences, software, semiconductors and IT. It was founded in July 1992. The Park is huge, and contains some 3600 companies, 110 R&D institutions and over 100 000 workers. Some in China call it China's "Silicon Valley". Major global companies have a presence in ZJ Park, including Novartis, Pfizer, AstraZeneca, IBM, Citibank, eBay, Infosys, SAP, SMIC, Dow, Dupont and Sony.

We chose to focus on ZJ Park and its innovation ecosystem, for several reasons. First, it would be misleading to try to map an overall innovation ecosystem for China. As Dan Breznitz and Michael Murphree note in their book *Run of the Red Queen* (2011), there are at least four different key economic regions in China, each of them very different from the other. Second, in many ways ZJ Park represents the spearhead of Chinese innovation efforts, because it seeks to foster private start-ups and encourage their growth. Third, we were fortunate to gain the full cooperation of ZJ Park, in assembling a broad cross-section of experts who could help us piece together the fascinating puzzle of Chinese innovation, in an authentic and veracious manner. The 21 participants in our Experts Workshop, include entrepreneurs, managers, scientists, and officials.

Data Analysis

Anchors and processes
This section provides a summary of raw inputs collected at the ZJ Park Experts workshops (see methodology in Chapter two), conducted by the General Manager of Zhangjiang Science Park in Pudong, Shanghai. The list of anchors provided by workshop participants is shown in Table 9.3 and the list of processes in Table 9.4. These lists are rather unusual, and require some preliminary explanation.

Our instructions to the Experts Workshop participants were very clear. We sought their wisdom in listing key *existing* anchors and processes, underlying the innovation ecosystem. At the ZJ Park Workshop, we felt

Table 9.3   List of 24 ZJ Park innovation anchors

Number	Anchor Name
1	Talent pool
2	Young people/innovative spirit
3	Focus: priority of central government (direct) (national)
4	Research/high-quality hospitals/manpower
5	World class education institutions
6	Demand/market
7	Openness of the market to new ideas
8	Open system for entrepreneurs
9	Network/group thinking
10	Capital funding (including government)
11	Willingness to take risk
12	Cluster
13	Government policy/funding/encouragement
14	Risk-reduction platforms (R&D Israel/Shanghai)
15	Atmosphere/state of mind (luxury center)
16	Tax incentives income tax exempt/software
17	One-stop shop/staff from business (at ZJ Park)
18	International city and park(worldview) (from outside China)
19	Environmental challenges
20	Government supports activity OUTSIDE China
21	(Demand) – based on existing services/products
22	Venture capital: key role (lack VC group)
23	Culture: everything is possible, nothing is easy same rules for all
24	Comfortable not having fixed framework/protection

Table 9.4   *List of identified processes fostering ZJ Park (Shanghai) innovation, ranked by importance and classified by market side (supply, demand, or both)*

Ranked Number	Process Name	Demand side (D), Supply side (S), Both (D S)
1	Protection for innovation/appreciation/reward	S
2	Incentive (investors) (tax credit) (matching)	S
3	Innovate to survive	S,D
4	Gap between innovation and commercialization	S,D
5	Market of early adapters	D
6	Services (available at incubator)	S
7	Tolerance of wild ideas	D
8	Incubator process/	S
9	Passion/just do it	S,D
10	Lack of loyalty in company (turnover)	S
11	Market condition: allow start-ups to survive	D
12	Guidance/(Beijing)	S,D
13	Procurement	D,S
14	Leadership/project leadership	D
15	Think local/think social	S,D
16	Discipline/intellectual property, knowhow, confidentiality	S
17	Respect, admiration for start-ups (including failures)	S,D
18	Incentive: innovation is normal work	S,D
19	Languages/English	S,D
20	Balance/flatter structure/not age-based	S
21	Lack of cultural baggage/pragmatism	D
22	Appreciation of innovation	D
23	European crisis	D
24	Radical	D

that what we received from the participants was a combination of what exists at present and what *will exist*, in the near or medium-term future. China is a dynamic rapidly-changing society, and hence it is perhaps to be expected that what our experts provided was some linear combination of what is already is in place and what will be in place, or what they would *like* to be in place, in the future. This is to be expected in a nation undergoing rapid change, in which the central government is capable of accelerating such change and implementing it, as it wishes.

As with the other nations we studied, an important group of the anchors corresponded with cultural factors. For instance: no. 23, "everything is possible", no. 11, "willingness to take risk", no. 2 "innovative spirit among young people", and no. 7 "openness of the market to new ideas". Some of the anchors originate with the central and Shanghai governments: no. 3 "priority of central government", no. 16 "tax incentives", and no. 10 "government capital funding", and relate to public funds. Some of the anchors relate to the immediate ZJ Park environment: no. 5 "presence of a world-class business school, CEIBS", no. 4 "high quality hospitals", and no. 12 "the local 'cluster' of start-ups". No. 8 cites the "open system for entrepreneurs", even though the system is at present far from completely open, and no. 22, "venture capital", even though there is an admitted scarcity of it. A key anchor seems to be the international worldview provided by ZJ Park and Shanghai in general, no. 18. A very wide variety of entrepreneurs, managers, scientists and diplomats are in Shanghai, China's financial capital, and basically bring the outside world to the young Shanghai entrepreneurs.

Table 9.4 lists the two-dozen key innovation processes, in order of importance, and classified according to which side of the market (supply or demand) they are assigned to. (Recall that each participant receives 15 points, to allocate among the processes, according to importance.)

China is a materialistic society. So it is reasonable that the top-scoring processes, protection/appreciation/reward, and incentives, reflect the material rewards that innovators in China receive, both material and prestige. In third place is "survival", reflecting the participants' view that firms that fail to innovate will simply be shunted aside by those who do. Fourth is the technology transfer process, crossing the gap between basic discoveries and commercialization. This is a source, like many processes of both advantage and disadvantage – disadvantage, if done poorly, and advantage, if done well. ZJ Park is one of the centers where technology transfer occurs. The fifth-ranked process, early adopters (a term also mentioned in Geoffrey Moore and Regis McKenna's book *Crossing the Chasm* (1991)), reflects the fact that as a huge country, China has a small but significant market for radically new innovations. Predictably, the one-stop shop basket of services offered at ZJ Park is listed as an important contributing process, as is "tolerance of wild ideas", and "incubator process" (closely related to the sixth-ranked process). In some ways, tolerance of wild ideas, tied for sixth, is both wishful thinking and reality. In the hierarchical Chinese society, wild ideas are not always tolerated; but in entrepreneurial circles, they are. Chinese entrepreneurs, like entrepreneurs everywhere, are passionate about their businesses (ninth), but employees lack loyalty and turnover is very high, with key personnel jumping ship when they receive a better offer (tenth). In 11th place, "market condition" is the huge Chinese domestic market that enables start-ups to survive without necessarily going global from day one (see below, Lyceem case study). And 12th, "guidance from Beijing", reflecting the key role played by central government policy, funding, direction and planning, as, for instance, found in the regular Five-Year Plans.

Among the less important processes are: government procurement (which was highly important in the French ecosystem), project leadership, discipline, language ability, the non-hierarchical structure of innovative firms, and lack of "cultural baggage" (that is, replacing a rigid culture based on authority with one based on creativity and ideas). Once again, we stress that the processes listed in Table 9.4 reflect *both* what exists at present, and what is hoped will exist in the near future, simply because in the dynamic Chinese society, change is underway and a transformative shift to innovation is a major national objective.

Analysis of the Cross-Impact Results

The essence of an ecosystem is the interaction among its various components. The data generated in the ZJ Park brainstorming workshop were used as inputs for further and more elaborate analysis. A "cross-impact analysis" (the perceived links between various anchors and processes) was employed to create a bipolar five-point Likert scale ranging from strong negative link, score 1, to a strong positive link, score 5, for each cell in a 24x24 cross-impact matrix.

Factor analysis was employed on the list of processes (variables). The anchors serve as observations in order to group the processes into major factors according to the similarities in their linkages with the anchors. Tests of sample adequacy constituted the necessary preliminary conditions for conducting factor analysis and obtaining meaningful results. The Spearman correlation matrix among the processes provided the input for both the tests and the factor analysis. The linkage-pattern items obtained in the ZJ Park (Shanghai) workshop demonstrate good sampling adequacy at the overall (KMO = 0.611). The result of the Bartlett's sphericity test rejects the null hypothesis that the correlation matrix is an identity matrix (p = 0.000).

Exploratory principal axis factor analysis with subsequent orthogonal rotation (Varimax rotation with Kaiser normalization) produced six factors, that together explain 81.2 percent of the variance. The factor loadings are presented in Table 9.5. In order to facilitate factor labeling, the dominant items marked in bold in Table 9.5, were defined as those with an absolute value of the loading greater than 0.46. Through the factor analysis the processes divided up into five major groups, three of which

Table 9.5 *Factor analysis results for the ZJ Park innovation ecosystem*

Factor Name	Items (Processes)	Factors					
		1	2	3	4	5	6
Attitudes and policies that help and hinder	Guidance/(Beijing)	**-0.873**	0.024	0.005	-0.232	0.209	0.115
	Gap between innovation and commercialization	**0.793**	0.111	-0.015	-0.034	0.343	0.306
	Innovate to survive	**0.707**	0.433	-0.034	0.241	0.259	-0.127
	Government procurement	**-0.682**	-0.356	-0.167	-0.042	0.433	-0.218
	Incentive: innovation is normal work	**0.651**	0.511	0.162	-0.158	0.370	-0.190
	Think local/think social	**0.620**	0.090	0.431	0.281	0.154	0.083
Start-up culture	Languages/English	0.018	**0.867**	0.189	-0.088	0.115	-0.230
	Tolerance of wild ideas	0.183	**0.783**	-0.098	0.324	0.039	0.278
	Passion/just do it	0.346	**0.612**	0.278	0.269	0.138	0.020
	Respect, admiration for start-ups (include failures)	0.308	**0.518**	0.180	0.452	0.492	0.017
Direct government assistance	Services (available at incubator)	-0.022	0.122	**0.861**	0.130	0.000	-0.011
	Incubator process	0.070	-0.070	**0.837**	-0.014	-0.137	0.116
	Protection for innovation/appreciation/ reward	0.136	0.208	**0.678**	0.161	0.095	0.297
Open-market forces	Market condition: allow start-ups to survive	0.102	0.052	0.276	**0.900**	0.198	-0.002
	Market of early adapters	0.362	0.523	-0.131	**0.640**	0.026	-0.250
	Leadership/project leadership	0.153	0.293	0.452	**0.456**	0.382	0.221

Trust in human and intellectual capital						
Confidentiality of intellectual property (patents)	−0.006	0.104	−0.005	0.162	**0.865**	−0.074
Lack of loyalty in company (turnover)	0.378	0.390	−0.389	0.190	**0.534**	0.089
Tax incentives						
Incentive (investors) (tax credit) (matching)	0.027	−0.085	0.294	−0.054	−0.073	**0.913**
Percent of variance	19.7	16.8	14.9	11.3	11.1	7.4
Cumulative percent	19.7	36.5	51.4	62.7	73.8	81.2

KMO* = 0.611
Cronbach's Alpha = 0.812

explained between 15 percent and 20 percent of the overall variance and the remaining two, from 11 percent, and finally, a stand-alone factor, "tax incentives", explaining seven percent.

The main factor that presents both the supply side and the demand side of innovation was the one that related to "attitudes and policies" – including both government procurement and Beijing guidance, and key attitudes toward innovation ("normal work", "innovate to survive", etc.). The second related to the "start-up culture" (we recall that the culture aspect was a key element of nearly all the innovation ecosystems we mapped) and belongs to the demand side of innovation. The third factor was "direct government assistance", to be expected in a nation where central government policy is pervasive, powerful and massive, and obviously presents supply side of innovation. The fourth factor, "open market forces", reflect China's shift toward market-driven demand-pull innovation, from technology-push policy-driven innovation. The fifth factor, "trust in human and intellectual property", relates to how the patent system protects intellectual property. This is an area China has given huge attention to in recent years, in view of the widespread feeling that intellectual property has in the past been illegally appropriated by China, and the lack of trust in workers, who leave one job for another rapidly when offered incentives.

Overall, the cross-impact picture is one of an interesting blend between "soft" and "hard" factors: "soft" factors related to changing attitudes and cultural values, and "hard" factors related to government support, influence and policy. Our experts have clearly recognized that without fundamental changes in attitudes and values, massive government support for innovation will not be sufficient.

The next methodological step included the classification of anchors into groups. The classification of anchors into clusters did not involve a similar statistical procedure as was done with the processes and was based on logic. The anchors were grouped into five clusters as listed in Table 9.6: attitude and values, government policy, human capital, market process and finance.

CONSTRUCTION OF AN INNOVATION ECOSYSTEM MAP FOR SHANGHAI ZJ PARK

Structure of the System

In the final step of this methodological exercise, an innovation map was produced for the Shanghai ZJ Park ecosystem. Figure 9.7 presents

Table 9.6   List of anchors grouped into major clusters

Name of Cluster	Anchor Name
Attitude and values	Openness of the market to new ideas Network/group thinking Willingness to take risk Atmosphere/state of mind (luxury center) Culture: everything is possible, nothing is easy same rules for all Comfortable having fixed framework/protection
Government policy	Focus: priority of central government/(direct) (national) Government policy/funding/encouragement Risk reduction platforms (R&D Israel/Shanghai) Tax incentives income tax exempt/software One-stop shop/staff from business (at ZJ Park) Government supports activity OUTSIDE China
Human capital	Talent pool Young people/innovative spirit Research/high-quality hospitals/manpower World class education institutions International city and park (worldview from outside China)
Market process	Demand/market Open system for entrepreneurs Cluster Environmental challenges (Demand) – based on existing services/products
Finance	Capital funding (incl government) Venture capital: key role (lack VC group).

the ZJ Park, Shanghai, China, innovation ecosystem map. The interactions between the group of anchors (clusters) and the group of processes (factors) was computed based on a mathematical procedure for determining and weighting the direction and strength of link between the factors and clusters (see in detail in Chapter 2).

By nature the start-up culture is driven by both demand-driven and supply-driven forces. Trust in human capital and in intellectual property protection is purely supply-side driven, reflecting conditions in the market for patents and for skilled workers. Tax incentives play an important role and are by definition supply-related, as they are driven purely by central

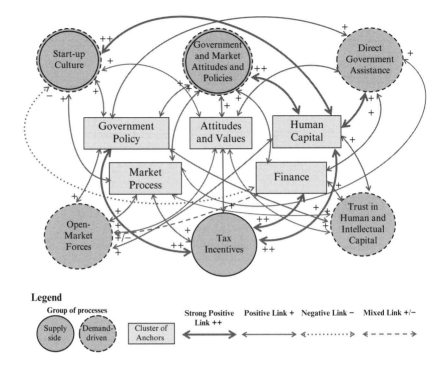

Figure 9.7   Shanghai's innovation ecosystem

government policy. Direct government assistance is another factor representing supply side of innovation. Attitudes and policies are driven both by central government actions, including the Five-Year Plan, and by processes that combine supply-side and market-driven forces (such as regarding innovation as part of normal everyday "work").

The human capital anchor cluster was found to be very important in the ecosystem with strong positive association with four of the factors: start-up culture, market and government attitudes and policies, as well as with direct government assistance and tax incentives that are by definition supply-driven related. China generates an enormous number of university graduates annually – to such an extent, that many are now encountering difficulty, for the first time, in finding employment. This is another reason why innovation has become so crucial for China – without a major increase in sectors that innovate; the enormous output of China's universities will not find suitable employment.

Government policy and finance anchor clusters obviously have a strong and positive relation with tax incentives processes factor, but weaker ties with all the other factors. Attitude and values as well as market processes have only weaker ties with all processes factors in the ecosystem. This is generally typical of an early-stage innovation and entrepreneurship ecosystem that has not yet had time to "ripen" and mature. In China, the industrialization process has been extraordinarily rapid, perhaps unprecedentedly so, but it may be true that building an innovation ecosystem with strong interactions takes much more time.

Some of the negative interactions are worth noting. The finance infrastructure may actually hinder the start-up culture, because bank finance seems reluctant to fund start-ups, preferring established companies. This is true of many other nations as well, but in China, is of especial importance, because in general bank finance is relatively plentiful for companies approved and fostered by Beijing. Finance may also hinder "open market forces", because many of the top banks are tightly controlled by the central government and their decisions are not always market-based.

The main differences, we believe, between China's ZJ Park innovation ecosystem and those of the other nations shown in this book, are two-fold. First, the ecosystem represents a subset of China's innovation, restricted to an admittedly huge (by world standards) but still relatively small (by Chinese standards) area, dedicated solely to innovation. Second, it must be admitted that the ZJ Park innovation ecosystem, drawn up to reflect innovation in Shanghai in general, contains an element of wishful thinking, representing the system that participants hope and trust will emerge, rather than the one that reflects reality as it is at present. We believe this is reasonable, because China has shown repeatedly in the past that it is capable of implementing sweeping visions and transformational change rapidly, and a transformation toward an economy built on innovation is definitely a key part of China's vision of the future.

Case Studies

These case studies reflect a very broad range of Chinese innovation, from start-ups to established firms, and product innovation to process innovation. "Attitudes and values" is an anchor at the heart of the ZJ Park innovation ecosystem; Lyceem Travel shows how the values and attitudes of young Chinese start-up entrepreneurs drive new enterprises. The Haier-Strauss case study reveals how market forces in China drive entrepreneurial ventures, in this case a partnership between a Chinese consumer electronics company and an Israeli food products multinational company. Taobao reveals how the combination of "start-up culture" and "market forces" can drive a unique and highly successful Internet business. The list of China's top ten innovators is a highly varied one, showing how innovation in China occurs in many parts of the innovation ecosystem. Finally,

BYD and BGI illustrate how superior human capital, led by scientific brilliance, can drive basic science breakthroughs into large fast-growing innovative enterprises. The concluding brief case study of Apple shows how US-China synergy benefits both nations, with Apple's breakthrough innovative designs finding a key partner in China's flexible, rapid and cost-effective manufacturing system.

Lyceem Travel Products Co.
Mary Zhu is the business development officer for Shanghai Lyceem Travel Products Co., which sells travel bags online. Lyceem is a start-up headquartered in the ZhangJiang Science Park. We observed a meeting of Lyceem's management and workers.

A college graduate, Mary's English is excellent. She told us how Lyceem grew from a dozen workers to 50 in only two months, and then quickly doubled again to 100 employees; such a rapid scale-up start-up in other countries would find challenging. Some of Lyceem's products are humdrum (like cosmetic cases) but some are innovative, like a lovely transparent waterproof bag for mobile phones, intended for use at the beach. Unlike many start-ups, which must think and act globally from day one, and aspire to reach distant markets, Lyceem can thrive solely in the domestic Chinese market – a huge advantage. This is especially true, as China shifts towards domestic consumption as its growth engine and seeks to expand personal spending.

We asked Zhu what her personal goals are, expecting to hear about the desire for wealth most young Chinese are allegedly seeking. "To be a good person," she said emphatically. "To be happy with my husband, my parents, my kids. To be an honest person. To develop my dream. Work is just a means to that." Like entrepreneurs everywhere, the Chinese start-up youth seem more enthralled with the process of launching a business than the fruits it yields them. And in many ways, they resemble entrepreneurs everywhere.

Haier-Strauss Water[5]
This joint venture illustrates how Chinese firms partner effectively with innovative foreign companies, for mutual gain and to help China move up the value chain.

Strauss Group is an Israel-based global food company focused on dairy, coffee and chocolate. Strauss Water is a kind of start-up operating within H2Q Water Industries, owned 87 percent by Strauss Group for making and selling water devices worldwide. Haier Group is a large Chinese global consumer electronics and home appliances company, headquartered in Quingdao, China; the Haier brand led the world market share in "white goods" (kitchen appliances) with 6.1 percent. Its annual revenue is an esti-mated 33 billion RMB (about $4.6 billion).

In October 2009, Strauss acquired Tana Industries, purchased by Strauss subsidiary H2Q for NIS 291 million (about $72 million). Tana Industries was owned by Kibbutz HaLamed Hai and made the Tami4 water purifying device. On 18 May 2011, Strauss Water and Haier Group launched their joint venture in Shanghai, to produce the home water filtra-tion device, with a $4 million marketing campaign featuring the mantra "Smart Water – Safe Home". The device is based on ten pending patents. The heart of the device is a high-tech filter known as MAZE, developed by Israeli entrepreneurs and produced in Israel. The high-tech purifier not only filters water, but also heats it to exactly the right temperature for making tea. Strauss and Haier each invested $20 million in the joint venture. The device will be sold initially in Beijing, Shanghai and Quingdao (headquarters of Haier), and later, in Shenzhen and Guangzhou.

Israeli entrepreneur Haim Wilder invented MAZE, together with Hebrew University Professor Avi Domb. MAZE is a unique water puri-fication technology and filter that works with zero water pressure and its technology is the core of the Haier Strauss device. The Tami 4 appliance itself will be manufactured in China. But the crucial high-tech MAZE filter is produced in Israel, at Kibbutz Netiv Halamed Hey.

Alibaba – Taobao

Alibaba is a Hongzhou-based group of Internet-based businesses that include B2B (business-to-business) online marketplaces, retail and payment platforms, shopping search engine and cloud computing services. Its CEO until recently was the legendary Jack Ma. Ma founded China Yellow Pages in 1995, China's first Internet-based company. He founded Alibaba. com in 1999, a B2B marketplace site serving 80 million customers in 240 countries. Alibaba's web-based trading platform is Taobao. Thousands of Chinese manufacturers use Taobao to find potential customers and transact with them directly. Taobao's platform embeds a large number of important innovations to facilitate these transactions. For instance, it has the capability to enable electronic fund transfers, and deal with the quirks of the Chinese banking system. Taobao's innovative system is driven by Alibaba's deep customer intimacy and understanding of its clients' needs; a quality that accounts for much of Alibaba's startling success. And, as Orr and Roth (2013) note, "customer intimacy" is a quality few Chinese companies have, as they are driven largely by a manufacturing mindset. This lack of customer intimacy may explain government failures, note Orr and Roth, to develop indigenous Chinese 3G protocol (TDS-CDMA) and an indigenous Chinese Wi-Fi protocol (WAPI).

China's top ten innovators
The business magazine *Fast Company* regularly publishes lists of the most innovative companies, by country. The companies are chosen by a panel of top experts. Here are China's top ten:

1. Tencent: China's Facebook, with more than 700 million users, $3 billion in revenue, $1 billion in profits, and is aggressively acquiring USA firms (Riot Games).
2. Greenbox: highly-styled children's clothing, for China's growing upscale middle class.
3. United Styles: an online retailer of children's clothing lets users design, order, share and preview their clothing through a Facebook interface. Garments are made by Chinese digital textile printers.
4. Lenovo: China's first truly global brand, after acquiring IBM's ThinkPad. After the acquisition, Lenovo signaled its global intentions by moving its headquarters to New York State.
5. Suntech Power: has made China a global solar power leader, after reacting to falling solar power demand at home in China by globalizing. China nonetheless aims to expand its solar power from 140 megawatts today to 20 000 megawatts by 2020, and Suntech will lead.
6. Renren: a "real name" social network, now listed on the New York Stock Exchange.
7. BYD (Build Your Dream): see below – electric cars.
8. Innovation Works: in-house coaching and funding for early-stage start-ups.
9. Alibaba (see above).
10. Huawei: mobile phone/telecom company, aggressively expanding abroad, using China's advantage of scale. Huawei has leveraged its skills learned in China's low-cost no-frills market, to drive similar markets overseas, while reinvesting resulting profits to move up the value chain.

BYD
What does BYD stand for? It stands for Build Your Dreams. And – it stands for an up-start car company that plans to be number one in China by 2015 and number one in the world by 2025, according to its President Wang Chuanfu. Wang is a genius. He invented a revolutionary battery that powers a third of the world's cell phones. And now, he has leveraged his knowledge of battery technology to build electric cars that can charge in as little as 15 minutes. Founded in 1995, BYD employs 170 000 workers in seven huge plants, and has 10 000 engineers and scientists in its R&D centers. Evidence that BYD is on the right track? An investor

named Warren Buffett bought a 9.89 percent interest for $230 million. How did BYD transition from making cell phone batteries for Nokia, to making cars? It bought a Chinese car manufacturer four years ago. Car production, according to BYD, is rather low technology. BYD uses its high-technology experience, to upgrade the technology of car production.

BYD is a sort of Chinese role model. Look for America and Europe to bring back home some of its manufacturing. Look for China to respond by moving up the value chain and upgrading its factories, to build branded high-quality high-technology products, like BYD's electric cars. This has been China's vision from the outset. As with all innovation, a major driver will be excellence in basic science (of the kind achieved by Wang Chuanfu), transferred across "the Valley of Death" to commercial applications by bold entrepreneurs, sometimes by the scientists themselves. China's enormous focus on its human capital, a key part of its innovation ecosystem, is typified by this small piece of data – a single Chinese university, Harbin Engineering School, now graduates more engineers annually than the entire ten-campus University of the Californian system.

BGI[6]

BGI, originally the Beijing Genomics Institute, is the world's biggest genetic sequencing company. It accounts for half of all global genetic sequencing capacity, and has mapped genomes for cancer cells, plants, insects, humans and the giant panda. Its co-founder Wang Jian recounts that BGI was originally a state-run research institute that was "kicked out" of Beijing and sent to Shenzhen, a manufacturing hub thousands of miles away. This refocused BGI on commercial products and led to partnerships with global institutions. It has now acquired a USA sequency company (Complete Genomics), and has as its goal to bring the cost of genetic testing to below $1000, cheap enough to incorporate into regular medical care. BGI recruits young creative researchers even before they graduate. Wang tells them, "come work for us and become world-class, why go back to school?" He seeks counter-culture Chinese, who rebel against authority rather than conform to it.

Apple

China is a key part of Apple's innovation ecosystem. Here is why, as explained by Dan Breznitz, in an interview with the *New York Times*, based on his book *Run of the Red Queen*:

> There's a white power supply box on the power cord [of Apple computers]. That box has been improved with continued R&D so it doesn't go up in smoke and so it will do what it does ever more efficiently. This is entirely done in China. The company that makes the power supplies is constantly doing

research to make them smaller, more efficient, cooler, cheaper and less energy intensive. This can only be done in China because firms can find high-quality engineers and tell them, "You will make power supplies better" and the engineers will oblige. What are the chances you can hire someone from an elite U.S. university . . .. to do that?[7]

SUMMARY AND CONCLUSION

In their informative article on Chinese innovation, two McKinsey principals based in Shanghai, Gordon Orr and Erik Roth, conclude:

> China hasn't yet experienced a true innovation revolution. It will need time to evolve from a country of incremental innovation based on technology transfers to one where breakthrough innovation is common. The government will play a powerful role in that process, but ultimately it will be the actions of domestic companies and multinationals that dictate the pace of change – and determine who leads it."[8]

China's government builds five-year strategic plans. The latest Five-Year Plan (2011–15) calls specifically for a transition from "made in China" to "created in China". The Science and Technology Development Plan calls for 2.5 percent of GDP to be spent on R&D by 2020. There is no question that China has vast resources to back its innovation policies. But are there tangible successes reflected in China's businesses? The 2012 China Innovation Survey canvassed more than 100 leading Chinese companies and multinationals in five sectors: industrials, automotive, health, consumer goods and chemicals and energy.[9] The results are rather surprising. According to the report (p. 2): ". . . many global companies already perceive Chinese companies as major innovation powers. Of the MNCs interviewed, 45 percent said some of their Chinese competitors were equally or more innovative than themselves." Among the advantages Chinese companies have over multinationals, in innovation, are (in order of importance): government support, faster decision-making, quicker to capture opportunities, higher speed to market, better stakeholder inclusion, better read of the market, more flexible. This reflects to some degree the ZJ Park innovation ecosystem presented above. According to the Chinese Innovation Survey, 86 percent of the Chinese companies surveyed, plan to expand their business abroad; and 66 percent (two-thirds) plan to extend their R&D presence abroad in the coming decade.

Our mapping of the ZJ Park innovation ecosystem hopefully sheds light on the fascinating transformation China seeks to implement, described by Orr and Roth; the entrepreneurs, inventors and managers in the Park represent the vanguard of Chinese innovation efforts. At present, Chinese companies excel in incremental innovation – improving what exists. As Professor Dan Breznitz notes:

> Chinese companies are extremely efficient at creating new versions, often simpler, cheaper and more efficient, of technologies and products shortly after they are invented and marketed elsewhere in the world . . . In novel-product innovation, China is very weak. . . . the political economic institutions and system in China make it so entrepreneurs can't make profit by developing novel innovation. But this same system makes process and second-generation innovation very profitable and successful.[10]

The ZJ Park innovation ecosystem offers a glimpse of what the future holds for China, a future driven much more by first-generation product innovation. The goal of the 2012 China Innovation Survey was to answer key questions about Chinese innovation. The results indicated that Chinese business leaders themselves see Chinese innovation as a key source of future competitive advantage, rather than just efficient low-cost manufacturing. This advantage exists in two separate areas, both of which find expression to some degree in the innovation ecosystem shown above: large-scale government support, and time-to-market: "ability to deliver products rapidly to markets via their decisiveness, speed-of-action and proximity-to-market". The study concludes (at p. 10):

> MNCs should be ready to face Chinese companies that possess strong – maybe even superior – innovation capabilities. Combined with the major cost advantages of these companies, and the way in which many are migrating upwards into higher market segments, MNCs will increasingly face these competitors not just in China, but also around the world – even in their home markets.

It will be fascinating to observe how this process – China's shift from made-in-China to invented-in-China unfolds. Whatever the case, the West should prepare itself for stiff Chinese competition, not solely in manufacturing but in radical innovation.

NOTES

*   With the assistance of Marta Garcia de Alcaraz, who organized the Experts Workshop for us, and Erica Huang, General Manager of Zhiangjiang Science Park, who provided hospitality and insights.
1. The exchange rate for China's renminbi (yuan), relative to the dollar, is about 6.23 yuan per dollar. This rate greatly undervalues the yuan. If market forces operated freely, the yuan would exchange for about 3.5 yuan per dollar, because the yuan is undervalued by nearly half (Source: *The Economist* (2013), "Daily chart: The Big Mac index", 31 January 2013, www.economist.com/blogs/graphicdetail/2013/01/daily-chart-18, accessed 19 February 2014). Thus, when converting China's GDP (in yuan) to GDP

in dollars, using the 3.5 exchange rate gives a much larger value than when the official exchange rate, 6.23 yuan per dollar, is used.

2. *The Economist* (2012), "Innovation in China: From brawn to brain", 10 March 2012, at www.economist.com/node/21549938, accessed 19 February 2014.

3. Gordon Orr and Eric Roth (2012), "A CEO's Guide to Innovation in China", *McKinsey Quarterly*, February 2012, at www.mckinsey.com/insights/asia-pacific/a_ceos_guide_to_innovation_in_china.

4. *The Economist* (2013), "How innovative is China? Valuing patents", 5 January 2013, www.economist.com/news/business/21569062-valuing-patents, accessed 19 February 2014.

5. This is based on an unpublished case study, Haier Strauss Water, by Shlomo Maital and Nama Sidi (Haifa, 2011).

6. See Leslie Hook (2013), "China wakes up to innovation", *Financial Times*, 11 February 2013, www.ft.com/cms/s/0/3d97c42e-7200-11e2-886e-00144feab49a.html, accessed 19 February 2014.

7. Dan Breznitz (2011), Book Chat: "Moving China Up the Value Chain", *New York Times*, 4 August 2011, http://economix.blogs.nytimes.com/2011/08/04/moving-china-up-the-value-chain/?_php=true&_type=blogs&_r=0, accessed 19 February 2014.

8. Orr and Roth (2012).

9. Booz & Co. (2012), "Innovation: China's next advantage? 2012 China Innovation Survey", June 2012.

10. Dan Breznitz (2011).

10. The Singaporean national innovation ecosystem*

INTRODUCTION

In this chapter, we present Singapore's innovation ecosystem. Singapore is almost unique, in the manner in which it rose from a small embattled nation in 1965, when it became independent from Malaysia, to a wealthy modern industrialized nation in 2013. We begin first by recounting some of Singapore's history, without which its success is difficult to comprehend. We then describe briefly Singapore's economy and its global competitiveness. Next, we survey Singapore's economic freedom, which contrasts rather starkly with its limited political democracy. Singapore's remarkable ease of doing business is presented next, suggesting that other nations would do well to benchmark Singapore's success in eliminating needless bureaucratic red tape. We then provide data on Singapore's innovation and entrepreneurship, relative to other globally competitive nations. The next section presents Singapore innovation ecosystem – as always, first listing the key anchors and key processes, then providing the results of a detailed factor analysis of the processes, and finally, using the factor analysis to construct the innovation ecosystem and discuss its implications. Several case studies of innovative Singaporean companies follow, including Singapore Airlines, Starhome and Creative. The chapter closes with a summary of the main findings.

BACKGROUND

The Republic of Singapore comprises a main island and 62 smaller islands, off the tip of the Malay Peninsula, with a total area of about 700 sq km; it is really a city state with some five million people. On 31 August 1963, Singapore declared independence from Britain and joined the Federation of Malaysia. In 1965, the Malaysian Parliament voted to expel Singapore, which became independent on 9 August 1965. This decision was preceded by race riots between ethnic Chinese and ethnic Malays. Malaysia felt that since Singapore was three-quarters ethnic

Chinese; it was best to eject it. Founding Prime Minister Lee Kuan Yew had a powerful vision for Singapore that he proceeded to implement, even though he later intimated, in his memoires, that at the time, in 1965, he had doubts whether little Singapore would survive as an independent nation (see Lee, 1999, 2000). The essence of Lee Kuan Yew's vision was simple: to endure and to prevail, Singapore, as a very small country distant from the world's power and financial centers, would have to excel in everything it did – airlines, ports, industry, education. It would have to aspire to be number one, and not only aspire but achieve. Excuses could not be tolerated. It is this aspect of Singaporean culture that endures to this day, and helps explain Singapore's world-class excellence in so many areas. An example is Singapore Airlines, conceived from the outset to be world leading in quality of service, newness of its fleet, and other key benchmarks. Singapore is often criticized for its lack of political democracy, stemming from the dominance of the PAP – People's Action Party and the suppression of opposition parties. This is partly unfair. The race riots that preceded Singapore's independence led Lee Kuan Yew to establish very clear "rules of the game" that would prevent mixed-race Singapore from descending into chaos. As shown below, Singapore's alleged lack of political democracy is tempered by its embrace of high-level economic democracy (competitive free markets), and as well, by its almost total absence of political corruption, which many so-called democratic nations envy.

Singapore's gross domestic product (GDP) is about $260 billion (2011), or a strikingly high $59 520 per capita, when measured in terms of purchasing power parity, one of the highest per capita GDP levels of any non-oil-producing nation. Its current account surplus is 22 percent of GDP; this is a key to understanding Singapore, because its economy is highly dependent on exports and its growth is driven by its export surplus. Foreign direct investment is very large, amounting to 25 percent of GDP (2011), or a cumulative total of $483 billion (International Institute for Management Development (IMD), *World Competitiveness Yearbook*, 2012).

Despite its tiny size, Singapore ranks 14th or 15th in the entire world in value of exports and imports.[1] It has the highest ratio of trade to GDP in the world; trade (exports plus imports) is over four times its GDP. Some 7000 American, Japanese and European multinational companies have a presence in Singapore, along with about 1500 each from China and India. Only about three Singaporeans in five are Singapore citizens. The remainder are permanent residents or foreign workers. Singapore has the world's highest proportion of millionaires – one of every six households has at least a million US dollars in wealth. The degree of inequality in the distribution of income is very high. Singapore's infrastructure is first rate, with its port one of the world's most efficient, and most busy, competing with Shanghai, Hong Kong and Shenzhen.

Singapore is a highly organized, even regimented society, for reasons noted above. This high degree of discipline makes Singapore's economy and society highly efficient, but is also inimical to individual entrepreneurship and creativity. A variety of central policies have been implemented to overcome this deficiency, with limited success.

SINGAPORE'S CAPABILITIES IN FREE MARKET COMPETITION

In this section we present four economic indices: global competitiveness, economic freedom, ease of doing business and innovation and entrepreneurship with regard to Singapore capabilities to cope with its challenges.

Global Competitiveness

Singapore is one of the most competitive nations in the world. Its ranking (in the IMD *World Competitiveness Yearbook*) ranged in recent years from 1st (in 2010) to 4th (in 2012). Singapore's competitiveness landscape (see Figure 10.1) consists almost solely of "peaks", with almost no troughs (an exception is "prices", owing to 5 percent inflation in 2011). In business efficiency and government efficiency, Singapore ranks second in the world. Despite its high wages, Singapore's high productivity keeps it globally competitive, showing that high wages need not be a barrier to cost competitiveness. At the same time, Singapore has no minimum wage, in principle, and a very large disparity in wages between low-paid and high-paid workers. And its ranking in productivity fell sharply, from 2nd in 2011 to 14th in 2012.

Among Singapore's main challenges are: improving productivity of its small businesses, adapting to slow population (and workforce) growth, high economic inequality, and building competitiveness in new industries – a perennial problem Singapore faces. Among the key attractiveness indicators are: stable predictable policy, competent clean government, low business taxes, an effective legal system, good infrastructure, overall friendliness toward business, and a strong educational system.

Economic Freedom

According to the Heritage Foundation, which computes an annual Economic Freedom Index for many nations, "Singapore's economic

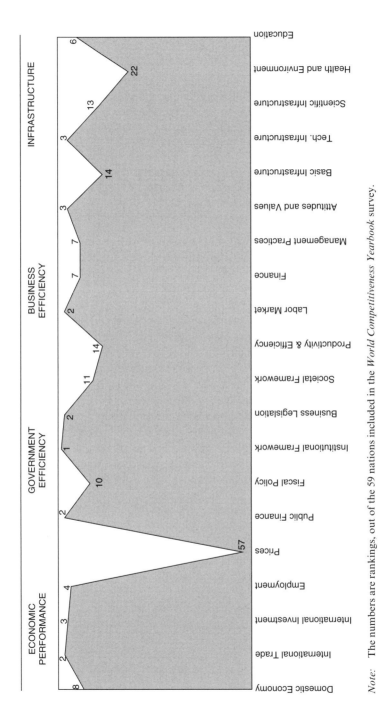

Note: The numbers are rankings, out of the 59 nations included in the *World Competitiveness Yearbook* survey.

Source: IMD, *World Competitiveness Yearbook 2012.*

Figure 10.1   Singapore's competitiveness landscape

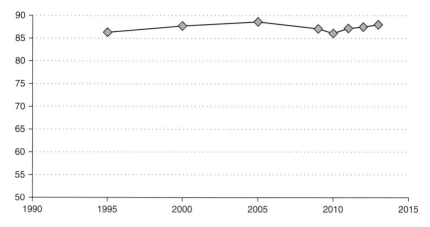

Source: The Heritage Foundation, Index of Economic Freedom 2013, see www.heritage.org/index/.

Figure 10.2 Singapore: Economic freedom score, 1995–2013

freedom score is 88, making its economy the second freest in the 2013 Index. Its score is 0.5 point higher than last year, with an advancement in financial freedom outweighing small deteriorations in five other economic freedoms. Singapore is ranked second out of 41 countries in the Asia–Pacific region." (See Figure 10.2.)

Among the reasons cited for this high ranking are a prudent macro-economic policy, well-secured property rights, zero tolerance for corruption and a strong legal system. The Heritage Foundation report for 2013[2] notes that: "Singapore's openness to global trade and investment has facilitated the emergence of a more competitive financial sector and continues to provide real stimulus and ensure economic dynamism. Competitive tax rates and a transparent regulatory environment encourage vibrant commercial activity, and the private sector is a continuing source of economic resilience and competitiveness."

Ease of Doing Business

According to the World Bank, doing business in Singapore is exceptionally easy (Figure 10.3). The latest global rankings list Singapore as 1st in the world (!) in ease of doing business. Broken down, Singapore ranks 4th in the world in ease of starting a business, second in getting a construction permit, first in "trading across borders", 5th in paying taxes, 36th in registering property, and 2nd in resolving insolvency. As the world's leading trading

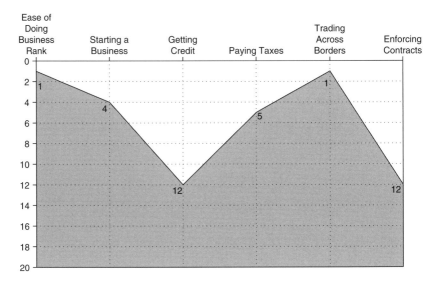

Source: Doing Business Project – The World Bank, 2012, see www.doingbusiness.org/ rankings.

Figure 10.3   Singapore: Ease of doing business, 2012

nation, Singapore has simply taken a high-level executive decision that everything related to trade must be smooth and efficient, from the port, to the regulations that govern trade. The country that ranks 2nd in the world is Hong Kong, which like Singapore lives and dies through its foreign trade.

Innovation and Entrepreneurship

In contrast to its excellent achievements in many economic indices as mentioned above, Singapore has recognized long ago that it has a problem with innovation and entrepreneurship. According to the IMD *World Competitiveness Yearbook*, Singapore ranks 23rd in the world in the subjective evaluation of experts that "entrepreneurship is widespread in business", ranking below the US (14th), Mainland China (15th), and Israel (2nd). For innovative capacity of firms to generate new products processes and/or services, Singapore ranks much higher, 8th. What this implies is that Singapore's innovative "style" is based more on innovation in existing large organizations than in garage-type individual entrepreneurship; in any event, the authoritarian Chinese culture that dominates Singapore is probably infertile soil for such entrepreneurship. This will become clearer when we view Singapore's innovation ecosystem.

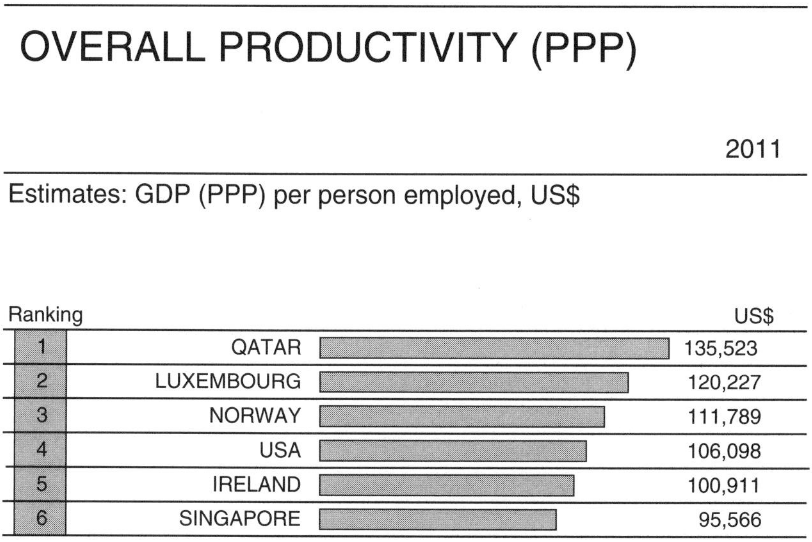

OVERALL PRODUCTIVITY (PPP)

	2011
Estimates: GDP (PPP) per person employed, US$	

Ranking		US$
1	QATAR	135,523
2	LUXEMBOURG	120,227
3	NORWAY	111,789
4	USA	106,098
5	IRELAND	100,911
6	SINGAPORE	95,566

Source: IMD, *World Competitiveness Yearbook 2012.*

Figure 10.4 Productivity ranking

Productivity

Singapore ranks only 14th in "productivity and efficiency" in the "competitiveness landscape" diagram (see Figure 10.1). But measured as GDP per worker, in purchasing power parity, Singapore ranks 6th, at $95,566; and if we disregard Qatar (oil and gas) and Luxembourg (highly-paid EU civil service jobs), Singapore ranks 4th (see Figure 10.4). This suggests that strengthening Singapore's innovative capability will be complemented by its ability to implement innovative ideas with speed and efficiency.

INNOVATION ECOSYSTEM

We convened a group of experts in Singapore, as our methodology requires, to define key innovation anchors and processes. Participants came from a wide cross-section of Singaporean society, including the Ministry of Education, start-ups, large multinationals, banks, higher education, etc.

Data Analysis

Anchors and processes
This section provides a summary of the raw inputs collected at the Singaporean Experts Workshop (see Chapter 2) conducted at NTU Nanyang Technological University. The list of 25 key anchors for Singapore that emerged from the workshop is given in Table 10.1.

A few of these anchors require explanation. The second and fourth anchors relate to China. Singapore manages its relations with its huge neighbor carefully, and leverages its own ethnic Chinese majority to

Table 10.1   List of innovation anchors for Singapore

Number	Anchor Name
1	Lack of market (small domestic market)
2	Proximity to China (cultural/language/historical/geography)
3	Lack of historical baggage (new nation)
4	Two pandas: gifts from China, political neutrality (especially regarding China)
5	Great leaders (beginning with Lee Kwan Yew) who learn from everyone, everywhere
6	Military service
7	Lack of corruption (in the context of the region)
8	Meritocracy (earn based on merit)
9	World class primary schools
10	Immigration of scientists
11	Cultural diversity
12	Cultural acceptance
13	S'English (Singapore unique spoken English, heavily accented)
14	Infrastructure: port/airport/broadband/IT/
15	Change and agility
16	Embracing new technology
17	Small nation (controlled environment, large lab)
18	Bilingual skills (English/China), bridge with India, etc. (understanding)
19	Free Trade agreements
20	Intellectual property protected
21	Government as client for innovation/civil service
22	Private/public partnership: culture of collaboration Singapore conversation
23	Singapore Master Plan (e.g. One North)
24	WDA – Workforce Development Authority
25	Safe environment

Table 10.2   List of identified processes fostering Singapore innovation, ranked by importance and classified by market side (supply, demand, or both)

Ranked number (by importance)	Process Name	Demand-side (D), Supply side (S) or both (D S)
1	Excessive rigid rules, lack of chaos (freedom)	D
2	Ease of doing business	S
3	Government grants	S
4	Coordinated processes, via master plan, for all government agencies	S
5	Top down central government decisions	S
6	Clear national goals and direction	S
7	Educating young children in innovation and entrepreneurship	S
8	Competitive spirit, fear of failure from early age	D
9	Tax incentive	S
10	Government schemes related to Housing and Development Board (HDB)	S
11	Government strategic direction	S
12	Online quick start of a business (e-Government)	S
13	NRS (National Research Foundation) grants	S
14	Skills, know-how focus of schools	D
15	Foreign students/scholarships/talent basket	S

gain advantage in trade and investment with China. (China gives pandas only to nations that it particularly favors; it gave two to Singapore.) The sixth anchor relates to the fact thet Singaporeans do compulsory military service, which is serious, highly organized and often strenuous (some infantry train in the jungles of Thailand). Singapore's official language is English (thirteenth anchor), a decision adopted from the outset, and one that gives it a major advantage in Southeast Asia; locals call it "S'English", for Singaporean English. Singapore is highly organized, with master plans for nearly everything, and this is seen as a possible anchor for innovation (twenty-third anchor). It has a skilled workforce, fostered in part by a governmental Workplace Development Authority.

Table 10.2 lists the key innovation processes identified by workshop participants, along with the point score of each (indicating their perceived importance). Again, some explanations are needed.

The first process in order of importance actually refers to Singapore's extreme level of discipline and organization, which expert participants identified as "lack of chaos", which they perceive as necessary for true creativity (especially in research). In general, innovation demands that the lamb of discipline lies down with the wolf of creativity. Participants apparently feel that Singapore's lack of creativity "wolves" may be in part due to the dominance of its "lambs" of discipline. Ease of doing business, and grants and funding, ranked second and third. The fourth most important process was, according to participants, the fact that government agencies and ministries are coordinated, through a master plan that is constantly revised and updated; this integration of policies is not very common in nations, where ministries battle over turf, budgets and influence. The top-down processes were cited, together with the comment that more bottom-up processes are needed to foster innovation. The existence of a process that shapes national goals and directions was mentioned, sixth in importance, as were programs to educate young children in innovation and creativity. Singapore is a competitive society; this was listed as a process important for innovation. Singapore has a single agency where capital can be raised very quickly, online, a kind of one-stop shop; finally, Singapore attracts foreign students, through generous scholarships, and participants felt this process brings talent and creativity.

Interaction among anchors and processes
The essence of an ecosystem is the interaction among its various components. The data generated in the Singapore brainstorming workshop were used as inputs for further and more elaborate analysis. A "cross-impact analysis" (the perceived links between various anchors and processes) was employed to create a bipolar five-point Likert scale ranging from strong negative link, score 1 to a strong positive link, score 5, for each cell in a 25x15 cross-impact matrix.

Analysis of the Cross-Impact Results

Subsequent exploratory factor analysis established the validity of the developed scales and helped to avoid redundant items and assured the association of each item to a single scale. Factor analysis was employed on the list of processes (variables). The anchors serve as observations in order to group the processes into major factors according to the similarities in their linkages with the anchors.

Exploratory principal axis factor analysis with subsequent orthogonal rotation (Varimax rotation with Kaiser normalization) produced four factors that together explain 73.5 percent of the variance. The factor loadings are presented in Table 10.3. In order to facilitate factor labeling, the

Table 10.3   Factor analysis results for the Singapore innovation ecosystem

Factor Name	Items (Processes)	Factors			
		1	2	3	4
Culture and entrepreneurial environment	Competitive spirit, Fear of failure from early age	**0.752**	−0.134	−0.040	−0.131
	Skills, know-how focus of schools	**0.745**	0.235	−0.193	0.351
	Excessive rigid rules, lack of chaos (freedom)	**0.720**	−0.104	0.173	0.286
	Government strategic direction	**0.677**	0.288	0.115	0.459
	Ease of doing business	**−0.653**	0.272	0.051	0.232
Government funding and early education	NRS (National Research Foundation) grants	0.103	**0.877**	0.148	0.012
	Educating young children in innovation and entrepreneurship	−0.217	**0.718**	−0.175	0.257
	Government grants	−0.500	**0.569**	0.185	0.112
Government directives	Coordinated master plan for all government agencies	−0.253	−0.004	**0.789**	0.168
	Tax incentives	−0.128	0.471	**0.758**	0.154
	Top-down central government decisions	0.421	−0.236	**0.738**	0.067
	Online quick start of a business (e-Government)	0.575	0.449	**0.576**	−0.023
Specific policies	Government schemes related to Housing and Development Board (HDB)	−0.019	0.022	0.241	**0.919**
	Clear national goals and direction	0.186	0.514	0.059	**0.679**
Percent of variance		24.7	18.5	16.5	13.8
Cumulative percent		24.7	43.2	59.7	73.5
KMO* = 0.561					
Cronbach's Alpha = 0.724					

dominant items, marked in bold in Table 10.3, were defined as those with an absolute value of the loading greater than 0.57.

Through the factor analysis we distilled the existing innovation process drivers down to four key factors. They are:

1. *Culture and entrepreneurial environment* (which accounted for about a quarter of the variance): competitive spirit; fear of failure from early age; skills; know-how focus of schools; excessive rigid rules; lack of chaos (freedom); government strategic direction; and ease of doing business.
2. *Government funding and early education*: National Research Foundation (NRS) grants; educating young children in innovation, entrepreneurship; government grants. This factor adds 18.5 percent to the explanation of the variance.
3. *Government directives*: coordinated master plan for all government agencies; tax incentives; top-down central government decisions; and online quick start of a business (e-Govt.). This factor adds 16.5 percent to the explanation of the variance.
4. *Specific policies*: government schemes relating to the Housing and Development Board (HDB); and clear national goals and direction. This factor adds 13.8 percent to the explanation of the variance

It is significant that despite Singapore being a highly regulated business environment, with strong government influence everywhere, culture remains the key, dominant process. Part of the culture factor includes the "lack of chaos" element mentioned earlier. Three of the four process factors (except the first) are intimately related to government, consistent with the highly regulated environment of Singapore. Expert participants in our workshop quickly identified this paradox – while many government programs exist to foster innovation, it may be that those very processes themselves impact innovation negatively by eliminating the free, open atmosphere necessary for creativity. The fact that it is easy to start a business is not sufficient to ensure high-level innovation, if the cultural environment is not one that fosters the open creation and exchange of new ideas.

CONSTRUCTION OF A NATIONAL INNOVATION ECOSYSTEM MAP FOR SINGAPORE

The next methodological step included the classification of processes and anchors into groups. The processes were grouped according to the results of the factor analysis. The classification of anchors into clusters did not involve a similar statistical procedure and was based on logic. The

Table 10.4   List of anchors grouped into major clusters

Name of Cluster	Anchor Name
Government direction	Great leaders (from Lee Kwan Yew) . . . learn from everyone Military service Infrastructure: port/airport/broadband/IT/ Government as client for innovation/civil service Singapore Master Plan (e.g. One North) WDA – workforce Development Authority Safe environment
Rule-based society	Lack of corruption (in the context of the region) Meritocracy (earn based on merit) Cultural diversity Cultural acceptance (S'English) Intellectual property protected Private/public partnership: culture of collaboration, Singapore Conversation
Small open nation	Lack of market (small domestic market) Proximity to China (cultural/language/historical/ geography) Two pandas: gifts from China, political neutrality (especially regarding China) Small nation (controlled environment, large lab). Free Trade agreements
Flexibility	Lack of historical baggage (new nation) Change/agility Embracing new technology Bilingual skills (English/China), bridge with India, etc. (Understanding)
Centers of excellence	World class primary schools. Immigration of scientists

anchors were grouped into five clusters as listed in Table 10.4: government direction; rule-based society; small open nation; flexibility; and centers of excellence.

In the final step of this methodological exercise, an innovation map was produced for the Singapore ecosystem. This can be seen in Figure 10.5. The interactions between the group of anchors (clusters) and the group of processes (factors) was computed based on a mathematical procedure for determining and weighting the direction and strength of link

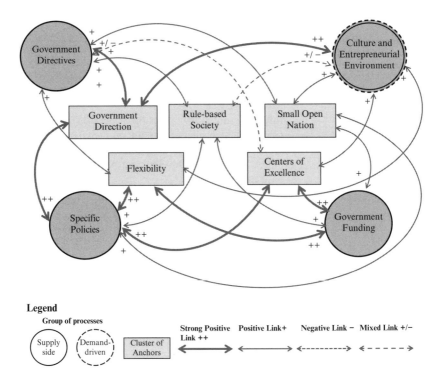

Figure 10.5   Singaporean innovation ecosystem

between the factors and clusters (see in Chapter 2). The results show that
the government directions cluster has strong positive association with
three process factors: government directives, specific polices, and culture
and entrepreneurial environment. The role of government direction in
the first two process factors is quite expected. Through its great leaders,
Singapore builds a world-class building national infrastructure (port/
airport/broadband/IT). It was done through the Singapore master plan
and workforce development authority, which determine clear national
goals, foster government top-down decisions, offer tax incentives and
online quick starts for new businesses. But this cluster has also a decisive
role in shaping Singaporean culture and entrepreneurial environment.
The Singapore government through its military service, on the one hand,
and by offering a safe environment, on the other hand, creates an entrepreneurial environment characterized by the existence of competitive
spirit, skills, know-how focus of schools, lack of chaos and ease of doing
business.

The anchor cluster, "rule-based society" plays only a secondary role in encouraging the process factors in the systems, and hence it has only a weaker positive association with all the identified factors. This is because of its ambivalence. On the one hand, it creates an environment of direction, purpose, system and efficiency. But on the other hand, since innovation is in part "intelligently breaking the rules", it may be anathema to individual creativity – a dilemma with which Singapore has struggled with for years. Government directives, government funding and specific policies are moderately positively influenced by lack of corruption, meritocracy, culture diversity and acceptance, culture of collaboration and S'English, as well as by lack of historical baggage, agility, embracing new technology and bilingual skills. The role-based society cluster has an ambiguous association with the culture and entrepreneurial environment factor.

Flexibility and centers of excellence anchor clusters have positive and strong relations with government funding and specific policies. It is clear that the existence of flexibility and centers of excellence in the Singaporean system, such as world-class primary schools and immigration of scientists, pushes the government to establish national research foundations, assist in educating children in innovation and entrepreneurship, and supply grants.

The Singaporean national innovation ecosystem map is unique and unusual. It reveals that in Singapore, innovation is largely supply side, dominated by government policies, programs and funding. But "like all", its culture and entrepreneurial environment play an important role; here, markets and demand play some role. The "flexibility" anchor seems to clash with rigid government regulation, and the "rule-based society" anchor, but in fact does not. Singapore's policy mechanism has "flexibility" built into it; every five years, a high-level task force is appointed, in the past headed often by the current President Dr Tony Tan, an MIT PhD in operations research, with the objective of redefining Singapore's main competitive advantage and reinventing Singaporean industries that are globally competitive. This committee has guided Singapore's evolution from manufacturing, to finance, to biotechnology and health tourism.

Underlying the innovation ecosystem for Singapore is a key element; its Central Provident Fund. Each worker in Singapore pays some 16 percent of gross wages into this fund, matched by an equal contribution from the employer. Thus, a third of workers' wages are compulsory saving. (One can argue that the entire one-third is worker funded, because if wages are roughly equal to marginal product, then in the absence of the required one-third contribution of employers, workers would receive the proceeds in their wage packet, in a competitive labor market.) This gives the Singaporean Government enormously deep pockets – enormous resources that can be employed to create, for instance, new biotechnology capabilities that previously did not exist a decade ago. For example, "Singapore's Biomedical Sciences Sector (BMS) spanning pharmaceuticals, biotechnology and medical devices is a key pillar of the economy, and accounts for 21 percent of total manufacturing output and over 5 percent of GDP" (UK Trade and Investment, 2013) (see case study below).

The innovation ecosystem shows that Singapore has embraced its own, unique path to innovation, leveraging its competitive advantages. Efforts by Singapore to foster "garage-based Silicon Valley individual entrepreneurship" did not succeed. The ecosystem indicates that there is room in Singapore to encourage far more market-based demand-driven innovation processes – without, however, blindly copying or imitating individualistic innovation approaches that contradict the dominant Chinese culture that is Singapore's trademark. Singapore's development of its biotechnology industry can serve as a model for other nations to benchmark, in "start from scratch" innovative investment.

The innovation ecosystem poses an interesting dilemma. Participants in the Experts Workshop indicated in a consensus view that "lack of chaos" (meaning, lack of freedom to "intelligently break the rules") was inimical to Singaporean innovation. Yet it is that very lack of chaos, a rule-based system that is smoothly and efficiently run and built on aligned national strategies implemented with vision and large investments, that currently drives Singapore's unquestioned success. It is a difficult problem to find ways to introduce more "chaos" without harming the very thing that drives and underlies national innovation in Singapore.

CASE STUDIES

In this section, we provide several case studies of innovation that help illuminate the dominant and often highly constructive role played by Singapore's government, as revealed in the above national innovation ecosystem map.

Singapore's Biomed Sector

According to the UK Trade and Investment Authority:

> In 2011, there were 284 biomedical entities registered in Singapore, of which 95 were foreign owned. Over 100 BMS (Biomedical Sciences) companies are engaged in cutting-edge manufacturing, R&D and strategic headquarters activities. Seven leading biopharmaceutical companies and 25 medical technology companies have manufacturing facilities, supplying to global markets. Over 30

leading biomedical sciences companies have established Asia Pacific headquarters in Singapore. The biopharmaceutical sector contributed £11.4 billion to the total BMS output in 2011. Singapore was the third fastest growing exporter of pharmaceutical goods from 2000 to 2010 (Datamonitor). Singapore aims to be the regional center for clinical trials and drug development. Major CROs [contract research organizations, that run clinical trials on a contract basis] are established and expanding, and run multi-country trials from Singapore's strategic location in Asia. The total CRO market in Singapore rose to US $132.6 million in 2010 (Frost & Sullivan)[3]. Singapore also offers a strong regulatory framework to support the industry. The World Economic Forum recognizes Singapore as the "Top Country in Asia for IP protection". It is the first Asian country to accede to the Pharmaceutical Inspection Co-operation Scheme (PICS) for global acceptance of pharmaceutical products made in Singapore. It also follows international GMP (Genetically Modified Product) regulations and is the APEC (Asia Pacific Economic Cooperation Forum) Coordinating Centre for Good Clinical Practice (GCP).

According to the UK Trade and Investment Center:

> Biopolis, Singapore biomedical sciences city, co-locates public and private research centres. The £50 million Phase four will add another 46 000 sq. meters by 2013, bringing the total to 300 000 sq. meters. It will be the base for Proctor & Gamble's Innovation Centre. Biopolis Phase five is under construction and will add 46 182 sq. meters of biomedical research facility.
> A dedicated pharma park, now in phase two, has attracted over £three billion in investment by pharmaceutical manufacturers. To further establish Singapore as a choice investment location for medtech companies, the 7.4-ha MedTech Hub was launched in May 2012.

With remarkable speed, and huge investments, Singapore's government has established a strong competitive advantage in the realm of biotechnology. It is a good example of how Singapore has attracted world class innovation (for example Procter & Gamble's Innovation Center) in lieu of developing its own home-grown variety, by leveraging the government's large pool of funding.

Starhub

Starhub Ltd is a Singaporean telecom company providing mobile, fixed and internet services. It is the second largest mobile operator in Singapore, with an annual revenue of over two billion Singapore dollars (about US $1.6 billion). Starhub is a young company, launched in May 1998 when the Singaporean Government first announced that the telecom sector would be liberalized and opened to competition in 2000. Part of the liberalization was removing the restriction on foreign ownership. Nippon Telegraph and Telephone (NTT), a huge Japanese telecom company, became a major shareholder. Starhub is a good example of how freeing a sector to competition can generate strong innovation. Starhub has introduced a strong series of innovative products and services, in recent years, including a secure wireless email platform for Blackberry (2010), fast mobile broadband (2010), HDTV (2010), surf-for-free Internet (2005), 100 Mbit speed (2010).

At the annual awards event of Singapore Advertising, Starhub won the "brand of the year" award as well as the "Product Innovation of The Year Award." Its winning entry, Birds & The Bees 2.0 for StarHub SafeSurf (Internet content filtering service), is "a user-configurable Internet block-page". It is described as an "innovative content control service creates opportunities for parents to play an active role in informing their children about sex and the appropriate use of the Internet". It is significant that Starhub's innovation is aligned with Singaporean culture, which seeks to limit access of impressionable children to pornographic websites available on the Internet.

Singapore Airlines

Singapore Airlines was founded in 1972, only seven years after the nation itself achieved independence. It began as a purely regional airline, serving destinations in Asia. But Singapore's founding Prime Minister Lee Kuan Yew had a vision, that Singapore Airlines would (like everything else in Singapore) lead the world, a vision that seemed megalomaniacal at the time, given Singapore's tiny population, tiny land area and meager resources. Singapore Airlines ranked third in the world among all airlines, in 2012, trailing behind only Qatar Airways and Asiana Airlines.

Singapore Airlines innovated in several key areas; it was first to offer free drinks and a choice of meals in Economy Class, and ranks first in the world in this aspect of air travel. It was the first to fly the Airbus 380, in 2007, and the first to operate the world's longest non-stop commercial flight (Singapore to Los Angeles) in 2004. It also introduced in-flight telephony by satellite, in 1991. Revenue for the fiscal year 2011/12 was $14.6 billion. Singapore Airlines' load factor, a key measure of operational efficiency, is consistently close to 80 percent.

SUMMARY

Every national innovation ecosystem is in at least some ways unique. Singapore's ecosystem is perhaps the most unique of all. Few nations, even China, have as extensive, well-funded, long-run government policy direction as does Singapore. In particular, Singapore's system of compulsory saving, through the Central Provident Fund, provides the government with massive resources equal to about a third of all the aggregate wages paid in Singapore. If the US had a similar compulsory saving system, then its "Central Provident Fund" would total about $3.3 trillion annually (one-third of total labor compensation of $10 trillion). This sum would exceed by a third of America's total annual gross domestic capital formation.

The combination of forward-looking long-range national policy planning, featured by regular Strategic Five-Year Plans, combined with the massive resources available to implement the results of that planning, give Singapore unique capabilities. But on the negative side, the highly regulated rule-based Singaporean system of governance may not be favorable for the kind of individual "garage entrepreneurship" common in, say, the US.[4] Like every nation, Singapore has been influenced by other nations' models of innovation and sought to implement some, with little success. Today Singapore seeks its own unique Singaporean approach to innovation; so far, the results have been better.

NOTES

*   With the assistance of J.D. Yap, VP, SME and Commercial Banking, Fullterton Financial Holding, Singapore.
1.   With typical thoroughness, Singapore has ensured it has an especially complete listing in Wikipedia, with 249 references! The data in this section come from http://en.wikipedia.org/wiki/Singapore, accessed on 19 February 2014.
2.   The Heritage Foundation, Economic Freedom Index, http://www.heritage.org/index/, accessed on 19 February 2014.
3.   "Contract Research Organizations (CROs) choose Singapore and China as gateways for future growth in Asia", www.innovationcorner.com, http://dduhamel.wordpress.com/2011/12/09/contract-research-organizations-cros-choose-singapore-and-china-as-gateways-for-future-growth-in-asia/.
4.   Apple was founded by Steve Jobs and Steve Wozniak in Jobs's parents' garage in California, in 1976. Since then, the mythology of the garage-based start-up has spread globally.

11. Conclusion: A comparison of national and regional innovation ecosystems

> Each person is like all other persons, some other persons, and no other person.
> Clyde Kluckhohn

INTRODUCTION

In this concluding chapter, we present a comparative analysis of the results obtained from our eight case studies – innovation ecosystem maps for Israel, Poland, Germany, France, Spain, Greater Toronto, Shanghai and Singapore, described in detail in the previous chapters. Employing the methodology we have developed (see Chapter 2) has generated the visual foundations that enable us to concretely portray of those nations' innovation ecosystems, always keeping in mind the main goal – to achieve consensual understanding of the innovation system, as a basis for building effective pro-innovation policies. We note as well that a major focus of this methodology is to distinguish between supply-side and demand-side innovation drivers.

The results obtained from the Experts Workshops conducted in each of the eight countries in our study provided data that was analyzed based on cross-impact analysis, as described in Chapter Two. The matrices that were produced from the analysis were used to construct the eight innovation ecosystem maps presented in the previous chapters. These maps show visually: (a) innovation anchors, essentially "stocks" of capabilities that drive innovation, and (b) innovation "processes", or flows (changes related to various anchors, or stocks), and the detailed and intricate manner in which they interact.

Based on these maps and related factor analyses and interaction analyses, we have constructed a comparison among these case studies, based on three layers of examination. The first layer refers to the list of key anchors identified in each of the participant countries based on four key innovation dimensions that have emerged:

- culture (shared values);
- context (scientific and technological infrastructure, structure of the economy);
- markets (demand, preferences);
- institutions (system of laws and regulations, written and unwritten "rules of the game").

COMPARATIVE ANALYSIS

In Chapter 2, we included a brief quote by the anthropologist Clyde Kluckhohn: "Each person is like all other persons, some other persons, and no other person." This concisely sums up our comparative results, which are shown in Table 11.1. The eight nations we examined are in some ways all alike in their innovation systems, and each is unique in some ways.

We now proceed to describe similarities and differences among the eight innovation ecosystems.

A. "Like All . . ."

Each of the eight innovation ecosystems had "anchors" in each of the four key dimensions listed above. The exceptions are Poland and Singapore that lacked a market-based anchor and Spain that lacked a market-based anchor and institutional anchors as well.

All eight have significant anchors that fall under "context", reflecting scientific and technological infrastructure, human capital, governance direction, transparency and accountability and technological structure that support innovation. Similarly most of them (with the exception of Spain) have anchors that belong to the "institutions" dimension, reflecting availability of capital to foster entrepreneurship and research and development (R&D), economic institutions, trade agreements etc. On the other hand, it is significant to note that the "markets" dimension was among the weakest of the four dimensions, overall. Three of the national innovation ecosystems totally lacked key anchors that belong to the market dimension and the others display only few anchors.

One of our most unexpected results was related to "culture". Though the Experts Workshops were largely comprised of those with management and technology or science backgrounds, the cultural aspect of innovation features prominently in all eight of the innovation ecosystems. In the end, it appears, it is the individual energy of entrepreneurs and innovators that drives the innovative ecosystem, which in turn flows from the culture and history of their nation.

Table 11.1 Comparison of innovation "key anchors" among eight case studies

Key Innovation Dimensions	Israel	Poland	Germany	France	Greater Toronto, Canada	Spain	Singapore	Shanghai, China (ZJ Park)
Culture (shared values)	"Out of the Box" thinking Entrepreneurship Culture Culture of empowerment Cultural diversity	Entrepreneurship Culture of empowerment	Pro-innovation culture	Education, mobilization	Culture and entrepreneurship Global	Pro-innovation culture	Rule-based society Flexibility	Attitude and values
Context (infrastructure, economy)	Scientific and educational infrastructure	Human capital structure	Technology capabilities Government Institutional infrastructure External effects	Corporate policy	Science and technology infrastructure Governmental infrastructure	Technological and entrepreneurial infrastructure Human capital Leadership	Government direction	Human capital

Markets (demand, preferences)	Competitive structure	—	Market structure	Demand-side Policies	Finance	—	Market process / Finance
Institutions (regulation, laws)	Economic institutions	Financial, regional systems	Availability of human capital	Public policy, intervention and regulation	Human capital	Small open nation	Government policy
		Economic institutions				Centers of excellence	

In Table 11.2 a comparison of innovation key processes is presented with respect to their supply or demand side. Each of the eight innovation ecosystems had key processes representing the demand or the supply side of innovation. Half of the key processes purely fall under the supply side, while only eight key processes depict purely the demand side; none of them belong to Greater Toronto, Spain and Singapore. In regard to the mixed aspect of innovation, the data reveal that of the 20 innovation processes linked with demand, 12 fully combine aspects of both supply and demand (such as "joint public-private initiatives", "public-private cooperation", "culture and entrepreneurial" and "labeling and awareness").

We believe that the "Valley of Death" identified by Jackson, where basic research crosses the "desert" of resource scarcity toward commercial exploitation, exists in all eight countries under study, because it is market forces that "pull" innovative ideas through this barren territory towards full implementation and global scale-up. The eight innovation ecosystems indicate that this "demand-pull" force can fruitfully be strengthened in each of the eight case studies under study, in particular in Spain, Singapore and Greater Toronto.

B.   "Like Some . . ."

There are aspects of the innovation ecosystems that exist in some, though not all, of the eight countries. All eight systems are complex, as one might anticipate, though the French, Polish, Spanish and Singapore ecosystems appear rather simpler than those of Israel, Germany, Greater Toronto and Shanghai (see the eight individual country innovation ecosystem maps in the previous chapters).

Poland's ecosystem is simple probably because it is in its early stages. Poland's system features growing "awareness" of the vital importance of innovation. It seems that for Poland, the Experts Workshop identified a clear need to create a culture of innovation, which we believe is quite typical of a transition economy shifting from state planning to a market-driven economy based on private initiative. Spain features "local and regional initiatives". Israel's culture of "empowerment" and "out-of-the-box" thinking is vital, while Germany features "cluster strategies". France's system stresses the key role played by government procurement policies. Shanghai's science park and related innovation incubation system reflect China's abundant capital (China leads the world in gross capital formation as a proportion of gross domestic product (GDP)[1]) and strong focus on exports. Canada, specifically Greater Toronto, in the health innovation ecosystem, stresses abundant government support programs and a business environment in which it is easy to start and run businesses.

Table 11.2 Comparison of innovation "key processes" among eight case studies

Supply/ Demand Side of Innovation	Israel	Poland	Germany	France	Greater Toronto, Canada	Spain	Singapore	Shanghai, China (ZJ Park)
Demand-driven innovation	Demand in the private sector	Private sector attractiveness	Market-driven forces Cluster strategies	Lead markets and consumer policies	—	—	—	Start-up culture Open market forces Trust in human and intellectual capital
Supply side of innovation	National Research Funds Government investments in human capital Government programs	Increase awareness of innovation Government policies to foster innovation implementation Government programs	Key skills development Tax, subsidy policies	Standards and regulations Public procurement	Government direct funding Mentoring	Local and regional incentives Targeted public programs Public funding of private entities	Government funding Government directives Specific policies	Direct government assistance Tax incentives

Table 11.2 (continued)

Supply/Demand Side of Innovation	Israel	Poland	Germany	France	Greater Toronto, Canada	Spain	Singapore	Shanghai, China (ZJ Park)
Both supply and demand side of innovation	Private and public-sector activities Public-private cooperation	Encourage technological independence	Standard-ization	Labeling and awareness raising industries	Specific tailored programs Human capital Clinical training Awards visibility	Joint public-private initiatives Human capital develop-ment	Culture and entrepre-neurial environment	Attitudes and policies that help and hinder

Singapore focuses on its disciplined rule-based system, the strong guidance of government and like China, its abundant capital resources.

The third "layer" of our comparative analysis of the eight innovation ecosystems is related to the existence and strength of linkages between anchors and processes (see the ecosystem maps in the previous chapters). A comparative analysis of the linkages is shown in Table 11.3. The table was constructed to identify and isolate the most important linkages for each of the eight case studies. For each of the four key dimensions common to all the ecosystems, we listed (for each case study) the main processes that were most strongly linked to anchors comprising the four dimensions, as listed in Table 11.1. In this manner, it can be seen which dimensions of the inno-vation ecosystems contribute most to fostering innovation-supporting processes, which processes are "innovation accelerators", and what are the major differences across countries. Note that groups of processes may appear in more than one dimension. For example, for Israel, public-private sector cooperation links closely with both the culture dimension and with the infrastructure dimension.

The meaning of the empty cells in Table 11.3 is that no groups of pro-cesses were identified that were strongly linked with the anchors included in a particular dimension, but only weakly or bi-directionally linked. It is clear that the dominant dimensions of the innovation ecosystems are, on the one hand, the culture dimension, and on the other, the infrastructure dimension, which together form the foundation anchors for developing the processes that drive the innovation systems. The influence of the other two dimensions – the market dimension and the institutional dimension – is much smaller. The relative weakness of the market dimension is especially striking, which contributes significantly to creating innovation-supporting processes only in Germany, France and in Shanghai, among the eight nations. One of the main findings emerging from our analysis is the need to greatly strengthen market-driven demand-originating innova-tion in the countries under study. The linkages between the institutional anchors and innovation-supporting processes are weak in Israel, in France and in Spain. There is awareness of this issue in the EU, as the Innovation Union Report cited in Chapter 1 shows.

Comparative analysis between the eight nations, based on the tables, indicates there is a strong contribution by the culture dimension to innova-tion processes in Greater Toronto, Spain and in Israel. This is expressed in the manner culture drives processes for collaboration between public and private sectors, and for launching new government programs to encourage innovation, R&D and human capital. Culture is less important in France and in Germany; Poland in particular appears to need to create and strengthen an innovation culture, as it is a transition economy. This is true

Table 11.3 Comparison of innovation

Key Innovation Dimensions	Israel	Poland	Germany	France	Greater Toronto, Canada	Spain	Singapore	Shanghai, China (ZJ Park)
Culture (shared values)	Creating demand in the private sector Public-private cooperation Government Investments in Human Capital Government programs for supporting innovation Government programs for supporting innovation	Private sector attractiveness Private sector attractiveness	Market-driven forces Key skills development Standardization	Lead markets and consumer policies Labeling and awareness raising industries	Specific tailored programs Human capital Clinical training Awards visibility Government direct funding Human capital clinical training	Joint public-private initiatives Targeted public programs Human capital development Public funding of private entities	Specific policies Government funding Culture and entrepreneurial environment	— Attitudes and policies that help and hinder

	Private sector attractiveness	Key skills development	Awards visibility	Specific policies	Direct government assistance / Tax incentives
Markets (demand, preferences)	—	Cluster strategies	Lead markets and consumer policies / Labeling and awareness raising industries	—	Tax incentives
Institutions (system of laws and regulation)	Key skills development	Specific tailored programs	—	Specific policies / Government funding	Tax incentives

even more with respect to Shanghai in China as a nation that led great economic transition in the past decade. In all eight countries studied except France, the infrastructure dimension supports processes that contribute to innovation driven by the public sector and the private sector alike. France notably appears to lack processes driven by this dimension.

C.   "... and Like None ..."

Each innovation ecosystem has unique features found only in that country. Through the process of best-practice benchmarking, it is useful for nations to explore these special innovation drivers, and to find ways to adapt them to their own innovation systems. Here are a few of the more significant features in each of the eight countries we analyzed:

Israel

In Israel the important role of cultural characteristics and assets in driving and nurturing Israeli innovation is clear. Evidence shows that strong ties exist between cultural anchors and supply- and demand-driven processes. Pure supply-side processes such as government support for the defense industries and the establishment of military R&D programs (such as Talpiot) were found to exert significant spillover effects on innovation infrastructure (for example entrepreneurial and applied technological skills). The existence of a strong scientific and technological base (such as research universities) and solid entrepreneurial infrastructure (for example emphasis on the teaching and development of entrepreneurial and applied technological skills at a young age) seems to be one of the key drivers of the Israeli innovation ecosystem.

The strongest catalysts of the Israeli innovation ecosystem are the joint demand and supply processes, focusing on government and public policy measures, private sector activities and dual private-public initiatives. A variety of institutions exist that leverage defense-related R&D into civilian innovation, especially indirect ones, for example, young engineers who develop technology-intensive projects within the military use their knowledge and experience later to launch startup companies. Another notable example is the Office of the Chief Scientist (OCS) within the Ministry of Economy, which plays a key role in R&D by leveraging a large budget to support technology-intensive projects. The OCS also supports: (a) MAGNET, in which commercial firms and at least one research institution collaborate on developing generic technologies; (b) MAGNETON, which funds two-thirds of the R&D cost of an existing partnership between a company and an academic institution; and (c) Nofar, which funds 90 percent of later-stage applied academic research, in bio- and nano-technologies, to bring the research to sufficient maturity to interest a business partner in investing in it. An extensive Public Incubator Program at its peak had some 30 government-sponsored incubators spread throughout Israel, each with 10–15 projects, offering basic funding for two years for each (see Maital et al., 2008).

Poland

The Polish innovation ecosystem seems to be in its initial stages of development. This is understandable. As a transition nation, Poland's economy is still a "work in progress," shifting from a planning model to a free market one. As a result, there is low connectivity and loose ties between the various factor and cluster groups. The demand-side interactions in the system are much more significant than the supply-side interactions. This conclusion, however, must be qualified by the fact that the demand-side aspect is based on only two true demand-side processes.

We believe that the embryonic nature of Poland's innovation ecosystem is a distinct advantage. Poland begins the work of painting its own innovation portrait on a clean canvas. It can benchmark other nations, learn from their experience, and build its own system unencumbered with baggage collected in the past. It can embrace and adapt all the innovation policies that have proved successful in other nations, and reject those that have failed. In this sense, Poland's innovation ecosystem shows great promise for the future.

Germany

The German innovation ecosystem is highly interconnected, with many strong links between processes and anchors. It is significant that three of the five key processes that drive German innovation are demand-driven. This suggests that for nations interested in strengthening demand-driven innovation, Germany is a country that could and should be benchmarked with useful results.

Technological capabilities and the existence of economies of scale (in the market structure cluster) seem to have a profound impact on processes that foster innovation in Germany. Cultural ("pro-innovation culture") and public policy anchors (in the availability of capital and government culture clusters) also play a vital role in driving these processes. Labor unions provide a good example. Outside Germany, it is widely thought that the strong labor unions hinder innovation and growth. In fact, they are likely to contribute, as we see to Germany's innovate *kurzarbeit* policy that kept experienced SME workers in the *mittelstand*. In several places in the map, the term "SME" (small and medium-sized enterprises) is seen – this reflects the German *mittelstand* SMEs, a rather unique and important feature of German innovation. But on the other side, Germany has important industrial "clusters", specifically the automotive cluster surrounding the city of Stuttgart, with major installations of Bosch, Mercedes and Porsche. Such clusters comprise agglomerations of complementary capabilities and are actively supported by tax and subsidy policies. Germany's vocational training schools provide valuable skills that support its *mittelstand* SMEs that produce precision machinery. Germany also has a unique chain of R&D labs, the Fraunhofer Institutes, that provide fast and efficient technology transfer.

France

What is remarkable about this map is not just what it reveals, but what it fails to reveal. Indeed, this is a major use of innovation ecosystem mappings – to compare them with those of other nations, in order to reveal key weaknesses and lacunae. Many countries, such as Israel, have innovation systems built crucially around the role of leading world-class science and technology universities, with a network of linkages to and from those institutions. France has such top science and technology universities, Ecole des Ponts et Chausees, Ecole des Mines, some of which date back to 1747.

French engineers and scientists are known worldwide for their excellence and creativity, particularly in civil engineering but increasingly in electronics and in biology. Yet these universities do not play a prominent role in the French innovation ecosystem. We speculate that this is perhaps an extreme case of the "Valley of Death" noted in Chapter 1 – the enormous gap between the production of basic research in science and technology, and the successful rapid and profitable commercial exploitation of such research.

The dominant role of public policy and government budgets in France's innovation ecosystem is striking. We are led to wonder whether France can define a new type of pro-innovation policy, in which government procurement policies specifically, clearly and persistently award contracts to smaller innovative businesses and startups, in light of the very high weight awarded by the French experts to "public procurement". Such policies have been implemented elsewhere, by governments, to help develop peripheral underdeveloped regions. Why not employ them to strengthen underdeveloped entrepreneurship?

Spain

The Spanish innovation ecosystem is highly interconnected, and is mainly characterized by moderate positive links between processes and anchors. It is significant that four of the five key processes that drive Spanish innovation are supply-driven. The country has a number of local and regional incentives for innovation worthy of further study, especially those surrounding Valencia and Andalusia. Spain also has a number of "acronym" programs that are of interest, including PROFIT (university-industry research), and two other public-private initiatives (CENIT, CDTI). This finding accentuates the importance of strengthening targeted demand-driven policies in Spain. What we also learned about Spain, significantly, was the highly regional and local nature of Spanish innovation. Catalonia, for instance, is recognized as an autonomous region and as a "nationality". Its capital is Barcelona and its population totals some 7.5 million. It is the center of the Catalonia Innovation Triangle. The Basque Country, another unique Spanish region, also has its own language and culture, and has like Catalonia a strong, but different, entrepreneurial drive. As a result, we observe that not only does Spain itself have a unique innovation ecosystem, but also several unique Spanish regions.

Greater Toronto

This innovation ecosystem differs from the seven others, in that it is solely focused on healthcare and related innovation. But it does reflect Canada's unique approach, which is to identify issues that deserve and require government support, and then to create a virtual blizzard of such programs, which somehow seem to coordinate and cooperate, even though at first glance they seem scattered and unorganized. The combination of these innovation support programs, entrepreneurial energy and culture, proximity to the USA (as a potential market), strong infrastructure and excellent healthcare centers and human capital and training, combine to create an effective system – though it is doubtful if it is one that can be widely imitated.

Shanghai, China (ZJ Park)

In many ways, building an innovation ecosystem map for ZJ Park was the most interesting of our eight workshops. Its focus was not solely on what now exists in Shanghai, and in China, but on what will be in the future – in China's future innovation ecosystem, as its policymakers envision it. In some ways, Shanghai, ZJ Park and the entrepreneurial incubator we visited, are spearheads of that new system. We observed, indirectly, in the workshop, China's massive efforts at creating human capital; China leads the world in the OECD Programme for International Student Assessment (PISA) scores for reading, maths and science. We also indirectly observed China's R&D focus, in which the vast majority of R&D is both financed and performed by business and the private sector, rather than by government-sponsored institutions as in the EU (China ranks sixth in the world as regards the proportion of R&D financed by business, and seventh, in the proportion of R&D performed by business). We also understood the principle of the "long tail". In a nation as huge as China, with a normal distribution of talent, creativity and independent thinking, even if the mass of the population reflects a hierarchical culture that is subservient to authority, there will always be the "long tail"; the small percentage who rebel, who create, who innovate, and who think differently. They naturally gravitate to places like ZJ Park, where they find advice, financing and management expertise. And this small percentage, when multiplied by a large population (1.4 billion), comprises a very large number. This is China's version of the Law of Large Numbers, when applied to innovation.

Singapore
When Singapore was founded by Lee Kwan Yew, in 1965, the ethnic composition of the nation did not bode well for its wellbeing or survival, with ethnic Chinese, Malays and Indians competing for scarce resources and jobs. President Lee understood that for Singapore to endure and prevail, it would need a highly-disciplined, rule-based culture that would counteract strong centrifugal forces. This unique system has proved a boon, though widely criticized for being undemocratic (there is, for instance, a single dominant political party). In some ways this discipline fosters innovation, because every five years, a Singaporean Government Task Force re-examines Singapore's competitive advantage and seeks to reinvent and redesign it. This has led to large and rapid changes in Singapore's competitive focus, and to some innovation, as this remarkable, wealthy city state, shifts from manufacturing to finance to communication and biotechnology. This type of innovation is the polar opposite to the garage entrepreneurship of the USA, but in its own way it is effective, and is suited to Singapore's history and culture. Again, it is doubtful that other nations can imitate it, though perhaps they might adopt some aspects, like the five-year task force to re-examine the nation's competitive strengths. Singapore's challenge is to maintain its rule-based discipline, while at the same time providing more freedom for individual creativity – not an easy task, but one Singapore is tackling.

Best practice benchmarking
One of the most effective management tools is known as best-practice benchmarking – exploring far afield to discover, what is the very best global practice, for a particular process, procedure or management function? Benchmarking is best done beyond one's own industry, where most managers are highly familiar with conventional ways of doing business. We believe there is great and mostly untapped potential for best-practice

benchmarking in innovation and pro-innovation policies – a process in which countries adapt and import ideas that have been successful in other countries in strengthening innovation, while carefully tailoring them to their own values, culture, personality and history. Every nation seeking to be more innovative can learn from every other nation, including the eight nations and regions we described above. This learning should be tempered and conditioned on a deep understanding of the nation's own innovation ecosystem, and the culture that underlies it. As management consultant Jim Collins has observed, every business has a yin-yang foundation – the "yin" of values that can never be changed, and the "yang" of ideas, products and processes that must be changed continually. There is continual ongoing tension between these two forces. And they exist in countries, too. Managing the difficult conflicting "yin" and "yang" and differentiating between the two is the challenge of shaping effective innovation policies.

SUMMARY AND CONCLUSIONS

If a country is a business, then like a business, every country requires strategic direction and vision, that provide a clear answer to the question, what does our country do better than other countries – in which products and industries can we excel, so that we can produce and export, in order to generate jobs, income, wealth, exports and dynamic sustained growth, even in the face of weak global markets? And how can this competitive advantage be sustained and maintained, in the face of fierce global competition in world markets? How can our country develop new skills and new technologies, to remain competitive? In an age when macro-economic policy is often dominated by the ongoing global financial and economic crisis, and is inherently short run, the long-run dimension of national competitive strategy and national innovation policy is essential, if only to provide citizens with a vision of the future other than austerity.

Such strategic planning is normally regarded as "top down", driven by the country's political and business leadership. But our analysis of national innovation ecosystems has revealed, we believe, the crucial importance of combining "top-down" strategic innovation policies with "bottom-up" policies driven by the infrastructure of existing capabilities. These capabilities find expression in the innovation "anchors", in our analysis, which differ widely across countries in their impact on the evolution of innovation ecosystems and their ability to implement national strategic goals. These anchors, and the dimensions to which they belong, comprise the foundation on which nations can build their strategic innovation policies, by strengthening innovation-fostering processes that are closely linked to national objectives. Each nation, therefore, must design its own unique, specific national innovation policy, according to the strengths and weaknesses identified in its innovation ecosystem – its innovation accelerators, that help the country achieve its goals for improving the wellbeing of its citizens.

It is the combination of effective top-down innovation policies, integrated closely with bottom-up market-driven initiatives and energy that create effective innovation ecosystems. It is an over-simplification to assign top-down policies to "supply-side", and bottom-up initiatives to "demand-side", yet, it is probably true in general that market forces are more of a "bottom-up" nature.

The importance of constructing visual innovation ecosystems goes well beyond their specific content. Effective consensual innovation policies rest crucially on an economy-wide understanding of the innovation system and its drivers. We envisage a two-stage process, in which experts from all parts of society meet to engage and interact on understanding and mapping the ecosystem, and only after reaching consensual agreement on how the system works (and why perhaps it does not), debating how policy interventions can be most effective. By achieving a deep understanding of national innovation ecosystems, and by studying those of other nations, we hope that innovation policies will be more innovative, more effective in their national impact and more integrative in their worldwide design. A widely-employed slogan in global corporate strategy is "think global, act local". We believe this slogan is applicable to national strategic innovation policy as well.

NOTE

1. See the Global Innovation Index (2012), p. 204.

Epilogue: Systems mindset as foundations for policy

We close our book with a few observations and insights gleaned from our research, and some suggestions for future directions in innovation research.

The insight that motivated our research on national innovation ecosystems was primarily the fact that in countries in which we live and which we studied, pro-innovation policies are afflicted by two ailments. One is political fragmentation, in which government ministries and departments frame their own policies, almost independent of other ministries, vigorously protecting their "turf" and seeking political capital, even when ministers are all from a single-ruling political party. The second is the lack of a systems mindset, where analysis of the impact of pro-innovation policies is based on implicit or explicit partial equilibrium analysis, that fails to take into account feedback, interactions and secondary effects. These two "ailments" are of course related. If government ministries and departments shared a common systems mindset, along with a common consensual view of the innovation ecosystem, perhaps innovation policies could be made more effective.

The widespread awareness of the key role innovation plays in promoting economic growth and development has led to a massive effort to quantify innovation indicators at the national and regional level. Two such examples are the Global Innovation Index 2012, often cited in the preceding chapters, and the European Commission's Innovation Union Scoreboard 2013. There are numerous other databases that supply supplemental country data on infrastructure, economy, education, society and other indicators related to innovation, such as the World Development Indicators of the World Bank, the International Monetary Fund (IMF) economic indicators, the *World Competitiveness Yearbook* compiled and published by the International Institute for Management Development (IMD), and the World Economic Forum (Davos) database on global competitiveness, including innovativeness.

All these rich data sources provide deep and important insights into the level of innovation, by country, its components, and its change (rise or fall) over time. But they all are characterized by a common difficulty – they

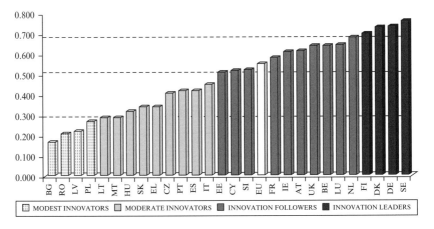

Note: Codes: SE = Sweden, DE = Germany, DK = Denmark, Fl = Finland, NL = Netherlands, LU = Luxembourg, BE = Belgium, UK = United Kingdom, AT = Austria, IE = Ireland, FR = France, EU = European Union (average), Sl = Slovenia, CY Cyprus, EE = Estonia, IT = Italy, ES = Spain, PT = Portugal, CZ = Czech Republic, EL =Greece, SK = Slovakia, HU = Hungary, MT = Malta, LT = Lithuania, PL =Poland, LV = Latvia, RO = Romania, BG = Bulgaria.

Source: European Commission, Innovation Union Scoreboard 2013.

Figure E.1   Innovation rankings for 27 EU nations

reflect in general a basket of individual variables, without an understanding of how those variables interact and combine to generate innovative products, exports, jobs and global competitiveness.

Figure E.1 shows the rankings for 27 European Union (EU) nations in innovation, based on 25 detailed innovation indicators, for the period 2010 and 2011 (European Commission 2013). Among the four EU nations we mapped, only Germany is in the top four "innovation leaders". France is in the next group of ten "innovation followers"; Spain and Italy are in the group of nine "moderate innovators" and Poland is in the last group of four "modest innovators".

The detailed data underlying Figure E.1 are doubtless highly useful. The 25 indicators used to create the rankings are logically divided into three groups: "enablers", "firm activities" and "(innovation) outputs". The methodology is not radically different from that of the Global Innovation Index 2012.

Many of the anchors and processes found in our eight innovation ecosystem maps are also found in the innovation databases described above. Our modest contribution, we believe, is the attempt to understand the complex system that links all these indicators and variables, parts of an intricate complicated machine that when it runs smoothly, generates new products, services and processes that world markets find attractive and that create economic wellbeing. How is it that Poland, which ranks only 24th (out of 27) in innovation is able to create an impressive innovation ecosystem that generates leading medical innovations? And why is it that France's 11th ranking finds little reflection in entrepreneurial activity or startup creation? The answers, we believe, can be found only in these nations' innovation ecosystems – in the interactions among the many variables that enable, drive and enhance innovation.

We believe that the state of research into innovation and innovation policy resembles that of early research in thermodynamics. Thermodynamics, the study of the relationship between energy and power, began as an attempt to improve the efficiency of steam engines. The four laws of thermodynamics, while theoretical, have driven major innovations; the steam engine invented by James Watt changed the world by initiating the first Industrial Revolution. The search for a better steam engine drove research into thermodynamics, and thermodynamic theory itself drove better machines.

What are the key laws of innovation? Are there such laws? What are the principles that drive innovation systems? At present no such "laws" exist. The very concept of Laws of Innovation violates one of our favorite definitions of innovation – intelligently breaking the "rules"; the very notion of laws that show how to break "laws" is paradoxical, or even internally contradictory.

To make matters worse, innovation systems are a subset of all complex systems. And according to a leading expert on the theory of complexity, Geoffrey West (2013, p. 7):

> What makes a "complex" system so vexing is that its collective characteristics cannot easily be predicted from underlying components: the whole is greater than, and often significantly different from, the sum of its parts.

This is why the rich data sets on innovation indicators help raise interesting questions, we believe, but stop short of providing effective answers. The "whole" of the innovation system in a nation or region is, as West notes, significantly different from the sum of its parts. He continues:

> A city is much more than its buildings and people. Our bodies are more than the totality of our cells. This quality, called emergent behavior, is characteristic of economies, financial markets, urban communities, companies, organisms, the Internet, galaxies and the health care system.

And, he might have added, emergent behavior is also characteristic of national innovation ecosystems.

For years, scientific research became fragmented, with increasing specialization. Lately, major breakthroughs (for example, in nanotechnology) occur when pioneering scientists are able to combine chemistry, physics, engineering, and other disciplines, creating a synthesis of scientific disciplines. Perhaps this will be true of innovation research as well. Fragmented research on innovation, focused on such aspects as culture, finance, technology, policy, regulation and creativity, may now be merging into a grand synthesis, in which all these elements combine and interact.

"Complexity theory," notes West, "is groping toward a more unified holistic framework for tackling society's big questions." Perhaps innovation theory and the theory of pro-innovation policy are as well. There can be no question that the question, how can innovation be fostered, magnified, expanded, and enhanced, is indeed one of society's big questions. In a resource-scarce future, creating more value with fewer resources will be essential. Our understanding of innovation systems will crucially determine our ability to shape a better future for humanity.

References

Acemoglu, D., Gancia, G. and Zilibotti, F. (2012), "Competing engines of growth: innovation and standardization", *Journal of Economic Theory*, **147**(2): 570–601.

Acworth, E.B. (2008), "University-industry engagement: the formation of the knowledge integration community (KIC) model at the Cambridge-MIT Institute", *Research Policy*, **37**(8): 1241–54.

Afuah, A. (2000), "How much do your co-opetitors' capabilities matter in the face of a technological change?", *Strategic Management Journal*, **21**(3): 397–404.

Aghion, P., Bloom, N., Blundell, R., Griffith, R. and Howitt, P. (2005), "Competition and innovation: an inverted u relationship", *The Quarterly Journal Economics*, **120**(2): 701–28.

Alderman, L. (2012), "Challenging France to do business differently", *New York Times*, 19 December 2012, www.nytimes.com/2012/12/20/business/global/challenging-france-to-do-business-differently.html?pagewanted=all&_r=0, accessed 9 May 2013.

Alesina, A. and La Ferrara, E. (2005), "Ethnic diversity and economic performance", *Journal of Economic Literature*, **43**: 762–800.

Ambos, B. and Schlegelmilch, B.B. (2008), "Innovation in multinational firms: does cultural fit enhance performance?" *Management International* Review, **48**(2): 189–206.

Ardagna, S. and Lusardi, A. (2008), "Explaining international differences in entrepreneurship: the role of individual characteristics and regulatory constraints", *NBER Working Paper Series*, Vol. w14012.

Ashford, N.A., Ayers, C. and Stone, R.F. (1985), "Using regulation to change the market for innovation", *Harvard Environmental Law Review*, **9**(2): 419–66.

Azoulay, P. and Jones, B. (2006), "Innovation and Early Stage Ideas", presentation to Generating Ideas: Academic and Applied Research Conference, Tinbergen Institute, 20 December 2006, http://pazoulay.scripts.mit.edu/docs/generating_ideas.pdf, accessed 5 May 2013.

Baland, J.M. and Francois, P. (1996), "Innovation, monopolies and the poverty trap", *Journal of Development Economics*, **49**(1): 151–78.

Bercovitz, J. and Feldman, M. (2006), "Entrepreneurial universities and technology transfer: a conceptual framework for understanding knowledge-based economic development", *Journal of Technology Transfer*, **31**: 175–88.

Berliant, M. and Fujita, M. (2008), "Knowledge creation as a square dance on the Hilbert cube", *International Economic Review*, **49**: 1251–95.

Blind, K. (2004), "New products and services: analysis of regulations shaping new markets", Fraunhofer Institute for Systems Research, European Commission, www.innovation.lv/ino2/publications/studies_new_products_and_services_analysis_regulations_final.pdf, accessed 16 July 2012.

Booz & Co. (2012), "Innovation: China's next advantage. 2012 China innovation survey", June 2012.

Bottazzi. L. and Peri, G. (1999), "Innovation, demand and knowledge spillovers: theory and evidence from European regions", Working Paper, Universita' Bocconi, IGIER and CEPR.

Breznitz, D. and Murphree, M. (2011), *Run of the Red Queen: Government, Innovation, Globalization, and Economic Growth in China*, New Haven, CT: Yale University Press.

Cahill, B. and Maital, S. (2012), *Britain's Productivity Challenge: Toward an Operations Innovation Revolution*, London: Trinity Horne.

CAHO (2013), www.caho-hospitals.com/about-us/vision-values/, accessed 15 February 2013.

CECR (2013), www.nce-rce.gc.ca/NetworksCentres-CentresReseaux/CECR-CECR_eng.asp, accessed 15 February 2013.

Charles, E. (ed.) (1997), *Systems of Innovation: Technologies, Institutions, and Organizations*, London: Pinter.

Chen, F.F. (2008), "What happens if we compare chopsticks with forks? The impact of making inappropriate comparisons in cross-cultural research", *Journal of Personality and Social Psychology*, **95**(5): 1005–18.

Ciccone, A. and Papaioannou, E. (2007), "Red tape and delayed entry", *Journal of the European Economic Association*, **5**(2–3): 444–58.

CIHR (2013), www.cihr-irsc.gc.ca/e/193.html, accessed 15 February 2013.

Dobbs, R., Lund, S. and Schreiner, A. (2011), "How the growth of emerging markets will strain global finance", *McKinsey Quarterly*, December 2011.

Dumas, A. (2008), "The alchemy of innovation: how to leverage research", *Actualite Chimique*, **320–21**: 122–7.

Dutta, S. (2012), *The Global Innovation Index 2012: Stronger Innovation Linkages for Global Growth*, Fontainebleu, France: INSEAD.

Edersheim, E.H. (2006), *The Definitive Drucker: Challenges for Tomorrow's Executives – Final Advice From the Father of Modern Management*, New York: McGraw-Hill.

Edler, J. (2007), "Demand-based innovation policy", Manchester Business School Working Paper, No. 529.

Edler, J. and Georghiou, L. (2007), "Public procurement and innovation–resurrecting the demand side", *Research Policy*, **36**: 949–63.

Edquist, C. (ed.) (1997), *Systems of Innovation: Technologies, Institutions and Organizations*, Hove: Psychology Press.

Erumban, A.A. and de Jong, S.B. (2006), "Cross-country differences in ICT adoption: a consequence of culture", *Journal of World Business*, **41**(4): 302–14.

Etzkowitz, E. and Leydesdorff, L. (2000), "The dynamics of innovation: from national systems and 'Mode 2' to a triple helix of university–industry–government relations", *Research Policy*, **29**: 109–23.

European Commission (2012a), "Regional innovation scoreboard 2012", Brussels, http://ec.europa.eu/enterprise/policies/innovation/index_en.htm, accessed 15 May 2013.

European Commission (2012b), "Regional innovation scoreboard 2012. Methodology report", Brussels, http://ec.europa.eu/enterprise/policies/innovation/index_en.htm, accessed 15 May 2013.

European Commission (2013), "Innovation Union Scoreboard 2013", http://ec.europa.eu/enterprise/policies/innovation/facts-figures-analysis/innovation-scoreboard/index_en.htm, accessed 25 May 2013.

European Commission, Directorate-General for Research and Innovation (2011), "Innovation union competitiveness report", Luxembourg: EU Publications Office.

European Commission, Gallup Organization (2009), "Innobarometer 2009 – Analytical report", http://ec.europa.eu/public_opinion/flash/fl_267_en.pdf, accessed 20 July 2012.

EXCITE (2013), www.marsdd.com/aboutmars/partners/excite/, accessed 15 February 2013.

Feller, I., Ailes, C.P. and Roessner, J.D. (2002), "Impacts of research universities on technological innovation in industry: evidence from engineering research centers", *Research Policy*, **31**(3): 457–74.

Forrester, J.W. (1969), *Urban Dynamics*, New York: Pegasus Communications, Inc.

Forrester, J.W. (1958), "Industrial dynamics: a major breakthrough for decision makers", *Harvard Business Review*, **36**(4): 37–66.

Freeman, C. (1974), *The Economics of Industrial Innovation*, Cambridge, MA: MIT Press.

Freeman, C. (1987), *Technology and Economic Performance: Lessons from Japan*, London: Pinter.

Frenkel, A., Maital S., Leck, E. and Israel, E. (forthcoming, 2014), "Demand-driven innovation: an integrative systems-based review of the literature", *International Journal of Innovation and Technology Management*.

Frenkel, A. and Shefer, D. (2012). "University-industry technology transfer: fostering and hindering factors and programs", in A. Frenkel, P. Nijkamp and P. McCann (eds), *Societies in Motion: Innovation, Migration and Regional Transformation*, Cheltenham, UK and Northampton, MA, USA: Edward Elgar Publishing, pp. 139–65.

Frenkel, A., Shefer, D. and Miller, M. (2008), "Public vs. private technological incubator programs: privatizing the technological incubators in Israel", *European Planning Studies*, **16**(2): 189–210.

Fujita, M. and Weber, S. (2004), "Strategic immigration policies and welfare in heterogeneous countries", FEEM Working Paper No. 2.

Gallois, L. (2012), "Pacte pour la compétitivité de l'industrie Française", Commissaire general a l'investissement, Paris.

Getz, D., Peled, D., Buchnik, T., Zatcovetsky, I. and Even-Zohar, Y. (2010), "Science, technology and innovation indicators in Israel: an international comparison", Samuel Neaman Institute, Technion-IIT, Haifa, Israel.

Getz, D. and Segal, V. (2008). "The Israeli innovation system: an overview of national policy and cultural aspects", Samuel Neaman Institute, Technion-IIT, Haifa, Israel.

Gordon, R.J. (2012), "Is U.S. Economic Growth Over? Faltering Innovation Confronts the Six Headwinds", Boston, MA: National Bureau of Economic Research, Working Paper 18315, August 2012, www.nber.org/papers/w18315, accessed 5 May 2013.

Gordon Orr, G. and Roth, E. (2013), 'China wakes up to innovation', *Financial Times*, 11 February 2013, www.ft.com/cms/s/0/3d97c42e-7200-11e2-886e-00144feab49a.html#axzz2nNEbzBGB, accessed 23 November 2013.

GSK (2013), www.gsk.ca/english/index.html, accessed 15 February 2013.

Guiso, L., Sapienza, P. and Zingales, L. (2006), "Does culture affect economic outcomes?", *Journal of Economic Perspectives*, **20**(2): 23–48.

Hair, J.F., Anderson, R.E., Tatham, R.L. and Black, W.C. (1998), *Multivariate Data Analysis*, Upper Saddle River, NJ: Prentice-Hall, pp. 87–135.

Hansen, T.M. and Birkinshaw, J. (2006), "The innovation value chain", *Harvard Business Review*, **85**(6): 121–30.

Henderson, R., Jaffe, A.B. and Trajtenberg, M. (1998), "Universities as a source of commercial technology: a detailed analysis of university patenting, 1965–1988", *The Review of Economics and Statistics*, **80**: 119–27.

Heritage Foundation (2013), World Index of Economic Freedom, www.heritage.org/index/ranking, accessed 15 May 2013.

Herndon, T., Ash, M. and Pollin, R. (2013), "Does high public debt consistently stifle economic growth? A critique of Reinhart and Rogoff", Working Paper No. 322, PERI, University of Massachusetts, Amherst.

Hofstede, G. (1994), "Management scientists are human", *Management Science*, **40**(1): 4–13.

Hofstede, G., Hofstede, G.J. and Minkov, M. (2010), *Cultures and Organizations: Software of the Mind*, 3rd edn, New York: McGraw Hill.

HQO (2013), www.hqontario.ca/about-us, accessed 15 February 2013.

HTX.ca (2013), www.mri.gov.on.ca/english/programs/htx-Program.asp, accessed 15 February 2013.

ICES (2013), www.ices.on.ca/webpage.cfm?site_id=1&org_id=26, accessed 15 February 2013.

IMD (2012), *World Competitiveness Yearbook*, Lausanne, Switzerland: IMD.

INSEAD (2013), *Global Innovation Index 2012*, Fontainebleu, France: INSEAD.

Jackson, D.J. (undated), "What is an innovation ecosystem?", National Science Foundation, Working Paper, www.erc-assoc.org/docs/innovation_ecosystem.pdf, accessed 16 July 2012.

Jänicke, M. and Jacob, K. (2004), "Lead markets for environmental innovations: a new role for the nation state", *Global Environmental Politics*, **4**(1): 29–46.

Kim, J.O. and Mueller, C.W. (1978), "Introduction to factor analysis: what it is and how to do it", Paper 13, London: SAGE Publications.

Kreiser, P.M., Marino, L.D., Dickson, P. and Weaver, K.M. (2010), "Cultural influences on entrepreneurial orientation: the impact of national culture on risk taking and proactiveness in SMEs", *Entrepreneurship Theory and Practice*, **34**(5): 959–84.

Kuhlmann, S. (2001), "Future governance of innovation policy in Europe–three scenarios", *Research Policy*, **30**: 953–76.

Lach, S., Parizat, S. and Wasserteil, D. (2008), "The impact of government support to industrial R&D on the Israeli economy", Applied Economics Ltd – research and consulting in economics, marketing and social sciences, Tel Aviv, Israel.

Landes, D. (1998), *The Wealth and Poverty of Nations: Why Some are So Rich and Some So Poor*, New York: W.W. Norton.

Lee, Y.K. (1999), *The Singapore Story: Memoirs of Lee Kuan Yew*, Englewood Cliffs, NJ: Prentice Hall.

Lee, Y.K. (2000), *From Third World to First: The Singapore Story: 1965–2000*, New York: HarperCollins.

Li, J. (2012), *Cultural Foundations of Learning: East and West*, Cambridge: Cambridge University Press.

Lichtenthaler, U. (2010), "Intellectual property and open innovation: an empirical analysis", *International Journal of Technology Management*, **52**(3–4): 372–91.

Lundvall, B-Å. and Johnson, B. (1994), "The learning economy", *Journal of Industry Studies*, **1**(2): 23–42.

Maital, S., Ravid, S., Sesadri, D.V.R. and Dummanis, A. (2008), "Toward a grounded theory of effective business incubation", *The Journal for Decision Makers*, **33**(4): 1–13.

Maital, S. and Seshadri, D.V.R. (2012), *Innovation Management: Strategy, Tools and Concepts for Growth and Profit*, 2nd edn, New Delhi: SAGE.

Malerba, F. (2005), "Innovation and the evolution of industries", *Journal of Evolutionary Economics*, **16**(1): 3–23.

MaRS (2012), "Public and public-private programs that support health care innovation: MaRS 2011/12 Annual Report", www.marsdd.com/wp-content/uploads/2012/12/MaRS_Annual-Report_2011_2012.pdf, accessed 15 February 2013.

Meadows, D.H., Meadows, D., Randers, J. and Behrens III, W.W. (1972), *The limits to Growth: A Report for the Club of Rome's Project on the Predicament of Mankind*, New York: Universe.

Merk (2013), www.merck-animal-health.ca/, accessed 15 February 2013.

Metcalfe, S. (1995), "The economic foundations of technology policy: equilibrium and evolutionary perspectives", in P. Stoneman (ed.), *Handbook of the Economics of Innovation and Technological Change*, Oxford, UK and Cambridge, USA: Blackwell Publishers.

Ministry of Science and Technology, Government of Spain (2011), "Spanish innovation strategy", www.mineco.gob.es/stfls/MICINN/.../Spanish_Innovation_Strategy.pdf, accessed 12 May 2013.

MIT Skoltech Initiative (2013), "Technology innovation ecosystem benchmarking study: key findings from phase 1", MIT, Cambridge, MA, January 2013, www.rhgraham.org/RHG/Recent_projects_files/Benchamrking%20study%20-%20Phase%201%20summary%20.pdf, accessed 14 May 2013.

Mitacs-Accelerate (2013), www.mitacs.ca/accelerate, accessed 15 February 2013.

Moore, G.A. and McKenna, R. (1991), *Crossing the Chasm: Marketing and Selling High-tech Products to Mainstream Customers*, New York: HarperCollins Publishing.

Mowery, D. and Rosenberg, N. (1979), "The influence of market demand upon innovation: a critical review of some empirical studies", *Research Policy*, **8**(2): 102–53.

Mowery, D.C. and Shane, S. (2002), "Introduction to the special issue on university entrepreneurship and technology transfer", *Management Science*, **48**(1): v–ix.

Muczyk, J.P. (undated), "Stages of transition from a planned to a free-market economy: Poland as a case study", Working Paper, Graduate School of Logistics and Acquisition Management Air Force Institute of Technology.

Munoz, E., Espinosa de los Monteros, J. and Diaz, V. (2000), "Innovation policy in Spain: technology, innovation and economy in Spain – national and regional influences", 20 January 2000, Grupo de Ciencia, Tecnologia y Sociedad Working Paper 00-03.

Nga, J.K.H. and Shamuganathan, G. (2010), "The influence of personality traits and demographic factors on social entrepreneurship start up intentions", *Journal of Business Ethics*, **95**(2): 259–82.

Niebuhr, A. (2010), "Migration and innovation: does cultural diversity matter for regional R&D activity?", *Papers in Regional Science*, **89**: 563–85.

Niosi, J., Saviotti, P.P., Bellon, B. and Crow, M. (1993), "National systems of innovation: in search of a workable concept", *Technology in Society*, **15**(2): 207–27.

OBI (2013), www.braininstitute.ca/what-we-do, accessed 15 February 2013.

OCE (2013), www.mri.gov.on.ca/english/programs/OCE-Program.asp, accessed 15 February 2013.

OECD (1997), "National Innovation Systems, Executive Summary", Paris.

OICR (2013), "Annual Report 2011/12", http://oicr.on.ca//files/public/OICR_Annual_Report_2011_12.pdf, accessed 15 February 2013.

Osborn, A.F. (1963), *Applied Imagination: Principles and Procedures of Creative Problem Solving*, 3rd rev. edn, New York: Charles Scribner's Sons.

Polish Academy of Sciences (2012), Tadeusz Baczko (ed.), "Report on innovativeness of the health sector in Poland in 2012", www.innovation-in-healthcare.pl/en/companies/, accessed 9 May 2013.

Porter, M. (1990), *The Competitive Advantage of Nations*, London: MacMillan.

Reinhart, C.M. and Rogoff, K.S. (2010), "Growth in a time of debt", Working paper 15639, National Bureau for Economic Research, Cambridge, MA.

Romer, P. (1987), "Crazy explanations for the productivity slowdown", in S. Fischer (ed.), *NBER Macro-economics Annual*, Cambridge, MA: MIT Press, Vol. 2, pp. 163–210.

Rosenberg, N. (1969), "The direction of technological change: inducement mechanisms and focusing devices", reprinted in N. Rosenberg (1976), *Perspectives on Technology*, New York: Cambridge University Press, pp. 108–25.

Saviotti, P.P. and Pyka, A. (2011), *Generalized Barriers to Entry and Economic Development*, Berlin: Springer.

Schein, E. (1996), "Three cultures of management: the key to organizational learning", in B. Bertagni, M. La Rosa and F. Salvetti (eds), *"Glocal" Working: Living and Working Across the World with Cultural Intelligence*, Milano, Italy: FancoAngeli, pp. 37–58.

Schmookler, J. (1966), *Invention and Economic Growth*, Cambridge, MA: Harvard University Press.

Schumpeter, J. (1934), *The Theory of Economic Development*, Cambridge, MA: Harvard University Press.

Schumpeter, J. (1942), *Capitalism, Socialism and Democracy*, New York: Harper.

Scott, M. (2013), "Technology start-ups take root in Berlin", *New York Times*, 29 April 2013, http://dealbook.nytimes.com/2013/04/29/technology-start-ups-take-root-in-berlin/, accessed 20 May 2013.

Senor, D. and Singer, S. (2011), *Start-up Nation: The Story of Israel's Economic Miracle*, 12th reprint edn, New York: Barnes & Noble.

Sharf, S. (2012), "Europe's most innovative companies, 2012", *Forbes magazine*, www.forbes.com/sites/samanthasharf/2012/09/05/the-ten-most-innovative-companies-in-europe/print/, accessed 14 May 2013.

SIM-one (2013), "Annual Report, 2012", www.sim-one.ca/Portals/0/Templates/SimOne/SI12-0543%20SIM-one%20AR%20Public%20Fin.pdf, accessed 15 February 2013.

Solow, R. (1957), "Technical change and the aggregate production function", in M.G. Mueller (ed.), *Readings in Macroeconomics*, Hinsdale, IL: Dryden Press, pp. 111, 323–36.

SR&ED (2013), www.fin.gov.on.ca/en/credit/ordtc/index.html, accessed 15 February 2013.

Sterman, J. (2000), *Business Dynamics: Systems Thinking and Modeling for a Complex World*, New York: McGraw Hill/Irwin.

Suárez, F. and Utterback, J.M. (1995), "Dominant designs and the survival of firms", *Strategic Management Journal*, **16**(6): 415–30.

Task Force on American Innovation (2012), "American exceptionalism, American decline? Research, the knowledge economy and the 21st century challenge", www.futureofinnovation.org, accessed 12 May 2013.

Taylor, M.R., Rubin, E.S. and Hounshell, D.A. (2005), "Control of SO2 emissions from power plants: A case of induced technological innovation in the U.S.", *Technological Forecasting and Social Change*, **72**(6): 697–718.

Tinbergen, J. (1942), "Zur Theorie der Langfirstigen Wirtschaftsent-wicklung", *Weltwirtschaftliches Archiv*, **55**(1): 511–49; reprinted in English translation in Jan Tinbergen, Selected papers, North Holland.

UK Trade and Investment (2013), www.ukti.gov.uk/export/countries/sectorbriefing/388440.html, accessed 24 February 2013.

UNCTAD (2008), Conference on Trade & Development, Issues paper on "Science, technology and engineering for innovation and capacity-building in education and research", Santiago, Chile.

Utterback, J.M. and Abernathy, W.J. (1975), "A dynamic model of product and process innovation", *Omega*, **3**(6): 639–56.

Vossen, R.W. (1999), "Market power, industrial concentration and inno-vative activity", *Review of Industrial Organization*, **15**(4): 367–78.

West, G. (2013), "Wisdom in Numbers", *Scientific American*, May 2013.

White, A. (2007), "A global projection of subjective well-being: a chal-lenge to positive psychology", *Psychtalk*, **56**: 17–20.

Wiener, N. (1961), *Cybernetics: or Control and Communication in the Animal and the Machine*, Massachusetts: MIT Press.

World Bank (2013), "Ease of doing business rankings", www.doingbusi-ness.org/rankings, accessed 10 May 2013.

Yergin, D. and Stanislow, D. (2002), *The Commanding Heights: The Battle for the World Economy*, New York: Free Press.

Index